THE AUTHOR: Tetsuo Sakiya was born in Tokyo in 1926. He graduated from the law faculty of the University of Tokyo in 1953 and started working for the *Asahi Shimbun* newspaper as a journalist, eventually becoming senior editor and writer for the *Asahi Journal*, a national weekly news magazine. He is now a professor of international relations at Musashino Woman's University. Among his books are *Biggu surii to kogatasha senso* (The "Big Three" and the Small Car War), 1979; *Honda cho-hasso keiei* (The Unique Management of Honda Motor Company), 1979; *Nihon keizai shitatakasa no kozo* (The Inner Strength of the Japanese Economy), 1981; *Nagoya shoho no himitsu* (Nagoya Business Practices: The Secret Behind Their Success), 1984; and *Tsukuba kenkyu gakuen toshi* (Tsukuba Academic New Town), 1985. He is the co-author, with Daniel Bell and Ezra F. Vogel, of *Kanosei no Nihon* (The Future Prospects of Japan), 1979, and translated *The Real World War*, 1982, by Hunter Lewis and Donald Allison, into Japanese. His hobbies include palying the piano, carpentry, astronomy, and repairing the family car.

Translated by Kiyoshi Ikemi   Adapted by Timothy Porter

HONDA MOTOR

The Men
The Management
The Machines

TETSUO SAKIYA

KODANSHA INTERNATIONAL
Tokyo and New York

Note: Superscript numbers refer to the list of sources on page 218.

Distributed in the United States by Kodansha Internation-
al/USA Ltd., 114 Fifth Avenue, New York, New York
10011. Published by Kodansha International Ltd., 2-2
Otowa 1-chome, Bunkyo-ku, Tokyo 112 and Kodansha
International/USA Ltd., 114 Fifth Avenue, New York, New
York 10011. Copyright © 1982 by Kodansha International
Ltd. All rights reserved. Printed in Japan.
LC 82-80983
ISBN 0-87011-697-5
ISBN 4-7700-1197-0 (in Japan)
First edition, 1982
First paperback edition, 1987
Third printing, 1989

CONTENTS

PREFACE

In 1946, when Japan was still in a state of total devastation from the war, Soichiro Honda set up a tiny ramshackle plant, called it the Honda Technical Research Institute, and started manufacturing small engines and motorbikes. Two years later, the firm was incorporated under the name Honda Motor Co., Ltd.—the beginning of a long struggle to become an internationally known motorcycle manufacturer, and eventually a world enterprise.

There is no denying that Honda's rare technological ingenuity was the driving force behind this success. But that is not the whole story, for the unique management philosophies of Takeo Fujisawa were an equally significant element. He joined Honda Motor in 1949 as a member of its board of directors, and thereafter Fujisawa and Honda worked together as partners and were responsible for making the company grow to what it is today. They are, indeed, the co-founders of Honda Motor Company. Both men come from poor families, and neither of them has any academic qualifications to speak of. Yet this did not deter them from becoming among the most successful business figures in postwar Japanese history.

The first purpose of this book is to provide a detailed description of these two entrepreneurs and the forces of history that shaped their lives. The way in which these men made the company grow was innovative: there was a complete division of responsibilities between them, with Honda devoting himself to technology and Fujisawa to corporate management. Their relationship was not that of superior and subordinate; rather, it was one of completely equal partnership, in sharp contrast with the stereotyped Western corporate structure where the president or the chief executive officer reports to the chairman of the board. After the company was firmly established, they seldom met or consulted; instead, they wielded near-dictatorial power within

7

their respective areas of responsibility. This, however, did not result in the corporate leadership of Honda Motor being split, for their thinking was similar and they shared common corporate goals. Even in Japan—where the coherent and homogeneous society makes it easy for its members to identify with a common purpose—the kind of relationship that existed between Honda and Fujisawa is unique.

Secondly, I have attempted an in-depth analysis of Honda Motor's corporate management and strategies, vis-à-vis Japan's cultural traditions and the radical political, economic, and sociological changes the country has undergone during the past century.

The third element in this book is Honda Motor's history following the retirement of its co-founders. Honda and Fujisawa gradually retreated from the day-to-day affairs of the corporation and delegated authority to four senior members of the board of directors, who formed a type of "collective leadership." When they were convinced that the four had sufficiently matured, the two retired together in October 1973, naming Kiyoshi Kawashima as the new president. Under Kawashima's leadership, Honda Motor made greater progress than ever before toward becoming a multinational enterprise. Honda and Fujisawa, who had from the very outset avoided stressing their ownership of the company, have totally refrained from interfering or meddling in corporate affairs since their retirement. In Japan, though perhaps to a lesser extent than in the West, it is most unusual that an entrepreneur voluntarily gives up the ownership of an organization he has created. In this sense, Honda Motor and its co-founders are unique by any yardstick.

Finally, this book would not have been complete without some description and explanation of the products that came from Soichiro Honda's technological ingenuity. These include numerous motorcycles, cars, and other products that have made "Honda" a household word.

In preparation for writing this book, I interviewed a number of the past and present executives and engineers of Honda Motor, including Soichiro Honda, Takeo Fujisawa, Kiyoshi Kawashima, Hideo Sugiura, Shigeru Shinomiya, Takao Harada, Kihachiro Kawashima, Michihiro Nishida, Tadashi Kume, Tasuku Date,

Kimio Shinmura, Shizuo Yagi, Yoshio Nakamura, and Taizo Ueda, just to name a few. Mr. Honda and Mr. Fujisawa were particularly generous in spending so much time with me.

I have also been assisted by Kiyoshi Ikemi, who undertook the translation into English, Timothy Porter, who adapted and edited it, and Jules Young and Shinji Ichiba of Kodansha International Ltd.

My deepest gratitude goes to all those whose names are listed above, and to many, many others, without whose cooperation and support this book could not have become a reality.

TETSUO SAKIYA

Tokyo, May 1982

Preface to the Paperback Edition

At the time of the first edition of this book in 1982, only two members of the Japanese automobile industry had invested directly in production in the United States: Honda Motor started manufacturing compacts in Marysville, Ohio, in November 1982; and Nissan Motor was constructing a plant in Smyrna, Tennessee, aiming to start the production of small trucks in the summer of 1983. Other major Japanese automakers, like Toyota, were making similar preparations but were working out how to minimize the risks involved.

Five years have passed since then, and the international situation as regards the Japanese automobile industry has changed dramatically. The meeting in September 1985 of the finance ministers and central bank governors of the so-called Group of Five—Britain, France, Germany, Japan, and the United States—produced agreement to readjust exchange rates, which brought about a rapid increase in the value of the Japanese yen against other major currencies. As major Japanese automakers had been heavily dependent on exports to the United States, the rising value of the yen against the dollar seriously weakened the competitiveness of their products. The Japanese government, meanwhile, extended the original three years of "voluntary" restraints of passenger car exports to the United States, initiated in April 1981. The result has been a conspicuous increase in the number of cars entering the United States from the Republic of Korea and other new auto-producing countries. Such developments have prompted Japanese automakers to rush to begin production in the United States.

According to the "International Automobile Program" sponsored by the Massachusetts Institute of Technology, the world automobile industry has experienced three major transformations, the first being the assembly line production system introduced by Henry Ford I in the 1910s, the second being the diversification leading to the development of products with new technology, such as compact engines, in Europe after World War II, and the third being the organizational innovations in production instituted by the Japanese, such as just-in-time systems and quality control with direct participation of the work force. The MIT program asserts that the world auto industry is now entering the period of the fourth transformation, which emphasizes new technology for flexible production systems, electronics, and new materials. New organizational structures will be indispensable if such new technology is to elevate the quality and quantity of automobiles. Although Japanese automakers at present are beset with difficulties resulting from the high value of the yen, organizational innovations will likely prove their strong suit.

In October 1983, Tadashi Kume succeeded Kiyoshi Kawashima as president and chief executive officer of Honda Motor. Kume, the engineer responsible for the development of the Life and Civic passenger cars, is pursuing the international corporate strategies initiated by his predecessor. In the Postcript to this edition I have outlined the main developments on the international front. In preparing this new section, I received the help of many Honda Motor executives and scholars such as Daniel Roos, James P. Womack, and Harry C. Katz at MIT and Daniel T. Jones at the University of Sussex in England, to whom I would like to express my gratitude.

T.S.

Tokyo, May 1987

1

A Blueprint for the 1980s

As individuals, Japanese often lack dominant personalities, but they usually establish a very strong identity as part of a group—whether that be a family, a corporation, or a nation. This group consciousness is rooted in the culture of a farming society that has traditionally found its source of spiritual identity in small rice-growing communities. In the West, a corporation is seldom more than an organization seeking profits, whereas Japanese corporations also have an inherent tendency to become "communities" serving their employees. One distinct characteristic of a typical corporation in Japan is that, with few exceptions, executives and the board of directors are chosen from among the long-time and senior staff members of the company. Corporate management thus consists of a community of "elders," and both management and employees have an equal sense of working together for the growth and prosperity of their "community." In this way, the unique characteristics and traditions of Japanese corporations represent a form of "corporate culture" nurtured in the nation's past.

In his novel *Anna Karenina*, Tolstoy says that while all happy families are alike, every unhappy family is different. Likewise, successful and growing companies in both Japan and the United States have many things in common, such as long-term employment systems, job rotation within the corporation, and long-range personnel policies. Because of the basic cultural differences between Japan and the West, it is true that American corpora-

11

tions follow a system of individual responsibility, while group responsibility is more common in Japanese enterprises. Yet many leading American companies, such as IBM, Eastman Kodak, Proctor & Gamble, Hewlett-Packard, and Texas Instruments, have management systems similar to those found in Japan.

According to the product cycle model of Professor Raymond Vernon at Harvard University, a corporation goes through periods of new product introduction, rapid growth, maturity, and decline. The multinationalization of corporations is thus aimed at maintaining an advantageous share of the market during the period of rapid growth and competition with other companies mass-producing consumer products. When a corporation launches a unique product and therefore enjoys a competitive edge over its foreign counterparts, it initially exports finished products—and will eventually multinationalize on the strength of cheaper capital and this technological lead. This is the path that has been followed by the multinationals in both North America and Europe.[1]

Many of the multinational automobile manufacturers in the West have now lost their international standing and are going through a difficult period of re-evaluation. The root of their problem lies in the fact that the automobile business has become a mature industry. Automobiles were first developed in the early days of the twentieth century, and since then the industry has not experienced the same technological revolutions that have characterized such fields as semiconductors, integrated circuits, computers, and telecommunications. As a result, the management of the automotive industry tended to be cautious about investing in new facilities, and placed greater emphasis on short-term profits than on long-term strategies. Meanwhile, production facilities were becoming obsolete and productivity improvements more difficult to implement. These factors have been the major reason for the decline in the competitive power of the car industry in the West. The American automobile industry in particular, which for decades had relied on large-sized vehicles, could not adapt quickly enough to an increasing worldwide demand for more compact cars, which was especially strong after the 1973 oil crisis. Initially, Detroit feared the loss of high profits from the production and marketing of large-sized cars; and by the time the industry tooled up for the mass production of small cars, it was already too late. The current plight of the automobile industry in the West has stemmed not from the poor quality of labor, as is often thought, but rather from a failure on the part of management to institute long-range strategies and to modernize production facilities.

Japanese automakers have always specialized in the production of compact, fuel-efficient cars. During the early 1950s, the Ministry of International Trade and Industry (MITI) adopted a policy of developing the automotive sector as a strategic industry. They believed this move would strengthen Japanese industry as a whole, thus overriding the opposition of the Bank of Japan, which insisted on limiting incentive financing to more basic industrial areas. In 1955, MITI announced that the auto industry should develop a mini-sized car for the masses; it would seat four passengers, have a maximum speed of 100 km per hour (63 mph) and be priced under 250,000 yen ($694). This policy took into consideration such factors as Japan's relatively low per capita income, high gasoline prices, small land area, and highly developed public transportation system. Since then, Japanese automakers have continued to implement advanced technology in the field of compact cars. When the first oil crisis of 1973 hit Japan, many people, including automakers, thought the automotive industry would be seriously damaged, for automobiles were the very symbol of a modern industrial society based on petroleum. But they soon discovered that because of the oil crisis, Japanese compact cars had now found a virtually insatiable worldwide market. By 1980, the production volume of cars and trucks in Japan was the highest in the world, surpassing even that of the United States.

Japan's auto exports increased sharply in the 1970s, contributing to an already serious economic situation in the United States, which then accounted for some 40 percent of Japan's car export market. The hardships faced by the American auto industry were further aggravated by the serious crisis which hit the Chrysler Corporation. In the car manufacturing center of Detroit, the auto and related industries seemed to be in a state of permanent recession.

By 1978, the share of Japanese cars in the U.S. market had reached 12 percent, rising to 16 percent in 1979, then to 21 percent in 1980. Serious auto trade friction between Japan and the United

States was inevitable. The American mass media played this story primarily as a domestic economic issue, reporting on the serious plight of the American auto industry, the poor showing of car sales in the U.S., the closure of plants, layoffs, the recession suffered by such related industries as steel, glass, and rubber, and the histrionics of Japanese imported cars being publicly destroyed with hammers. These problems were basically the result of the industry's miscalculation about the future demand for large-sized cars. Toward the end of the 1970s, most Detroit automakers forecast that the public would return in droves to the big domestic cars they had always been accustomed to owning. This has hardly proved to be the case, but large corporations rarely admit to error, and the Japanese auto industry provided a credible scapegoat.

The U.S. International Trade Commission concluded in November 1980 that increased auto imports to the United States had not been the cause of the American automotive industry's crisis. In fact, while the production volume of American domestic passenger cars dropped by 2,058,000, Japanese car imports to the U.S. increased by only 153,000 units. Japanese cars, which are all compacts, were preferred by many American users, however, because the American automakers simply could not satisfy their needs. Against this backdrop, Douglas Fraser, president of the UAW (International Union, United Automobile, Aerospace and Agricultural Implement Workers of America), visited Japan in February 1980 at the invitation of the Japan Federation of Automobile Workers Unions. He conferred with Japanese government leaders, including the late Prime Minister Masayoshi Ohira and also met with top executives of the major Japanese automakers. Fraser strongly advised both Toyota and Nissan to set up car assembly plants in the United States, reminding them that Volkswagen and Honda Motor Company were already building such plants to create new employment opportunities. President Eiji Toyoda told Fraser that Toyota was seriously considering the construction of an auto plant in the U.S., and President Takashi Ishihara replied that Nissan had still not reached a final decision in this regard. Fraser was somewhat less than satisfied by these seemingly evasive attitudes.

The auto trade problem had begun to assume serious political implications, which led the Japanese government to "voluntarily" limit car exports to the United States for three years, beginning in April 1981. The total quota for Japanese car exports to the United States during the first year was set at 1,680,000 units, as opposed to the 1,803,300 cars exported to America during the preceding year. Ironically, the Japanese automotive industry was thus assured of an enormous export volume to the United States, with Washington's guarantee of no further cutbacks. The United States, which in 1950 accounted for 76 percent of the world's total automobile production, was producing only 30 percent by 1980. The American automotive industry, which had profited so handsomely from international free trade, was now in the embarrassing position of having to ask the Japanese to curtail their auto shipments. Similarly, as regards the countries of the European Economic Community, export restraint programs were negotiated or import quotas were imposed.

Under these circumstances, it was only natural for Japanese automakers to set up operations in Europe, the United States, and other advanced industrialized countries, opening the way for these companies to become multinational corporations. As of the beginning of 1982, Nissan was building a truck plant in Tennessee, undertaking a joint venture with Alfa Romeo of Italy, and had decided to acquire a 36 percent equity in Motor Iberica of Spain. General Motors had acquired 34.2 percent of Japan's Isuzu Motors, which was then supplying GM with transaxles and other major components for their "J" cars. GM also entered into a collaboration with Suzuki Motor Company by acquiring 5.3 percent of their shares in a major step toward the development, production, and marketing of the GM "S" cars. Ford had 25 percent of Toyo Kogyo (manufacturer of Mazda cars and trucks), and the latter was already providing Ford with the transaxles and other important components for its "world cars," which they planned to produce jointly in Japan. Chrysler Corporation had acquired 15 percent of Mitsubishi Motors, but when Chrysler ran into serious difficulties their collaboration was re-evaluated, and in 1981 it was agreed that (1) Mitsubishi would supply Chrysler with new compact cars during and after 1982, (2) Mitsubishi would resume supplying Chrysler with engines for their "K" cars, and (3) the sales agreement, which gave Chrysler the exclusive right to market Mitsubishi cars in the United States, would be amended so that during and after 1983 Mitsubishi would have its own dealer network in America. In the spring of 1982, Mitsubishi started negotiations with Chrysler on a scheme to jointly produce compact cars in the United States with a view to assisting Chrysler's recovery program.

In June 1980, Toyota Motor Company, Japan's largest automaker, had proposed to Ford Motor Company that they jointly manufacture compact cars in America. Although talks on this proposal continued for a year, no agreement was reached, mainly because Toyota was afraid that a tie-up with Ford, which is on the "black list" of the Arab nations for having a production base in Israel, might lead to a boycott of Toyota products by the Arabs.

In March 1982, Toyota announced that it had started negotiating with General Motors concerning collaboration to produce compact cars in the United States. By May, they had reportedly reached agreement on jointly producing the new Toyota-designed Corolla, a front-wheel drive model powered by a 1,600cc engine; production would start from 1984 with an annual volume of 200,000 units. The biggest bottleneck to their negotiations is said to concern the form of collaboration. While Toyota is reportedly very anxious to set up a joint venture with General Motors, it is feared that such a venture between the two companies, which occupy the first and second positions in the motor industry worldwide, might constitute a violation of Article 7 of the Clayton Anti-Trust Act of the United States, which forbids mergers, joint ventures, and mutual equity holding between corporations that could significantly reduce competition or create a monopoly. While the Reagan administration is bent on giving added impetus and vitality to the private sector and is becoming increasingly tolerant of mergers and joint ventures between a manufacturer and a distributor, it still maintains a strict vigilance over collaboration between manufacturing firms that could reduce competition. These circumstances have given rise to two alternatives. Under the first alternative, Toyota would establish a wholly owned subsidiary in the United States, which in turn would purchase one of GM's idle plants to produce small passenger cars with marketing and technical collaboration with General Motors. The second alternative would call for General

Motors to produce Toyota-designed cars under license from the Japanese firm. It is likely that Toyota, which has already made known its willingness to make direct investments in the United States, will choose the first of these two alternatives in the event that a joint venture with General Motors incurs objections from the U.S. government.

General Motors has learned, meanwhile, that its first subcompact "J" cars, which had been designed with a view to competing with foreign imports, could not match the quality of Japanese-made automobiles. This has led the Detroit giant to seek to introduce technology for developing and producing high-quality subcompacts not only from its Japanese partners, i.e., Isuzu and Suzuki, but also by collaborating with Toyota. All these events point to a new reorganization of the automobile industry on a global scale.

The strong competitive power of the Japanese automotive industry rests on two major achievements. One is in the area of technological superiority: the Japanese have always specialized in compact cars and, with a long history of technological innovations, are now experts in the field. The other achievement is superiority in production: management has invested wisely in modern and streamlined production facilities, hired a high-quality work force, adopted up-to-date production tooling, maintained close and cooperative relations with suppliers, promoted the workers' sense of participation in the company, and achieved high production efficiency and quality improvements. However, it is primarily superior production techniques that have made the Japanese auto industry the most competitive on the global market.

The next question is to what extent this superiority in production techniques can be adopted when a Japanese automaker establishes overseas plants as a multinational corporation. In the West, corporations have achieved multinationalization on the strength of cheaper capital and a technological lead. Japanese companies, especially in the automobile area, have multinationalized based largely on their competitive edge in production techniques. Many observers expected Japan to follow a path of multinationalization quite different from that of the West. Conventional wisdom also dictated that Japanese multinationals would be successful abroad by adopting Japanese ways of management to the greatest degree possible. Some disagreed with such an analysis. Professor Vernon, for example, has stated that if a Japanese corporation attempted to multinationalize solely on the strength of its management system, its lead would be fragile, and he doubted whether such a corporation could survive in the United States.

In 1976, General Motors Corporation launched a full-scale program of "downsizing" its automobiles in response to a historic shift in demand from large to smaller cars during the aftermath of the oil crisis. This giant firm is now in the process of developing front-wheel drive cars with good fuel economy, maneuverability, and interior comfort—at a development and retooling cost which exceeds the budget of NASA's first Apollo program. General Motors has also adopted a system of improving the quality of working life (called QWL) to ensure high production standards and efficiency. This system originated in the United States to overcome the dehumanizing production techniques that had been established under the name of "scientific management" at the beginning of the twentieth century. American management consultant Frederick W. Taylor was an early exponent of this type of management system, which forced men on the production line to engage in repetitive, monotonous tasks as minute parts of a huge machine. The QWL system centers around enhancing workers' participation in corporate management and is aimed at raising morale and making work life more worthwhile. Japanese-style management is now modeled on such a system, although it has evolved in a homogeneous and group-oriented society quite different from that of the United States. In 1973, General Motors concluded an agreement with the UAW for the introduction of such a system, which has now been adopted by many of its factories and is said to be producing good results.

Ford and Chrysler are also preparing for full-scale production of "downsized" cars, but they are faced with serious financing problems. The entire American automobile industry is undergoing major changes, and it is anticipated that General Motors will further strengthen its dominant position. For GM, the current investment program means the rapid replacement of obsolete machines and tools with the most up-to-date equipment. As of 1980, the average age of its plant facilities was reported to be around forty years, as opposed to approximately fifteen years in the Japanese automotive industry. It is this "age difference" that has been a decisive factor in competitive power. If Japanese manufacturers had failed to invest in new production tooling, their position vis-à-vis General Motors would most certainly have been reversed. GM is introducing corporate management systems similar to those now existing in Japan, and the success of these programs would almost certainly diminish the competitive edge now enjoyed by the Japanese auto industry. Many Japanese automobile manufacturers are also concerned about the extent to which their production system will be competitively ahead of their foreign counterparts in and after the mid-1980s, when General Motors will be in full-swing production of compact automobiles.

Honda Motor's "Company Principle" reads, "Maintaining an international viewpoint, we are dedicated to supplying products of the highest efficiency at a reasonable price for worldwide customer satisfaction." Interestingly enough, this is not just an empty slogan describing an unrealistic goal for the company. This principle was adopted in 1956, at a time when the company was still very small. Honda Motor's policy has never been one of simply trying to export because the domestic market was saturated, nor of investing or building plants abroad because it was so requested by foreign countries. For example, in 1959 the company became one of the first in Japan to establish an overseas subsidiary, American Honda Motor Co., Inc. in Los Angeles. This subsidiary was to play a key role in exploring the potential market for motorcycles in the United States. And in 1962, Honda Benelux N.V. was founded in Belgium to assemble mopeds, making Honda Motor the first in the entire Japanese manufacturing industry to make direct investment and establish a factory in an advanced nation of the West.

In 1981, Honda Motor's total motorcycle production reached some 3.5 million units, and of those, one-third were produced and sold outside of Japan. Many of the self-proclaimed world enterprises and multinationals of Japan have high ratios of exports, but their percentage of overseas production is usually low, which indicates that large Japanese corporations are still hesitant about making direct investment in manufacturing plants abroad. Honda Motor has already become a world enterprise in the true sense of the term, for its products are being turned out at forty-three plants in twenty-eight countries outside of Japan. Starting out with motorcycles, Honda Motor has become the internationally dominant company in the field of two-wheeled vehicles. On the basis of this achievement, the company continues to pursue its own unique blend of international strategies, even though it is one of the most recent entrants into the field of cars and trucks and is certainly not the largest vehicle manufacturer in Japan.

In a speech delivered at the Center for International Business, held in Dallas, Texas, in January 1982, Hideo Sugiura, executive vice president of Honda Motor, said that the company's fundamental management policy, based on its "Company Principle," can be explained in four parts:

(1) Creating New Markets
We should not try to sell things just because the market is there, but rather we should seek to create a new market by accurately understanding the potential needs of customers and of society, and fully utilize our technology to develop and manufacture products satisfying such needs.

(2) Employee Participation in Management
We believe that good corporate management must be based on trust. The management and employees should share a sense of pursuing a common goal, so that each individual will play a specific role and the corporation as a whole will be working in unison to achieve that goal. And this thinking is both understood and supported by our work force, as a way to enhance their individual capabilities and *raison d'être*.

(3) Internationalization and Local Community Relations
As our activities expand internationally, we believe that, as a prerequisite to successfully establishing our overseas operations, we must not only make our products acceptable but also make ourselves well accepted as good corporate citizens in the communities where we operate.

(4) Direct Approaches
In achieving goals and solving problems, we have made it a cardinal rule to make direct approaches with straight think-

ing—free from precedents, customs, or popular views. Thus, we have pursued methods different from those of other companies, based on our own way of thinking, and by reinforcing this difference, we have consolidated our own corporate identity.

In December 1980, Honda of America Mfg., Inc. began construction of a car manufacturing plant in Marysville, Ohio, a suburb of Columbus. The ground-breaking ceremony, held in Marysville on December 2, was attended by many dignitaries, including Hónda Motor's President Kiyoshi Kawashima and Ohio Governor James A. Rhodes, who in his speech was obviously pleased that Honda Motor would be contributing to the economic development and employment opportunities in Ohio. Adjacent to the eastern edge of the automobile plant site, Honda of America had built a $30 million motorcycle manufacturing factory, which started operating on September 10, 1979. This plant looks much like Honda Motor's clean and well-designed production facilities in Japan and was very popular with the local community even before it was completed. When the company sought to hire 100 people, it received job applications from some 3,000 men and women. Today, the plant has a work force of 500, and is producing large-displacement motorcycles at a rate of 60,000 per year for sale in the United States and for export to twenty-five other countries.

Personnel management policies adopted by Honda Motor's Ohio motorcycle plant attach great importance to the system of job rotation. Not only has this policy helped avoid the repetition of monotonous work but it also insures that workers acquire a wide range of production skills. Therefore, they receive basic training as skilled workers, rather than remaining simple, unskilled laborers. Foremen have also been brought up through this system, and they now form the core of the production line. Many of these skilled workers are expected to work in the new automobile plant. Thus, they have a good chance to move to better jobs with their improved skills. The work incentive of the employees is stimulated in this way, their morale heightened, and their sense of participation in the management strengthened. As a result, the turnover rate of the workers is very low. The

Motorcycle assembly lines in the Suzuka plant (*top*) and in the Honda Motor plant in Ohio (*bottom*).

automobile plant will cost some $200 million and the target date for production start-up is toward the end of 1982. The first automobile to roll off the assembly line will be the 1983 Honda Accord, and ultimately the plant will employ 2,000 people and produce 150,000 cars per year. The Ohio car plant will mark Honda Motor's first full-fledged automobile manufacturing operation outside of Japan. The motorcycle and car plants in Ohio will become Honda Motor's production base in the United States, and the policy of obtaining as many components locally as possible is expected to help the economy of the entire region.

BL Limited (formerly British Leyland), Britain's largest car manufacturer, which is owned by the government, decided to produce one passenger car model under license from Honda Motor. The agreement for this technical collaboration was signed in Tokyo on December 27, 1979 by BL Chairman Sir Michael Edwardes and Honda President Kiyoshi Kawashima. In this case, Honda Motor sold a technical license to BL, marking the first time Japanese cars were to be built in an advanced nation of the West under license. The principal points in the agreement were that:

(1) Honda Motor grants BL a license to produce and sell in the European Economic Community under a BL marque one of the new passenger car models currently being developed by Honda.

(2) BL will have the exclusive right to market the model in the nine member nations of the EEC. Honda Motor intends to produce the same model at its own factory and market it under a Honda marque outside the EEC.

(3) BL will purchase some production tooling and receive such technical assistance from Honda Motor as is necessary to produce the model.

(4) Initially, Honda Motor will provide BL with certain components such as engines and transmissions. The local content ratio will be increased as much as possible.

(5) BL will produce the model at its Cowley plant, located on the outskirts of Oxford.

(6) The summer of 1981 is the target date for BL's commencement of the production of the model.

(7) BL's production volume is targeted at approximately

85,000 units per year.

(8) Production of the Honda car in the United Kingdom is the first step towards further mutual programs.

On August 26, 1980, Honda Motor unveiled a new four-door, hatch-back sedan, called the Ballade, and announced this as the model to be built by BL under the license agreement. In December of the same year, BL disclosed that the model to be produced at its Cowley plant would bear the name Triumph Acclaim. In what was regarded as the tightest engineering schedule in the history of the automotive industry, the Triumph Acclaim was launched in Britain in October 1981 without a single day's deviation from the original target.

BL is a company formed through the merger of such British auto manufacturing firms as Jaguar, Austin, Rover, and Triumph. Following the 1973 oil crisis, its profit picture deteriorated rapidly due to such factors as sluggish market demand and many labor disputes. This led the British government to take over BL in 1975. It is said that BL decided to enter into a technical collaboration and licensing agreement with Honda Motor in order to obtain immediate relief from the lack of a compact car model range. This is reminiscent of the years following World War II, when some Japanese automakers introduced production techniques from the advanced countries of Europe. For example, Nissan produced cars under license from Austin of Britain, Isuzu from Hillman of Britain, and Hino from Renault of France. Now, the situation is completely reversed.

Encouraged by the great success of working together on the Triumph Acclaim project, Honda Motor and BL announced the second stage of their collaboration in late 1981. This called for the companies to jointly develop and manufacture a new car model. With a target date of 1985, Honda Motor will be making two versions of this model at its factory in Japan—its own version for sale through Honda Motor's dealers in Japan and the BL version, which will be sold through the BL network in Japan. Similarly, BL will produce two versions at its plant in Great Britain—its own version to be marketed through its dealers in Europe and Honda Motor's version for sale through Honda Motor's dealer networks in European countries.

At an international meeting held in London in January 1982 under the sponsorship of *The Economist*, Executive Vice President Sugiura said:

> Europe is different from the United States, as Europe already has a large number of car manufacturers and is a mature market for compact automobiles. If a Japanese manufacturer were to invest in a new automobile plant in Europe, that would affect the production capacity of the existing companies and could possibly pose a threat to their survival. While investment on the part of a Japanese manufacturer might have the desirable effect of creating new jobs, I am afraid it might further aggravate the situation of excessive production capacity of the automobile industry throughout Europe. Such being the case, Honda Motor has chosen the path of entering into a collaborative arrangement with a partner in Europe....
>
> Through our experience with BL, we have proved that it is possible for manufacturers of different countries to overcome cultural differences, language barriers, and geographical distance, and to collaborate with each other as long as there is the common intention of developing and marketing products that are for the good of the customers. The Triumph Acclaim project represents a good combination of the expertise of Honda Motor and BL.... This, I believe, is a mutual complementary relationship in the truest sense of the term.

Honda Motor has also entered into a collaborative agreement for the joint production of subcompact cars with the South African subsidiary of Daimler-Benz, the second largest German car manufacturer after Volkswagen. The partner is United Car and Diesel Distributors (UCDD), with its headquarters in Pretoria. Although a local bank is the largest stockholder, Daimler-Benz holds 27 percent of UCDD's equity. The largest auto firm in South Africa, UCDD produces and sells passenger cars and trucks for Daimler-Benz. The agreement between UCDD and Honda Motor was signed early in 1981, and contains the following major provisions:

(1) Honda Motor grants to UCDD the right and license to manufacture one model of its passenger cars and sell it in South Africa under a Honda Motor name. UCDD also has the exclusive right to sell that model in Lesotho, Botswana, Namibia, and Swaziland.

(2) Honda Motor will provide UCDD with major production jigs and dies as well as production know-how.

(3) Although certain components, such as engines and transmissions, will initially be imported by UCDD from Honda Motor, the local content ratio will be at least 66 percent (in terms of weight), as required by the South African government.

(4) The start of production is targeted for the latter half of 1982, with a projected annual production volume of 10,000 to 12,000 units.

The size of the car market in South Africa is between 300,000 and 400,000 units per year. Of late, demand is growing rapidly, especially for small, fuel-efficient automobiles. Yet Daimler-Benz, whose model range consists mainly of luxury cars displacing 2,000cc or more, lacks small, popular-sized cars. The German manufacturer is therefore aiming at strengthening its South African production base and broadening the model range by letting its subsidiary launch joint production with Honda Motor. For Honda Motor, which is already marketing motorcycles but has not yet started selling its cars in South Africa, the collaboration with the Daimler-Benz subsidiary will facilitate market exploration in that country.

In addition to South Africa, Daimler-Benz has production facilities in Brazil, Argentina, Spain, Nigeria, and Iran, while Honda Motor does not. If joint production in South Africa progresses well and proves to be mutually beneficial, it is not unlikely that the Daimler-Benz–Honda Motor joint production schemes will spread to other areas.

On April 16, 1982, Honda Motor entered into major collaborative arrangements with Cycles Peugeot, France's leading manufacturer of two-wheeled motorized vehicles, by signing two agreements, both aimed at further expanding the markets in Europe for mopeds and scooters. Under the "Manufacturing

Agreement," the French firm will undertake to manufacture and supply to Honda Benelux two kinds of engines to be incorporated in mopeds under production by Honda Benelux at its plant in Aalst, Belgium; the projected annual volume is 50,000 units. Thus, the production source of the Honda Benelux moped engines will be shifted from Japan to France, significantly increasing the local content ratio of the Honda Benelux mopeds. The other agreement, meanwhile, licenses Cycles Peugeot to manufacture and market 50cc and 80cc scooters, both with engines of Honda Motor's design, throughout Europe under Cycles Peugeot's brand name. Production is scheduled to get underway in the spring of 1983 with a target volume of 20,000 per year. Honda Motor hopes eventually to start producing its own scooters at the Aalst plant with engines to be purchased from Cycles Peugeot. Both companies are confident that these collaborative arrangements will be instrumental in strengthening and further developing the two-wheeled vehicle industry in France.

Honda Motor has also established a joint venture for engine production with Mio Standard of Yugoslavia. The Yugoslav government gave its formal approval to set up the joint venture in December 1981. The new company, Mio Standard Motors, is located in Osijek, some 200 kilometers (120 miles) northwest of the Yugoslav capital of Belgrade. The initial investment in the joint firm is about $6 million, with Honda Motor contributing nearly $1 million worth of production facilities and technical know-how. Production will start in December 1982 at an annual rate of 24,000 engines, which will be raised to 30,000 per year in 1985. These engines will be installed in farming implements, compact power generators, and agricultural pumps, all of which are in large demand. This is the first time that a joint venture for engine production has been agreed upon by a socialist state.

Honda Motor has also signed a technical collaboration agreement regarding motorcycle production with the Chinese state-run Jialing Machine Factory in Chungching, Szechwan Province. The agreement has now been given Chinese central government and Szechwan provincial government approval, and went into effect on December 24, 1981. This is a broad-ranging agreement on technical collaboration, whereby Honda Motor will supply

Jialing Machine Factory with quality improvement know-how and production technology for mass production, and will also cooperate with Jialing Machine Factory in the production of new models in the future. In return, Honda Motor will receive royalties, and will supply production equipment, machinery, and certain parts.

Currently, motorcycle production in China is on a small scale, with manufacturing facilities at approximately twenty-five locations and a total production which was estimated at around 80,000 units in 1981. Jialing Machine Factory, which has 8,000 workers and a 50,000 unit annual production, is the largest firm to manufacture motorcycles. Since the Chinese central government adopted its economic readjustment policy, motorcycle production has tended to be more restricted. Despite such difficulties, Jialing's plan to improve its standing and introduce new models has received the strong support of the Chinese central government; and Honda Motor, by this agreement, is thus able to gain a strong foothold in the large potential Chinese market. The negotiations began in early 1981, when Jialing approached Honda Motor with a request for technical assistance, and were followed by exchanges between the respective technical teams. Executives from Honda Motor then visited China, leading to a satisfactory agreement within just one year.

Honda Motor is carrying out a wide-ranging program of international strategies, supported by the company's spirit of independence and a policy of not imitating others. This international outlook is motivated by the company's confidence in the future of technology. Kiyoshi Kawashima, president of Honda Motor, says, "We did not mean to do anything particularly unique. It is only that we thought about these problems from a serious, broad, and long-range viewpoint." In a speech before the Foreign Correspondents Club of Japan in October 1981 he added:

> Our current project of constructing an automobile plant in Ohio is based on this principle. We launched a feasibility study of this project many years before the Japanese–American auto trade friction problem became apparent. We started our study back in 1974, decided on building a motorcycle plant in Ohio in 1977, and resolved to go ahead with

car plant construction in December 1979. Needless to say, the experience we gained in Belgium has played an important role in bringing about the success of our Ohio motorcycle plant in such a short period of time. This has also been a principal factor in enabling us to become the first Japanese automaker to embark on passenger car production in the United States.

Our total investment in the motorcycle and car plants in Ohio will come to nearly $250 million, which is comparable to the cumulative total of about $260 million we have invested outside of Japan during the past twenty years. By comparing these figures, you will understand, I trust, the degree of commitment we are making in the United States....

The circumstances surrounding the automobile industry are becoming increasingly severe. The so-called automobile trade friction, which has become a political issue between Japan and the United States and between Japan and Europe, is symbolic of the circumstances in which our industry finds itself. I do not think it is necessary to go into details of what has happened and what the results are. I cannot help but say, however, that it is a matter for regret that the Japanese government, out of political considerations, has decided to voluntarily restrain car exports to the United States, despite opinions from many quarters that the plight of the American auto industry was not directly related to a sharp increase in car imports from Japan. I say so because we had long before made our own independent decision in the spirit of international cooperation to produce cars in the United States, and this decision was part of our long-term vision based on the assumption that the principle of free trade would be maintained. Although we have no choice but to obey the government's decision, I would like to reconfirm our position that this export restraint is no more than a temporary measure....

As exemplified by the tripartite collaboration among General Motors, Isuzu, and Suzuki, I anticipate that moves toward collaboration among automakers will be further stepped up as a means of ensuring their survival in the competition for developing energy-conserving compact cars that are growing in demand the world over. Honda Motor does not remain indifferent to such moves. We will not close our doors to an opportunity for co-existence and co-prosperity if that can be achieved on a mutually beneficial basis with another manufacturer of whatever country. Honda Motor will continue to carry out independent corporate management on the principle of equality, complementation, and mutual respect of identity. And this will form the basis of our overseas projects.

In the automobile industry, success is usually a matter of scale. Since a large capital investment for research and development, plant equipment, and tooling is necessary before the introduction of a new model, the more cars of the same type that are manufactured, the lower the per unit production cost. If a new model sells poorly, the production cost for each car will increase, and the automaker will therefore suffer. For this reason, the automobile industry has been governed throughout its history by "the law of the jungle"—where the weak perish and the strong become even stronger.

As a result of saturated markets, the automotive industry rushed into a new era of global reorganization in the early 1980s, after having enjoyed a large increase in demand caused by the rapid motorization in Europe during the 1960s and in Japan in the 1970s. Every automaker is now scrambling to survive in this "jungle" by trying to secure a larger share of the market, which now appears generally to have stopped growing. The focus of this global reorganization is in the field of compact cars, where a growing demand can be expected, despite the finite size of the international market. Under these circumstances, special attention is being paid to the global marketing of the "world cars." The international strategy of the major automotive companies now centers around how to achieve an efficient, uniform production standard of such vehicles through the international division of labor and how to reduce the per unit cost through a high level of production. The success or failure of the "world car" will, to a great extent, determine the future of these corporations. For this reason, most of the major international automakers are now trying to escape from their present difficulties by investing capital in foreign counterparts or by cooperating in the fields of R & D, production, and sales. In the past, when the world automobile market was growing rapidly, the major automotive companies totally dominated the less powerful firms and at the same time jealously protected their corporate and product image. Now even the strong can no longer enjoy such isolation and must try to survive through international "marriages of convenience."

In Japan, the domestic automobile market reached a point of saturation in the late 1970s, and Japanese automakers have since been growing mainly by increasing their exports. The Ministry of International Trade and Industry used to regard the promotion of automobiles as one of Japan's most important industrial targets. However, as the increasing export of Japanese automobiles began to cause political problems in the West, MITI has changed its policy and is now in favor of export restraint in the automobile sector. Japanese automakers began to "voluntarily" cut back their exports to the United States, Canada, and the European Economic Community beginning in 1981, and there remains little hope of this situation changing. Thus, the Japanese automotive industry can prosper in the future only through the promotion of multinationalization and by cooperating in the global reorganization of the industry. In order to survive in the present global market, an automaker must have technological advantages in R & D and in production processes, especially in the field of compact cars; without such an edge, even the ability to raise capital will be limited. Japanese automakers can make great contributions in these fields, and many automakers of the West are now trying to strengthen their small car divisions by tying up with Japanese counterparts.

Where compact cars are concerned, the R & D capabilities of the Japanese automotive industry are generally one step ahead of automakers in other countries. However, many new technologies are now required, the most important being that of improving fuel economy. In addition, better exhaust emission control, new safety features, and alternative fuel engines must be developed along with such related areas as ceramics, plastics, and high-strength low-alloy steel—materials which will be essential to the success of these new technologies. Electronics will also be an important feature in the international automobile market of the 1980s. Competition in all areas of R & D will become intense.

The drama of the global reorganization of the automobile industry is still unfolding, and each player is trying to appeal to the audience by concentrating on such roles as the procurement of capital, R & D, and production processes. No one can guess exactly how this play will end, but there is little doubt that Japanese automakers will be there for the final curtain call. To understand why, it is necessary to go back to the first act and meet two of the principal characters in the original script—Soichiro Honda and Takeo Fujisawa, the founders of Honda Motor Company.

2

The Good Old Days

The 1868 Meiji Restoration put an end to the feudal system under the Tokugawa Shogunate and marked the beginning of Japan as a modern, unified nation. With the promulgation of the Constitution of the Great Japan Empire in 1889, the country became the first constitutional monarchy in Asia, following along the lines of Prussia's national absolutism. The modernization of Japan was thus led by the state, resulting in the formation of a political system for the enhancement of capitalism.

The Meiji Restoration meant a switch from feudalism under the shogun to state absolutism under the emperor. Many people in Japan therefore believe that the Meiji Restoration was not a radical bourgeois revolution such as the 1789 French Revolution. This interpretation would be incorrect. As Takeo Kuwabara, professor emeritus of Kyoto University, says, the most important characteristic of the Meiji Restoration was that it was a complete cultural revolution.[2] Emperor Meiji personally took the initiative of introducing Western civilization, and he issued an imperial mandate encouraging the eating of meat (which, for religious reasons, had not been accepted before) and the adoption of Western hairstyles and clothing. By doing so, he tried to eliminate Japan's traditional culture and customs.

By the turn of this century, Japan was in the midst of a great industrial revolution. Imperialist forces of the major Western powers had already reached China, one of its closest neighbors, but Japan itself remained independent. The nation was thus able

33

to concentrate on internal development rather than having to divert manpower and resources to expel the "foreign devils," as was to be the burden of many Asian countries. Shortly after Japan's victory in the Sino-Japanese War of 1894–95, construction work began on the state-run Yahata steel mill. Under the guidance of German engineer Gustav Toppe, who was hired at a salary twice that of the prime minister's, the mill was completed in

The Yahata steel mill in the early 1900s.

European-style buildings near Ginza in the early twentieth century.

January 1901. The largest steel plant in the Orient, it produced 90,000 tons per year, and came to symbolize Japan's emergence as an industrial society.

Textile plants were built, and villagers started wearing factory-woven clothes. The railway system, which was inaugurated in 1872 between Tokyo and Yokohama, now covered much of the nation. Country people who traveled from distant villages to the

A Japanese textile factory around 1910.

Uniformed delivery boys of Japan's first department store, Mitsukoshi, which opened in 1910.

capital could scarcely hide their amazement at this modern, "Westernized" city. In Ginza, at the heart of Tokyo, new brick buildings, electric lights, and the latest European fashions proclaimed Japan's economic prosperity. Venerable old shops were becoming modern department stores, and motion pictures were shown for the first time in 1897. Using a machine invented by Thomas A. Edison and known as the "Vitascope," the program included scenes of Niagara Falls, New York City, and the burning at the stake of Joan of Arc. The Japanese audience was spellbound. And in 1899 the first beer hall in Japan opened in Shimbashi; Tokyoites were now able to contemplate the benefits of Western civilization over a cold glass of Nippon beer.

The most important diplomatic task for Japan was to amend a series of disadvantageous treaties. In 1853, Commodore Matthew C. Perry led American ships to Uraga (now called Yokosuka), and with the threat of this naval power demanded that the Shogunate open Japan to foreign trade. In 1858, the Tokugawa Shogunate signed treaties of commerce with the United States, the Netherlands, Russia, Britain, and France. These treaties contained provisions most unfavorable to Japan, specifically that foreigners residing in the country were given extraterritoriality and Japan was not given the right to establish import tariff rates on her own. The Meiji government was determined to amend these inequalities, and successfully concluded a new treaty with Britain in 1894, followed by similar treaties with other nations. All of these treaties took effect in 1899. At the time, both Britain and Russia were competing for the control of Asia. This led to a confrontation in Japan between the pro-Russian group, led by ex-Prime Minister Hirobumi Ito, and the pro-British group, led by Foreign Minister Jutaro Komura. The argument was finally settled pragmatically and in favor of Britain, on the grounds that Britain could prove to be a more formidable enemy than Russia. This cleared the way for the signing of the Anglo-Japanese Alliance in 1902. While the Japanese government was exhilarated at having thus concluded a treaty with the strongest power in the world, a war with Russia became increasingly inevitable.

"We beat the Russians!" The cry echoed throughout Japan as the country celebrated its victory in the Russo-Japanese War of 1904–05. Coming only ten years after victory in the Sino-

Japanese War, most citizens of Japan now felt that their country had become a major force in world affairs. And some were even conceited enough to believe that their nation had now joined the ranks of the United States, Great Britain, France, Germany, and Italy as a first-class international power.

Perhaps Soseki Natsume, a leading novelist of the time, understood the situation more clearly when he wrote, "If the war had continued much longer, we probably would have been defeated. It was a good thing we were able to put an end to it." To Soseki, who had just returned from two years of study in England, Japan still lagged behind the advanced nations of Europe in the areas of science and technology. Though it was unknown outside government circles, Japan had also nearly run out of money to pursue the war effort. At the beginning of the Russo-Japanese War, it was estimated that the conflict would cost around 500 million yen. When the fighting ended, this figure had increased to 1.8 billion yen. Over half of the war expenditure had to be raised through foreign loans, mainly in Great Britain and the United States. Neither of these countries were willing to extend further credit, for although they feared Russian supremacy in Asia, they also feared a decisive victory for Japan. It was only through the personal mediation of President Theodore Roosevelt that Japan agreed to an early peace.

On September 5, 1905, the very day the Treaty of Portsmouth to end the war was being signed, a mass rally was held in Tokyo by those who opposed peace with Russia. Militarists and politicians who were bent on toppling the government and who spon sored the rally demanded war reparations and the cession of Sakhalin Island from Russia. Jutaro Komura, the foreign minister and chief negotiator at the peace talks, was blamed for his "humiliating diplomacy" of seeking peace in exchange for only the southern half of Sakhalin Island and for failing to gain any war reparations. The sponsors were unable to control the thousands of demonstrators at the rally, which soon developed into a full-scale riot. They clashed not only with police, but also set fire to streetcars, police stations, and the homes of high government officials. Complete turmoil prevailed in the city, and martial law was finally proclaimed.

These riots were only the leading edge of a mass dissatisfaction over the heavy tax burdens imposed by the government to defray the horrendous costs of the Russo-Japanese War. Soon Japan was hit by a recession that followed the wartime economic boom, and large-scale strikes were staged at mines and factories. In 1907, the recession turned into a major depression as the stock market plummeted and many financial institutions went bankrupt.

Hideshiro Fujisawa, whose son Takeo was later to become the co-founder of Honda Motor Company, ran into serious business difficulties during this economic collapse. Heavily in debt, he farmed out his eldest daughter and ran away from his hometown with his wife and new-born daughter, hiding in downtown Tokyo during the winter of 1907, where he had to look for work in a city wracked by financial depression and icy winds. He finally became an apprentice at a house painting firm, but the family could barely survive on his small salary. By the time that Takeo was born three years later, in November 1910, the family's situation had improved somewhat.

The 1910s marked a period when Japan was able to enjoy the benefits of worldwide economic expansion. Moreover, the nation profited neatly from taking part in World War I. During the early days of the war, Japanese forces took possession of the German-held Pacific islands north of the equator (an area now called Micronesia) and Shantung Province in the Republic of China. On the strength of this latter territory, Japan forced China to accede

Jobless workers sleeping on benches in a Tokyo park around 1920.

to a twenty-one-point demand. As a result, southern Manchuria and eastern Mongolia were virtually annexed by Japan, who also took over German concessions in Shantung Province. In terms of both industrial output and foreign trade, the Japanese economy grew by a factor of nearly five during the war.

Hideshiro Fujisawa was then successfully running a small company called Jitsueisha. The firm was a type of advertising agency, specializing in the production of commercial slides shown at movie theaters during intermissions. Hideshiro also came up with the novel idea of showing movies on night trains, which he called "a mobile theater." Although this dream was turned down by the Ministry of Transport, business was stable and his son Takeo had a comfortable life during the first half of his elementary school years.

Those days of prosperity did not last, however, for the country was engulfed by yet another recession. Especially hard hit was the textile industry, which then formed the backbone of the Japanese economy. The situation was further aggravated by the Great Kanto Earthquake of 1923, the 1927 financial crisis, and the global depression triggered by the New York Stock Market crash of 1929. To make matters worse, the Japanese government followed a policy of monetary deflation, returning to the gold standard by re-evaluating the Japanese yen upwards. By the time this was effected in January 1930, the economic situation of the

Depositors, panicked by the many bank failures of the late 1920s, line up to try to withdraw their savings.

The Ginza area of Tokyo after the Great Kanto Earthquake of 1923.

nation was at an all-time low. More than half the graduates from the leading universities were unable to find jobs, and one out of every four workers was unemployed.

The Great Kanto Earthquake, so-named because it hit the Kanto Plain area centering around Tokyo and Yokohama, was of magnitude 7.9 on the Richter Scale. Some 140,000 people were killed or pronounced missing, a majority of them victims of fire. The first major tremor was recorded at 11:58 A.M. on September 1, 1923. This was immediately followed by a series of fires, which started at over a thousand different locations throughout Tokyo. The quake came just as many housewives were preparing lunch, and open flames in family kitchens were blamed as the principal cause of the fires. The flames and hot winds, igniting hundreds of thousands of wooden houses in the center of the city, spread quickly. The wind was so great that small boats on the Sumida River were lifted as much as twelve feet in the air. A giant black cloud, visible even from the suburbs, formed over Tokyo because of the smoke rising from the fires, and that night the city was bathed in a terrifying red glow. The earthquake completely destroyed Jitsueisha, and the elderly Fujisawa, who had been dependent on borrowing to operate his business, was not insured. After the disaster, he was hit by the heavy burden of having to repay his debts. Hounded by creditors, he scoured the city looking for people to lend him money, but to no avail. He finally rented a movie theater that showed foreign films, but this venture also went bankrupt in the midst of the depression. Thus, Takeo had to spend his middle school days in poverty.

"My father was a proud man, like the ancient warriors," Fujisawa later recalled. "He used to say that I should never think badly of myself, no matter how poor I was. He also taught me that all men are all equal, regardless of their social standing. What I learned from his philosophy was equality. And this served to encourage me a great deal, especially because I have no academic background."

Fujisawa read many novels in middle school, often borrowing books from his friends because the family was so poor. He was especially attracted to the works of Soseki Natsume, who was greatly influenced by Buddhism and wrote about the conflict between the ego and the renunciation of self.

"What I learned from Soseki," says Fujisawa, "was to put myself in other people's shoes when developing my thoughts. For example, if someone makes me a business proposition, I have to judge whether this proposition is sincere or is two-faced. And I can make that judgment if I put myself in his shoes." This philosophy was later to be applied with great success to his management of Honda Motor.

Fujisawa wanted to attend Tokyo Higher Normal School on a scholarship and become a teacher, but he failed the entrance examination because he had spent too much time reading novels instead of textbooks. When he graduated from middle school in 1928, the depression was so severe that he could not find work. He finally had to settle for a job writing addresses on envelopes and postcards. His father was ill, and Fujisawa now had to support the entire family.

In December 1930, shortly after turning twenty, he entered the 57th Infantry Regiment of the Imperial Army as a cadet. Every male citizen of Japan was obligated to serve in the Army or Navy for two years; but by volunteering to become a cadet, it was possible to get out of the service after only a year. Fujisawa's father decided his son should follow this path and managed, with difficulty, to collect the 240 yen needed for his enlistment. The regimental commander, Michitaro Komatsubara, was broad-minded and well versed in Russian affairs, and for these reasons he won Fujisawa's respect. Yet there was a strange and unpleasant incident while Fujisawa was serving under his command. Shortly after his enlistment, a noncommissioned officer punched a recruit on the head and emptied the contents of his bag. Finding some books, the officer put him under arrest, for the military regarded such a person as having thoughts dangerous to the nation. Witnessing this shocked Fujisawa. He had entered the army thinking that the military was there to protect Japan. But after this incident, he began to wonder.

After one year, he left the service and returned to his old job of writing addresses, a type of work that was looked down on. Fujisawa, unqualified for a job with any status because of his lack of education, felt totally humiliated in his work and was determined that if he were to rise to a higher position in the future, he would take care that anyone working under him should not have such feelings.

More than anything, Fujisawa hoped to become a merchant, and he spent several years looking for a suitable opportunity. In 1934, he finally found a job with Mitsuwa Shokai, a small-scale commission merchant dealing in steel, with a head office in Tokyo. His father was less pleased than his "merchant" son, because Fujisawa's salary for the first month was only 15 yen, about one-third what he had been making before. Yet Fujisawa felt he had made the right choice, since "you had to be a college graduate to work for a department store, but to sell things those stores did not handle, it was only your own effort that counted." Within the first year his monthly salary was increased to 80 yen, and by the end of the second year he was already the best salesman in the company and was earning 150 yen a month.

Many contradictions existed in Japanese society following the depression, for there was a great disparity in wealth between the *zaibatsu* (the large family-dominated industrial and business combines) and the workers, and between landlords and tenant farmers. According to newspaper accounts, Kichizaemon Sumitomo, head of the Sumitomo *zaibatsu*, had an annual income of 3 million yen in 1936.[3] While it is difficult to accurately translate this sum into today's currency, it would probably be close to $15 million. This *zaibatsu* had become the most profitable in Japan, surpassing Mitsui and Mitsubishi. Sumitomo was ruled by one man on a hereditary basis, whereas the Mitsui *zaibatsu* was owned jointly by eleven Mitsui families, and Mitsubishi by two families who were equal partners and descendants of the two founder-brothers, Yataro and Yanosuke Iwasaki. With the outbreak of the Sino-Japanese War in 1937, all of the *zaibatsu* started making huge profits. In 1938, for example, Hikoyata Iwasaki, the head of the Mitsubishi *zaibatsu* who made it the most profitable and who was grandson of its co-founder Yataro, earned 10 million yen.[4] When this was combined with the income of his father Hisaya and uncle Koyata, the total came to some 25 million yen, equivalent to over $100 million in contemporary terms. In contrast to these huge incomes, government statistics show that in the 1936–38 period, factory workers earned an average of 2 yen per day (less than $10). As a majority of the Japanese people were being paid at this level, a middle class was only just evolving during this period.

The plight of the farmers was equally miserable, for the basic cause of the worldwide depression that started in the early 1920s was an oversupply of agricultural products. The farmers in northeastern Japan were especially hard hit by poor harvests. In 1934, the rice harvest dropped to nearly one-half that of the previous year. A great famine devastated the countryside, and daughters of poor tenant farmers had to leave home to earn money elsewhere. Some found jobs at textile plants, others as maids for wealthy urban families, and many had to work in brothels. In that year alone, 58,000 women in northeastern Japan left their families. For those who worked in textile plants, it took between three and ten days to earn just one yen.

The majority of Japanese farmers were tenants operating on an extremely small scale, who had to give one-half of their rice crop to the landlord as a fee for using the land. It was this system that caused such great hardship, especially during times of poor harvests. Attacks on the *zaibatsu* and the big landowners came from both leftists and rightists. Even before Fujisawa's enlistment in the army, the establishment of the world's first communist regime following the 1917 Russian Revolution had been a great encouragement to the Japanese working class, whose leaders proclaimed that the working class would eventually rule Japan, too. As the depression of the twenties worsened, many intellectuals agreed with the communists that unemployment had been eliminated in Russia and that a wave of proletarian culture was replacing the "rotten bourgeois society." Fujisawa himself, however, had little sympathy with communism, and preferred his independence.

As the economic situation grew worse in the 1920s, the right-wing militarists began to gain in power, urging the Japanese people to unite under the emperor and to overcome what they called "the greatest crisis in the nation's history." The left-wing movement was suppressed, and by the end of the 1920s the Japanese Communist Party had been almost totally annihilated, to be replaced by the rightists as the major political force of the 1930s. The most radical of these rightists were young officers of the Imperial Army.

On February 26, 1936, these officers attempted a coup d'état. Among those murdered was Finance Minister Korekiyo Takahashi, who favored curtailing military expenditures. This attempted coup represented an internal power struggle within the army. The instigators, known as "imperialists," were young officers who thought the nation must be reconstructed in support of the emperor. After the coup was suppressed, their opponents, known as "disciplinists," took over political power. They insisted on tightening military discipline, and on mobilizing the nation's entire military force for external expansion. Japan's invasion of the Chinese mainland followed, and July of the following year marked the beginning of the Sino-Japanese War.

Two months after the war broke out, the owner of Mitsuwa Shokai was called up for military service and sent to the battlefields in China. While he was away, the management of the company was entrusted to twenty-seven-year-old Fujisawa. The war boosted the demand for steel, pushing up the price. Under Fujisawa's leadership, Mitsuwa Shokai made a profit of 200,000 yen in the final months of that year. As the war in China expanded in scale, the government tightened its control over the economy, making commercial profits difficult to achieve. This led Fujisawa to consider entering the manufacturing business. With an initial capital investment of 10,000 yen, he established the Japan Machine and Tool Research Institute in 1939 to manufacture cutting and grinding tools.

The government gave top priority to the production of war-related materials and goods, which resulted in inflation and a hard life for the common people. Fujisawa wrote several letters to the owner, reporting on the business and seeking permission to raise wages. The reply, which came shortly after the establishment of the Japan Machine and Tool Research Institute, instructed Fujisawa to maintain the current level of wages and bonuses until his return. Fujisawa was infuriated at the idea of freezing wages when the company was making such large profits. He saw the limitation of the owner's capabilities and made up his mind to become independent.

It was not until three years later that the Japan Machine and Tool Research Institute was able to manufacture satisfactory tools. The owner returned to Japan the same year, and Fujisawa told him that he wanted to become independent, promising he would repay the money he had borrowed from the company to establish the tool business. The owner, however, offered to let him keep the money as a bonus. Applying his commercial talents, Fujisawa was able to sell cutting tools to the military, and the enterprise made large profits and he paid his employees generously. His young workers were constantly haunted both by the fear of being drafted and by the uncertainty of their future, but the high wages were a great incentive and his employees reciprocated by working hard, which in turn brought even more profits to the company.

The war had already expanded from the Chinese mainland to the Pacific Ocean. Despite a major success at Pearl Harbor, the tide of war kept turning against Japan. On April 18, 1942, Tokyo was bombed for the first time in history by six carrier-based American B-25 bombers. Though damage was minimal, many residents of Tokyo now feared direct enemy attacks. In June, the Imperial Navy suffered a decisive defeat in a naval battle near Midway. Although Chester W. Nimitz, commander of the U.S. Pacific Fleet, went only so far as to say that the United States had reached the "midway" point in its efforts to avenge Pearl Harbor, America was now confident of ultimate victory in the Pacific.

Celebrating the German-Japanese Anti-Comintern Pact of 1936 (*left*); U.S.S. *West Virginia* and U.S.S. *Tennessee* on fire in Pearl Harbor, 1941 (*below*); in World War II, American flags were painted on Tokyo sidewalks to be trodden on by passersby (*opposite*).

Japanese Imperial Headquarters did everything possible to conceal this major loss, and three days later publicly declared that a major victory had been scored.

On November 1, 1944, an American B-29 heavy bomber from Saipan appeared over Tokyo. No bombs were dropped, as its mission was one of reconnaissance. But on November 24, seventy B-29s made what turned out to be the first of a long series of bombing raids on Tokyo. During the next three months, the bombers came in small groups and no serious damage was done. Yet the people began to realize that the war had entered a new and decisive phase.

On March 10, 1945, downtown Tokyo was hit by one of the biggest air strikes of World War II. One hundred and thirty American B-29 bombers, flying at low altitude, dropped incendiary bombs on the center of the city. The downtown area, crammed with wooden houses, was devastated more seriously than by the Great Kanto Earthquake of 1923. Some eighty thousand people were killed during the first day of air raids, and this was just the beginning of the fire bombings that were to destroy nearly all of Tokyo.

In June of that year, Fujisawa decided to move his company from Tokyo to Fukushima, in northern Japan, to escape the bombing. The machines and tools arrived in Fukushima on

抗戦を停止し母國を救へ

ビルマ戦線の敗残兵将兵諸士
に告ぐ

The scramble for anything edible in the period of starvation that followed the bombing of Japanese cities (*above*); one of the many propaganda leaflets (this one showing General Henry Arnold) dropped by American aircraft urging the Japanese people to surrender (*left*); listening to the emperor's declaration of surrender, August 15, 1945 (*below*).

August 15, which ironically turned out to be the day the war ended. Always practical, Fujisawa bought a forest, thinking that a great deal of lumber would be needed for the reconstruction of Tokyo.

In 1906, Japan was at peace, a prosperous future seemed assured, and the Honda family was blessed with their first son, Soichiro. His father, Gihei, was known as an honest man with the spirit of an entrepreneur. Coming from many generations of small farmers, he had fought in the Russo-Japanese War and later opened his own blacksmith shop, where he also repaired bicycles. Bicycles were becoming very popular in the big cities of Japan, and Gihei often went to Tokyo to buy used or broken-down bikes, which he then repaired and resold.

The family was poor and Soichiro, from the time he was a child, helped with his father's business. Even as a baby, he seemed fascinated by machinery. Several miles from his house was a rice polishing mill with a gasoline-powered engine, which was quite an oddity in those days. His grandfather would carry him there on his back and watching the motor became one of young Honda's favorite pastimes. In 1911, when he was in the second grade, he had a chance to see an airplane, piloted by Niles Smith. For the next month, Honda impersonated the illustrious pilot as best he could, by wearing aviation goggles fashioned from cardboard and terrorizing the village on a bicycle equipped with bamboo "propellers."

After finishing eight years of schooling, in 1922 Honda went to Tokyo at the age of fifteen to become an apprentice at Art Shokai (Art Automobile Service Station)—which, despite its grand-sounding name, was simply an auto repair shop. Having come from a small town in Shizuoka Prefecture, Soichiro was amazed to see as many as ten automobiles a day in Tokyo. In his native Komyo Village, he was lucky to see one a month.

This was a prosperous time in Tokyo, coming after Japan's stunning victories in World War I and before the Great Kanto Earthquake of 1923. Western-style buildings, housing the headquarters of fast-growing enterprises and trading companies, occupied the center of the city. The Imperial Hotel, designed by Frank Lloyd Wright, had just been completed the year Honda arrived. And while on the back streets *jinrikisha* (or "rickshaws" as foreigners often called them) were still a popular mode of transportation, down the main thoroughfares streetcars glided with quiet efficiency.

But the reality of Honda's job was many times removed from the excitement and glamour of the big city. The first task he was given was baby-sitting. Day after day, Honda had to carry the owner's young child around on his back, and his dream of becoming an expert auto mechanic seemed as far away as ever. He was miserable and would have packed his clothes and returned to Hamamatsu had he not been ashamed to face his parents. Honda's predicament was not an uncommon one at that time. Though Japan was now under direct imperial rule, liberalism favoring civil rights was mounting; however, the emphasis was placed on "a government for the people" rather than "a government of the people and by the people." At the same time, remnants of feudalism from the days of the Tokugawa Shogunate lingered on in the Japanese people, among them a strong sense of duty. For this reason, the society still willingly accepted a rigid apprenticeship system based on a strict master–servant relationship. Unlike many societies in the West, that of Japan was able to maintain an attitude of ambivalence, and no head-on clashes took place between the demand for broader rights and the sense of duty. This ambivalence, though substantially altered by post-war reforms, can still be found in Japan today.

Fortunately for Honda, the shop later found itself short-handed, and after six months of baby-sitting, he was ordered to assist with auto repairs. The 1923 earthquake, which devastated Tokyo and its vicinity, virtually destroyed Art Shokai, yet brought good fortune to Honda. Every employee of the company returned home except Soichiro and the senior apprentice. This enabled the two men to receive a thorough training in auto repairs. It was also Honda's good luck that Yuzo Sakakibara, the owner of the shop, was an ardent racing fan. At his suggestion, Soichiro used his free time at night to build a racing car. Honda's racer was powered by a Curtis-Wright aircraft engine that had been used by the military. The 8-liter, V-8 power plant had a maximum output of nearly 100 horsepower at 1,400 rpm. Other than the engine, Honda made everything himself, including the components and wooden wheel spokes. The car was fast and Honda won a surprising number of races.

After working at Art Shokai for six years, Honda was given permission by the owner to open his own business using the firm's name. Thus began, with high expectations but meager facilities, the Hamamatsu Branch Office of Art Shokai. Honda continued

Soichiro Honda in his early days in Tokyo.

The Art Shokai branch in Hamamatsu.

Honda in one of his first racing cars.

Honda's car crashing at the All-Japan Speed Rally, 1936

to devote his spare time to building racing cars. In those days, races in Japan were run counterclockwise, so Honda tilted a Ford engine to the left, making it easier for the car to execute left-hand turns. He also fitted the engine with a supercharger, which injected compressed air and improved fuel combustion. Unfortunately, the motor overheated and the exhaust valves became red hot. Honda attacked the problem with his usual flair, first by adding an auxiliary radiator to improve engine cooling, then by making valve seats from a heat-conducting metal, so that excessive heat would be dissipated when the exhaust valve was closed. The result was a racer with tremendous performance and an engine that did not blow up.

Honda was anxious to test his new design in an important race. He got his chance in July 1936, at the All-Japan Speed Rally held near the Tama River on the outskirts of Tokyo. Everything went according to plan, and as Honda neared the finish line he was out in front and moving at the incredible speed of over 120 kph (75 mph). Just then, a car that had been undergoing repairs edged out in front of him. They crashed. Honda's car was thrown into the air, landed with a screech of twisting metal, and rolled over three times. Honda was thrown free, but the left side of his face was crushed, his left shoulder dislocated, and his wrist bones were broken. His younger brother, who had been riding with him, was also seriously injured. All that he remembered before losing consciousness was the world turning upside down.

When he came to, he heard a nurse say, "How lucky you are to be alive!" Scars still remain above his left eye. In that race he set a new Japanese average speed record of 120 kph, which was not broken until more than ten years after the end of World War II. And although he did not win the race, he was given a trophy for this record. Honda once reflected that, "They used to say man lives for only fifty years. But with increased speed, man has been able to utilize time to expand his lifetime. Doctors are not the only ones contributing to longer life any more. We should no longer talk about distances, we should talk about time."

In 1937, Soichiro Honda embarked on a new business venture. "I made myself proud by launching a manufacturing business, but I soon realized that I had started a very difficult job." He had established a firm called Tokai Seiki Heavy Industry to manufacture piston rings. The problem was that he could not make them up to standard. He had already recklessly invested large sums of money to buy equipment, and unless something was done, fifty workers would have to be laid off and might well starve. The reason he chose this item was simple: a piston ring required only a small amount of raw material, yet it could be sold for a good price. In the late 1930s, a piston ring was worth more than solid silver of the same weight. Honda had every reason to believe these piston rings could be produced quite easily using the die-casting method.

When he was an apprentice, he had seen wooden car wheel spokes go up in flames during the inferno caused by the Great Earthquake. This motivated Honda to study metal casting after he became independent. He succeeded in making cast-iron spokes and was granted a patent. Placed on exhibit at an industrial fair, they caused a sensation. Honda thus considered himself to be an "expert"—but it was not quite that simple. By pouring molten iron into a die, he was able to make objects "shaped" like piston rings. Unfortunately, the trial products had almost no elasticity and were judged to be utterly useless. He sought lessons from the owners of foundries nearby, but was told that he would not be taught the secret of casting unless he became an apprentice.

Honda, who was the president of this fledgling company, and Miyamoto, the senior managing director, stayed at the plant day and night trying to discover these secrets on their own. The evenings were cold, and they drank warm *sake* before falling asleep beside the fire. On such nights, Honda would recall his better times with nostalgia. Then another day began, filled with trials and constant failures. He became a hermit, and his wife had to come to the factory to cut his long, straggling hair. Life became harder and harder, and he finally had to pawn some of his wife's belongings. Honda says he worked harder in those few months than at any other time in his life. Until then, he had thought that school education was without any value and strongly believed that theories come after inventions: "If a theory led you to an invention, all schoolteachers would become inventors." This time, however, he realized that he lacked even the most basic knowledge of casting.

Finally, he called on Professor Yoshinobu Fujii of Hamamatsu High School of Technology. Although the two had never met before, Fujii must have understood that Honda was very serious, and introduced him to Professor Takashi Tashiro of the same school. Tashiro analyzed one of Honda's piston rings and discovered that it did not contain enough silicone. "I didn't even know such a simple thing," thought Honda. So he went back to school. As a part-time student, Honda attended Professor Tashiro's lectures faithfully, all the time thinking about how to make a better piston ring.

Wearing two hats now, company president and student, Honda absorbed new theories in the classroom and then put them to use in the factory. By November, he was able to come up with a satisfactory prototype, nine months after making his first attempt. Meanwhile, the Sino-Japanese War was being felt even in small towns, where it was now common to see local people gathering to bid farewell to young soldiers being sent to the front. Although Honda continued to attend school, he did not show up for German lessons or the military training courses.

Both teachers and students commuted to school on foot. Honda was different; he went by car. He was the same age as Professor Tashiro, whom he often invited out for the evening. Given the rather strict nature of Japan's educational system at the time, the behavior of this part-time student became well known around the campus. One day, school principal Tei Adachi called Honda to his office and told him that he would not get a diploma because he had not taken the examinations. "Diploma? That's worth less than a movie theater ticket," Honda retorted. "The ticket guarantees that you can get into the theater. But the diploma doesn't guarantee that you can make a living." Principal Adachi was later promoted to head the Port Arthur Institute of Technology (in Liaoning Province, China)—a mecca for elite engineers. After the war, he was named President of the Yamanashi Technological University. Honda was by then a famous manufacturer of motor-cycles and Adachi, remembering their argument about diplomas, called his old adversary to confess, "I wish I had given you a diploma."

In 1941, the war spread from China to the Pacific and Tokai Seiki's business grew and prospered. The firm began supplying piston rings to Toyota Motor, which acquired 40 percent of the company's equity, and Taizo Ishida, former president of Toyota Motor, was named to Tokai Seiki's board of directors. Honda's company was now furnishing parts and machines to the navy and to the Nakajima Aircraft Company. By this time, most of Japan's young men had been drafted into military service and women started taking their places in the factories. Many production techniques were no longer suitable, and Honda invented automatic machinery to fabricate piston rings, which could be easily operated by these new workers. At the request of the military, he also invented machine tools for making aircraft propellers. During World War II, the propellers of large Japanese bombers were made of wood, and it took as long as a week to manufacture one propeller by hand. The new tools made it possible to grind the surfaces of two propellers at once, and the entire job took only half an hour. For this innovation, Honda received a letter of citation from the military authorities, and the newspapers praised him as an "industrial hero."

Located close to the Hamamatsu Air Base, Honda's factory was bombed toward the end of the war, and in January of 1945 the plant was almost completely destroyed by a severe earthquake. The war ended as Honda and his employees were trying to repair the machines.

Of the war, Honda recalls, "The American aircraft were so good that many Japanese planes were shot down. I thought we might lose the war. But we were told that Japan was a divine nation, and so I thought some divine miracle might occur. But we lost." Though it was a miserable experience for him to hear the voice of the emperor announcing Japan's surrender, Honda was not thrown into a state of despair as were many of the country's intellectuals. But he did feel that Japan was entering a period of great uncertainty and thought it safest to keep a low profile.

He sold Tokai Seiki's stock to Toyota Motor, which brought him 450,000 yen (equivalent to nearly $800,000 today), and announced that he was going to spend a leisurely year. This he proceeded to do with his usual vigor and unorthodox style. Honda thought that the Japanese were too agrarian-minded and knew of little else but hard work. Perhaps to demonstrate a more exuberant approach to life, he spent 10,000 yen (over $17,000 today) on a large drum of medical alcohol. The drum was installed in his house, where he made his own whisky and he spent the next year partying with friends and playing the *shakuhachi* (a Japanese wind instrument).

3

Starting from a Dream

In 1975, Bernard Krisher, former Tokyo bureau chief of *Newsweek* magazine, became the first foreign correspondent to interview the emperor, who was just about to visit the United States. "At the time of the termination of the war," the emperor told Krisher, "I made the decision on my own. That is because the Prime Minister failed to obtain agreement in the Cabinet and asked my opinion. So, I stated my opinion and then made the decision according to my opinion. Now, at the time of the outbreak of the war and also before the war, when the Cabinet made decisions, I could not override their decisions. I believe this was in accordance with the provisions of the Japanese constitution."[5]

Immediately after the war, the emperor remarked that Tokyo would never regain the prosperity it had once achieved. One of his aides is said to have replied, "Your Majesty, you should rest assured that Tokyo will return to what it once was in half a century." Ten years later the city had been rebuilt to the prewar level, and today it is virtually impossible to find any remnants of the wartime destruction. Yet, if the emperor had not decided to end the war on August 15, 1945, the Allied forces would most certainly have invaded the entire country, inflicting an undescribable degree of misery on the citizens. When soldiers of the Occupation forces first appeared on the streets of war-torn Tokyo, the Japanese people were astonished by their generally good behavior. They were also surprised by the soldiers' mobility as they roamed around the country in jeeps, dispensing chewing gum, chocolate, and democracy—all of which had been in short supply during the war years.

On September 2, Japan formally surrendered aboard the battleship U.S.S. *Missouri*. The United States government soon announced their basic Occupation policy for Japan, which included disarmament, the elimination of militarism, the punishment of war criminals, the promotion of a liberal democracy both politically and economically, and war reparations. General Douglas MacArthur, the Supreme Commander of the Allied Powers, issued a series of directives to deprive Japan of the ability to engage in war, the most important among them being the dismantling of the *zaibatsu* and the liberation of farmers.

On November 6, General Headquarters (GHQ) issued a memorandum calling for the dismantling of the four major *zaibatsu* of Mitsui, Mitsubishi, Sumitomo, and Yasuda. By this action, corporations belonging to these *zaibatsu* became totally separate entities, while the families owning the *zaibatsu* had their private assets frozen and heavily taxed. Farming villages also underwent drastic changes the following month when GHQ ordered sweeping land reforms, on the grounds that farming villages constituted a hotbed of militarism. Even before Japan's surrender, the Allied forces had held a meeting in the United States to discuss their

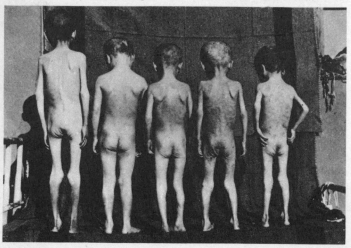

Postwar Japan suffered from a multitude of ills, among them malnutrition (*opposite*), a chronic lack of housing (*top*), and a thriving black market (*bottom*).

The reforms that came with the Occupation: Mitsui and Mitsubishi stock certificates being seized by the Occupation forces in October 1946 (*left*), under the policy of dissolving the *zaibatsu*; women casting their first vote on April 10, 1946 after they were granted suffrage (*below*); posters displayed in rural areas to inform tenant farmers that they could henceforth buy land of their own (*opposite*).

postwar policies. Because the Japanese militarists and ultranationalists would likely resort to guerrilla activities against the United States after Japan's surrender, it was proposed that the farmers should be liberated to discourage their support. In reality, though, most Japanese had already abandoned any such idea. The postwar Japanese government, however, feared that the economically depressed peasants might turn to communism. The liberation of farmers was thus carried out jointly by Japan and the United States; land was purchased from landlords at low prices and then sold to the tenants. Although this was done under the authority of the Occupation forces, the program turned out to be one of the most successful and radical land reforms in history.

Most of the policies of the Occupation forces were welcomed by Japanese, who were witnessing the disappearance of millionaires, big landlords, and monopolistic corporations. But while everyone hailed democracy, the specific type of democracy favored by Japanese varied greatly. One factor was constant: everyone was poverty-stricken. Edwin W. Pauley, head of the reparations mission to Japan, came to Tokyo on November 13, 1945 and issued a statement that the reparations policy of the Allied forces was to deprive Japan of everything that was not essential for the achievement of a minimal peacetime economy. The "minimal" meant that Japan would not be allowed to enjoy a standard of living higher than that of any country she had invaded. This led the Japanese to fear that they would never escape from poverty and near-starvation.

After 1943, Japan had faced critical shortages of virtually everything necessary for the war effort, and her military leaders were frantic to discover new sources of basic materials. One such venture was their attempt to fuel fighter planes with turpentine oil, and thousands of students were mobilized to dig up pine tree roots. Innovation went unrewarded and the novel scheme was a failure, but this idea also interested Soichiro Honda when he started a new business after the war. Gasoline was tightly rationed, and very little was allocated to each person, so Honda bought a pine tree forest and went into the production of turpentine oil.

More experienced with engines than with explosives, he set off dynamite at the root of a pine tree and inadvertently caused a forest fire. Honda did everything he could to control the flames, but most of his forest burned down. In spite of these early mishaps, turpentine oil did have certain advantages. When it was combined with gasoline that Honda bought on the black market, the mixture emitted a terrible smell of pine resin. If the police questioned him about where he had obtained the gasoline, he would say that the fuel was turpentine oil, which was outside government control—an impromptu excuse that apparently never failed.

For that matter, Honda's first real business after the war was also "impromptu." In October 1946, he established the Honda Technical Research Institute (the forerunner of Honda Motor Company) in Hamamatsu. The company's first project was to recycle small engines which had been used by the Japanese Imperial Army for communication purposes. The engines were bought cheaply, attached to bicycles, and sold at a high profit. When the war-surplus engines ran out, Honda started making his own, and bicycles fitted with those small engines became quite popular.

In the early days of the Occupation, Japan was faced with a serious food shortage. People in cities often had to travel to farm areas to buy the daily necessities of life. Train service had been badly disrupted, and the lines which did function were jammed with passengers, who even clung to the steam locomotives during the trip to the countryside. In this grim time, many died of hunger and nearly everyone suffered from malnutrition. Under these circumstances, Honda's motor-powered bicycles came in handy and many bike dealers and black market operators made the long journey to his factory with cash in hand. Always resourceful, Honda was also able to sell them his special blend of turpentine oil and gasoline.

The year Honda established his company also marked the first time that May Day had been celebrated in Japan since 1935. On May 19, thousands of hungry people gathered in front of the Imperial Palace to demand rice. One of the slogans at the gathering was a brutal parody of a prewar message from the emperor, "Imperial Edict: The Nation has been saved. I have plenty to eat. You citizens can starve and die!" The following year, a nationwide strike was planned, only to be called off at the last minute by order of GHQ.

Japanese society in the immediate postwar years was in a state of turmoil. While feeling uneasy about certain policies of the Occupation forces, a majority of Japanese reacted favorably to the efforts made by General Douglas MacArthur to democratize the nation. MacArthur had certain reservations of his own about Japan. Testifying before the United States Congress in 1951, he said that viewed from the development of science, art, religion, and culture, the Anglo-Saxon nations had already reached a level of maturity comparable to the human age of forty-five, and the same could be said of the Germans. The Japanese, on the other hand, were still in their schooldays, comparable to the age of twelve. These remarks caused surprise and disappointment among no small number of Japanese.

Japanese culture has inherited a pattern that is completely different from that of the West. As Professor Hayao Kawai of Kyoto University pointed out, Japanese culture is one of "eternal youth," meaning that Japanese seldom hesitate to import foreign cultures.[6] They become quite enthusiastic about popularizing these cultures among themselves, fully digest them, and make them their own. However, such enthusiasm dies out sooner or later, and people start looking for the excitement of introducing yet another culture from abroad. The pattern is repeated over and over again, enabling Japanese culture to retain its "eternal youth." This peculiar psychological characteristic of the Japanese people is termed "Protean style" by Professor Robert J. Lifton of Yale University.[7] Like the sea god Proteus in Western mythology, Japanese culture has the ability to assume different forms, constantly changing the objects and ideas about which the Japanese people are enthusiastic.

Many centuries ago, Japan was enthusiastically importing culture from China, and this culture became the people's spiritual "backbone" during the feudal period. During the days of the Meiji Restoration, they abandoned some of the traditions of the past, imported Western civilization, carried out a cultural revolution, and embraced a policy of modernization. Japan repeated the same process following the end of World War II, this time by abandoning militarism as something outmoded and adopting American democracy with a surprising degree of enthusiasm. This enthusiasm is now somewhat diminished, for Japan has attained its objective of catching up with the West.

In January 1946, on the occasion of the first New Year celebration after the war, Emperor Hirohito issued an imperial edict, personally denying his own divinity. The divinity of the emperor had, up until that time, been a matter of faith for the people of Japan. But they were now able to renounce this faith with few moral or ethical qualms, because they possessed a "Protean style" psychology. Professor Otis Cary, a historian at Doshisha University, read this imperial edict in an English-language newspaper, and had some doubts about the accuracy of the translation.[8] When he checked the Japanese original, he discovered that the straightforward word *haiboku* (meaning "defeat") was used instead of an ambiguous one like *shusen* (meaning the "termination of hostilities"). And more importantly, the word *kokumin* (meaning "people") appeared instead of *shinmin* (meaning "subjects"), which was used emphatically during the war to indicate that the Japanese were "subjects" of the emperor. Such a drastic change of attitudes in Japan came as a great surprise to many observers who did not know the country well.

Takeo Fujisawa was a frequent visitor to Tokyo around this time, often walking around the numerous black market areas to get a feeling for what was going on. He was hoping to get into a new kind of business with long-range prospects. Fujisawa thought often of the old Japanese saying "All is flux," and believed that one could not be successful in business without responding to the currents of the times. In Tokyo, Fujisawa noted that the economy was ruled by the black market and that young toughs were doing most of the business. Such scenes made him conclude it was premature for him to return.

In the summer of 1948, by pure chance, Fujisawa ran into his old friend Hiroshi Takeshima at a lavatory near the Yasukuni Shrine in Tokyo. Although it was mid-afternoon, there was no one else in sight. Surrounded by the remnants of burned-out buildings, they both felt lucky to have survived the war. Takeshima told Fujisawa that, "Tokyo will not be ruined like this for very long. It is certain to be reconstructed soon." Takeshima strongly recommended that he return to the city and Fujisawa decided to take the advice. When he arrived, people were beginning to recover from their shock at losing the war, and a popular song of the time, "Blue Mountains," seemed to express everyone's hope for a better, if somewhat distant, future. The Occupation forces were especially surprised by this unexpected vitality, and Fujisawa felt that he had made the right decision.

During the war, Takeshima had told Fujisawa about a brilliant young inventor in Hamamatsu by the name of Soichiro Honda. Somehow, that name had remained in Fujisawa's mind. And after their meeting in the summer of 1948, Takeshima told Fujisawa that Honda was looking for a backer. Fujisawa replied without hesitation, "I'll do that." He had always been a man who wanted to do business on his own, so he must have felt there was great potential in teaming up with Honda.

During the six years that Honda was in Tokyo as an apprentice, Fujisawa had lived nearby, but their first meeting took place at Takeshima's home in August 1949. "I looked for a financier in Hamamatsu, but all the potential investors want to recover their money quickly, and I don't like that," Honda said to Fujisawa, who replied, "I don't have the money now, but I will find what you need to launch your technology." After only a short conversation, they agreed to work together as a team; Honda was forty-two and Fujisawa thirty-eight. Fujisawa also told Honda, "I will work with you as a businessman. But when we part, I am not going to end up with a loss. I'm not talking only about money. What I mean is that when we part, I hope I will have gained a sense of satisfaction and accomplishment." At the meeting, the two men must have been trying to outdo each other in painting large, romantic pictures of the future—Honda in technology and Fujisawa in business.

Honda recalls the occasion well. "That was the time of do or die for everybody. When I first saw his face, I liked him. After talking for a little, I thought he was a wonderful guy because he possessed a personality totally different from mine. As we talked, I discovered that he was a romantic man. He was the type who, while having lofty ideas, translated thoughts into action with his own hands. I also felt strongly that he was a man who, if he did not do something himself, would have others do the job based on solid theories. If he had been a man who did nothing but chase dreams, I would not have been impressed."

Fujisawa, on the other hand, says, "I had no special impression. I simply thought, 'Here is Soichiro Honda, with whom I have decided to do business.' " After forming a team they often talked like two enthusiastic youths. And the more they talked, the more excited they became. Through these dialogues, Honda learned about Fujisawa's outlook on life and the knowledge he had gained from books, while Fujisawa learned about Honda's dominant personality and his enthusiasm for technology.

Honda recalls their early partnership as follows: "For example, assuming that reaching the top of Mount Fuji was the ultimate goal, both Fujisawa and I had the same goal. But I took one route, while he took another route because he had a different philosophy and personality. If we had been taking the same route, we might both have been finished off by an unexpected storm. We were able to communicate with each other because we were taking different routes. Fujisawa would say to me, 'I am at such and such a place, and I see a storm coming. So be careful!' Then I would be careful. We had heart-to-heart communication, although we were at different places and acted differently. Yet, we had the same goal of reaching the top of the mountain."

That feeling was certainly mutual, and Fujisawa recalls thinking later, "I had never met a terrific person like him. Nor had I read any novel or history book describing such a man." In Honda, Fujisawa seemed to have discovered a great untapped potential in himself, and he was both shocked and delighted.

Honda was then trying to develop a full-fledged motorcycle that would run much faster than a bicycle fitted with a clip-on engine. Joining the company in March 1947 was Kiyoshi Kawashima (now president of Honda Motor), who had just graduated from the Hamamatsu College of Technology. Honda was sitting at home on the straw mat floor with his legs under the foot warmer when he gave Kawashima his "presidential interview." After a short talk, he decided this was the right man for the job, perhaps because Kawashima was a fellow "speed demon" and wanted to design a high-performance engine.

The first prototype motorcycle was completed in August 1949. A celebration party was held in the office, with all the desks pushed into one corner. President Honda and his twenty employees had reason to be satisfied as they drank home-brewed *sake* and ate sardines and pickles. Someone said, "It's like a dream!" And Honda shouted, "That's it! Dream!" Officially, the motorcycle was called "Dream Type D," and was powered by a 98cc, 2-stroke engine with a maximum output of 3 horsepower.

Honda Technical Research Institute had been reorganized under the name "Honda Motor" in 1948. The following year, Takeo Fujisawa had joined the company as its managing director. From the start, Honda's way of doing business caught him by surprise. Honda spent most of his time at the factory and the research laboratory, teaching plant employees and engineers about technology, while Fujisawa devoted himself to sales and corporate management. Honda felt his life to be most worth living when his hands were covered with grease. But he could not manage alone, so he established a corporate organization. To him, the company was nothing more than a "'temporary building." For Honda's technology to be given the fullest opportunity for growth, Fujisawa did his best to make the "temporary building" a permanent one.

Honda Motor was now producing two types of engines, 50cc and 98cc. The 50cc was fitted to a bicycle by Honda Motor before being sold. The 98cc engine needed a body sturdier than a bicycle, and such a body was being manufactured by a company called

Kitagawa. Honda Motor's distributors placed separate orders for the body with this company and for the engine with Honda Motor, assembling them before sale. Fujisawa discovered a serious flaw in this simple distribution system.

While Honda Motor was delivering 100 engines per month to its distributors, Kitagawa curtailed its production to only 50 to 80 units. Naturally, the engines were in excess supply and Honda Motor faced difficulties in collecting its money. The distributors' payments tended to flow more smoothly to the body maker, and Honda Motor found itself at the mercy of this firm. Fujisawa was surprised that the Honda Motor's sales people were not aware of this production curtailment. Honda's reply was that, "Everybody is having problems," and he then tried to teach Kitagawa how to make better motorcycle bodies. Fujisawa was flabbergasted at Honda's behavior, which was tantamount to aiding the enemy.

When production of the Dream Type D started, Fujisawa planned to make it a strategic item in the company's expansion to Tokyo. He told the distributors that, "If you want to sell the Dream, we will not provide you with bare engines. And if you continue to do business with Kitagawa, we will continue to sell you our engines, but not the Dream." In other words, if they wanted to sell the Dream, they had to become exclusive distributors by cutting off their relations with the body manufacturer. This was an agonizing decision for Honda Motor's distributors, because Kitagawa's smart-looking pipe-frame motorcycles mounted with the Honda Motor engine were more popular than the Dream. Much confusion ensued, and some of the distributors even threatened their tormentor, Fujisawa, with knives.

This drastic measure taken by Fujisawa resulted in the loss of some distributors. But all was not lost, for as a certain number of distributors dropped out, open territories were created. As the company was following the principle of having one distributor in each territory, Fujisawa tried to fill these territories with new Dream dealers loyal to Honda Motor. The number of distributors, which had stood at around twenty, increased gradually to thirty and later to forty.

Today in Japan, motorcycles are marketed through both distributors and dealers. A distributor has an exclusive franchise in a given territory, and engages only in direct sales to retail dealers. This double-tier system started because only a small number of motorcycles were sold in Japan, and each dealer had customers in a very small territory and on an extremely small scale. This created the need for a distributor to control and coordinate these small dealers. The distributor not only sells motorcycles to its dealers, but also maintains large inventories on their behalf, and engages in a variety of other activities, such as giving driving safety instruction to customers and helping them obtain driving permits. Thus, the distributors are quite influential in the marketing of motorcycles, and also provide the manufacturer with information about what customers are looking for and what new models should be developed. In this regard, the method of selling motorcycles in Japan is quite different from that in the United States. Manufacturers in the United States sell their products directly to retail dealers, without going through distributors, because the scale is large, the dealers have sufficient capital and are capable of conducting business independently.

In March 1950, the Tokyo sales office of Honda Motor was established to serve as a controlling body for distributors in the Tokyo area. That autumn, the company purchased a sewing machine plant in Tokyo and remodeled it into a motorcycle factory. It was at this new plant that full-scale production of the Dream Type D got underway. The major problem was that the popularity of this model fell considerably below expectations. There were, however, some encouraging inquiries about the company's 50cc clip-on engine from abroad. In December 1950, Honda and Fujisawa invited a foreign visitor to Hamamatsu for a tour of their plant, and in the evening held a party for him. The next morning, it was discovered that in the course of the party, their guest had become sick from drinking too much *sake* and while throwing up in the toilet had dropped his false teeth. In those days, very few houses in places like Hamamatsu had modern plumbing systems, and the false teeth fell into a pile of filth. When Honda heard this, he immediately agreed to retrieve them. Taking off all of his clothes, he slowly climbed down the toilet. After a while, his fingers touched something hard. He triumphantly carried the teeth into the bath and carefully washed them as well as his body. Honda called a celebration party that same morning, bringing in *geisha* and *sake*. Always the clown, he held the false teeth in his mouth and danced, as the foreign visitor and the *geisha* roared with laughter.

When Fujisawa heard this story later, he literally shivered. "What would I have done in a situation like that?" he asked himself. "In the first place, money would have solved the whole problem without his going to that kind of trouble. But that man does not use money to motivate people. Besides, he even danced with those false teeth in his mouth to brighten the atmosphere. And that wasn't all. He proved that the teeth were sanitary. I couldn't have done that. He just beats me."

Recalling this incident, Honda says, "That was the embodiment of my belief that the man at the top of an organization must personally do things that others would hate to do most. You don't have to do it all the time; you must do it only once and that's the best way to make your subordinates follow you. The man holding the top position has the responsibility to be always prepared to do things that are most repulsive to others."

When the Dream was introduced to the Japanese market, few roads in that country were paved. As one cynic put it, "Japan has no roads, although there are plans for many." In the winter, the snow-covered roads often turned to mud. Because the Type D had only a narrow gap between the wheel and the fender, mud would get clogged there. This was its greatest weakness and the distributors would always bid farewell to Honda Motor in the autumn, saying, "We'll see you again next spring." In 1951, there was an unusually heavy spring snow and that year the future of the Dream looked as bleak as the gray April skies.

The Dream Type D was a sturdy motorcycle. Bikes with pipe frames were regarded as better-looking, but their shortcoming was that they broke easily at weld points. The Type D had a pressed body with reinforcements in places where stress was a problem. Because of the lack of popularity of the Type D, Fujisawa asked Honda to develop a new motorcycle. In those days, 4-stroke, side-valve engines were a common feature in most motorcycles. Fujisawa said to Honda, "The other bikes make pleasant sounds, while our 2-stroke engines make unpleasant, high-pitched noises. That's why ours are not selling." To this, Honda simply replied, "Theirs are no good." But he did, in fact, have a plan.

One morning in May 1951, Honda picked Fujisawa up at his house and drove him to the factory. The normally talkative Honda was silent as he drove. On arriving at the Tokyo plant, the two went to the designing room. On top of an old desk was a pencil drawing of an engine. Honda appeared to be in a trance as he explained the design to Fujisawa, who has never forgotten the expression on his partner's face. Next to them stood Kiyoshi Kawashima, who had made the drawing. It was the Type E engine, a 4-stroke, overhead valve (OHV) power plant displacing 146cc and having an output of 5.5 horsepower. It was a pioneering effort, because it was not for another ten years that OHV engines were popular among other motorcycle companies.

The testing of the Dream Type E was conducted on July 15 during a heavy rainstorm. Kawashima was the test rider, and he was to run the bike from Hamamatsu to the top of the Hakone mountains. Honda and Fujisawa followed him in a Buick driven by Honda. The Type E motorcycle left the automobile far behind, and was able to reach the mountain peak in top gear. "This is the first time I have felt happy being behind someone else," said Honda. When the two arrived at the summit overlooking Lake Ashi, Kawashima was already resting. There were very few motorcycles at the time that could climb such mountains without difficulty; the Type E made it at a remarkable average speed of 70 kph (about 45 mph) without any mechanical problems.

At the Tokyo factory, production of the Type E replaced that of the Type D. With the new model fast gaining popularity, the plant became almost chaotic. When an application was filed with the government for the construction of the Tokyo factory with a planned production of 300 units per month, officials of the Ministry of International Trade and Industry were suspicious, saying, "Are you really serious about such large-scale production?" Some even thought that Honda was beefing up the production plans only to obtain a larger allocation of gasoline. To the chagrin of Honda's critics, production at the plant increased rapidly, eventually reaching a monthly level of 900 units.

Honda Motor had no organizational structure at the time, nor did it have a sufficient number of workers. The company ran help-wanted ads in newspapers almost every day and hired nearly everyone who applied. They were assigned to the assembly lines from their first day. A worker who had entered the company two days previously might already be teaching newcomers. As the number of employees was only slightly over one hundred, Honda and Fujisawa knew every worker's ability and character. In those days, they could issue orders directly and know they would be carried out by the "community" of employees.

Honda himself often came down to the factory floor, wrench in hand, to help tighten bolts. A bolt that had been tightened by a young worker made two more turns when Honda did it himself. "You damned fool. This is how you're supposed to tighten bolts," shouted Honda as he hit his employee over the head with the wrench. Shouting in public was his way of education, and everyone became nervous at the mere sight of Honda holding a wrench. But his style of education seemed to have the desired effect, and it was through this "thundering method" that many Honda employees learned how to build motorcycles.

Honda Motor did not yet have adequate machinery and had to buy most of its parts and components from outside suppliers. As production increased rapidly, procurement became a great problem. Honda's mind was a repository of drawings for all sorts of components. As required, he would put the design on paper and send a young employee to the suppliers with an order to make the component. Even before the first messenger had arrived at the suppliers, Honda would tell another employee, "That first drawing was no good. Here's a new one. Have them follow this drawing instead." The suppliers were understandably upset. And when they asked the messengers when Honda Motor intended to pay, they were told, "Money is something else. Another man will come by to discuss that with you."

As the vehicles rolled off the conveyor lines, they were tested on the street in front of the plant. "If we did that today, we would be accused of noise pollution," admits Honda. The development of the Type E enabled Honda Motor to make a great leap forward beginning in the latter half of 1951. Fujisawa meanwhile kept working on the distribution network. While he was making the rounds of his distributors, one of them once said to him, "I want some new motorcycles. Here's the money. Take it with you." Fujisawa replied, "You send the money to me later." After his return to Tokyo, Fujisawa failed to receive any money, so he stopped delivering motorcycles to the distributor. When the distributor protested, Fujisawa said only that the money had not been received, so the deliveries had been stopped. The distributor panicked and came to Tokyo himself with the money.

Fujisawa told him, "You have been pocketing the money which customers have deposited with you. Who do you think you are? If you want to buy our motorcycles, you must advance me the money you collect from the customers!" This story soon spread to the other distributors. After that, Honda Motor was able to receive money for the Dream in advance.

At the Tokyo sales office, Fujisawa was virtually the only salesman and had little time for collecting money. But with the success of the Type E, money automatically started flowing in from the distributors. Moreover, those distributors who had chosen to do business with Kitagawa now decided they would rather sell the Type E. As the distributor network grew, the Tokyo sales office began to have complete control and started functioning as the corporate headquarters. It is normally the case that when a smaller enterprise grows to this extent, the management starts imitating larger companies by establishing a bureaucratic organizational structure and rigidly planning sales. This, however, tends to make the corporation lose its energy for further growth. For example, such a company tends to appoint more department or section heads than are needed to manage the firm, because the founder is satisfied with his success and issues many fancy titles to his employees to promote their social status. Many small companies are apt to be faced with such a crisis during this phase of their growth. To Fujisawa, Honda appeared to be a man who did not seek quick results. "That man Honda never said anything like that. There was no end to his pursuit of technology. And he possessed a grandiose dream. It was only natural that we had not reached any goal, because the two of us started out with something like a dream. If he had started talking about something like how much profit we would make next year, I probably would have been disappointed, because such talk would imply a concern about his personal income. He was a great person who played the leading role in this drama. So those of us who played supporting roles had to build a grand theater—a corporation—that would suit the leading actor."

One day, a meeting of the board of directors was held at Fuji-sawa's home in Tokyo. After the meeting was over, Fujisawa played a game of *shogi* (Japanese chess) with Honda. One of the board members started complaining to Fujisawa, who quickly became fed up and started shouting in a voice so loud that everyone was astonished. Honda showed no sign of being dis-turbed, but simply kept moving his pieces on the board.

"What a nice guy he is," thought Fujisawa. "He kept playing the game across the board from me. He was not disturbed at all. It looked to me as if he was saying to me, 'You too can shout all you want.' Perhaps that was because the game was not going in his favor."

The year 1950 was a turning point in Japan's postwar history. In June, North Korean forces, in a brilliantly executed surprise at-tack, invaded the Republic of Korea. Washington viewed the situation as a communist threat to the free world and enforced its "containment policy" against the Soviet Union. Parallel to adopt-ing this tough line against Moscow, the United States changed its overall policy toward Japan. Now, instead of being deprived of war capabilities, Japan was to return to the international com-munity and become an important element of the U.S. defense strategy for the Far East. In September 1950, President Harry S Truman issued orders to start preliminary negotiations for separate peace and security treaties with Japan. Prime Minister Shigeru Yoshida represented Japan, and in September 1951 the treaty was signed by Japan and forty-eight other countries. The Soviet Union declined to sign the peace treaty, although they were present at the conference. At the same time, a bilateral security treaty was concluded between Japan and the United States. The peace treaty took effect in April 1952. Japan had regained its independence, thus putting to an end the Occupation period, although under the provisions of the treaty it continued to provide military bases for American forces.

Strong domestic opposition was expressed against signing a peace treaty that did not include the Soviet Union and entering in-to a security treaty with the United States, for fear that Japan might be forced into an international power struggle. An opinion poll conducted shortly after the peace treaty came into force by the *Asahi Shimbun*, a major nationwide daily, showed that near-

The revitalization of Japanese industry was greatly aided by supplying jeeps and military trucks for the Korean War.

General MacArthur argued that the Japanese should be prepared to defend themselves and in June 1950 ordered the establishment of a police reserve force, forerunner of the Self-Defense Force.

ly one-half of the Japanese people either opposed or were critical of the treaty.[9] Public opinion was totally split, causing social uneasiness and political instability.

It was also around this time that the Japanese economy began to show clear signs of recovery. The people were no longer starving, but their living standards remained far lower than before the war. The per capita national income was only about 10 percent of that of the United States. Consumer goods were in short supply; automobiles, electrical appliances, and even the kitchen utensils used by Americans appeared to be symbols of a prospering civilization. These circumstances led the Japanese to work even harder to strengthen the industrial basis of the country.

The damage to the nation's wealth inflicted by World War II represented 25 percent of the gross national assets, not counting damage done to military property. In other words, all the assets accumulated by Japan during the ten years from 1935 to 1945 were lost. After the war, the government, though faced with various constraints by the Occupation forces, gave priority to the reconstruction of production facilities, which it was hoped would lead to higher living standards.

In February 1946, the government froze all individual savings and imposed rigid restrictions on personal spending. This made life all the more miserable, but the Japanese persevered. At the same time, the government adopted the priority production system, under which the entire economy was tightly controlled and top priority was given to increasing production of two basic materials—coal and steel—as a catalyst for the entire economy. For that purpose, the Reconstruction Financing Bank was established in January 1947. Japan faced an acute shortage of capital, and this new bank did not have sufficient funds, either. So, the newly established bank issued bonds, which were purchased by the Bank of Japan, in order to provide huge loans for the production of coal and steel. The Bank of Japan was simply printing money to loan to industry, and this naturally led to run-away inflation. This was a transfer inflation, whereby the people's income was forcibly diverted to finance production facilities. Besides coal and steel, this bank also provided funds to such industries as chemical fertilizers, electric power, shipping, and textiles.

This situation ended with the arrival of Joseph M. Dodge, president of the Detroit Bank, as economic and financial adviser to GHQ. On March 7, 1949, he issued the "Dodge Line," which observed that the Japanese economy was riding on a pair of bamboo stilts, one being American aid and the other domestic subsidies, and that if the stilts were made too long, the economy would fall down and break its neck. The "Dodge Line," aimed at stabilizing the Japanese economy, called for balancing the budget, reducing subsidies and price parities, stopping new loans by the Reconstruction Financing Bank, and adopting a fixed exchange rate of 360 yen to the dollar. At that time, the government was paying subsidies to offset price disparities of coal, fertilizers, and steel. Moreover exchange rates were fixed separately for different commodities and thus constituted an "invisible" subsidy. Under the "Dodge Line," the Japanese economy entered into a rapid deflation, bringing a sudden end to inflation. Another factor behind this shift in the economy was that production in mining and manufacturing industries more than doubled in the three years from 1946, due to a successful implementation of the priority production system.

In May 1949, a mission headed by American economist Carl S. Shoup arrived to study the Japanese taxation system. In September, Shoup issued a recommendation for a new system as a means of supplementing the "Dodge Line." What resulted was a system centering around direct taxes, which still forms the basis of Japan's taxation system today. By 1949, the Japanese economy had achieved a solid foundation for development in the international sphere. With the outbreak of the Korean War the following year, the Japanese economy got a great boost and was then able to overcome the "Dodge deflation" and enter a new era of expansion.

Japan's basic postwar economic policy centered around the fostering of heavy and chemical industries and the promotion of trade. The former was aimed at developing an industrial society capable of competing internationally by strengthening industries that were quite fragile in the prewar years. The latter was to promote exports and earn the foreign exchange needed to purchase the necessary food and raw materials for 100 million people living in a small country with very few natural resources of its own.

This basic policy achieved its initial target and then started to change in the 1970s.

The basis for implementing this policy dates back to the abolition of a controlled economy under the priority production system. The coal industry, which was under the government's direct control in the immediate postwar years, was returned to free enterprise. Electric power generation, which had been controlled by the government before the war, was reorganized to what it is today, with the country divided into nine regions, each with one electric power company that, as a private corporation, handles everything from the generation to the distribution of electricity.

Especially noteworthy is Japan's steel industry. Yahata Iron and Steel was originally set up as a state-run firm and later became semiprivate with the influx of private capital and assumed the name Nippon Steel. After the war, it became a private corporation, and was divided into two companies—Yahata Iron and Steel and Fuji Iron and Steel. (They merged again 1970 and became today's Nippon Steel.) This division gave an added impetus to competition among steelmakers. During World War II, the record for crude steel production in Japan was less than 8 million tons in 1943, when the comparable figure for the United States was 80 million tons. Japanese industrialists were led to believe that this difference in steel production caused Japan to lose the war, and that increasing steel output would be indispensable to the nation's economic development. Yataro Nishiyama, president of Kawasaki Steel, which was still a small-scale steelmaker, revealed a major plan, shortly after the end of the war, to build a huge waterfront integrated steel works in Chiba, east of Tokyo. The project did not get started until 1951 because of strong opposition from the Bank of Japan due to a shortage of funds. Yet, this scheme of building a giant plant by the ocean, with the benefit of reducing the costs of transporting raw materials and products by using ships, has become the foundation of the strong international competitive power of the Japanese steel industry at the present time.

While free competition among private enterprises was a direct result of the "Dodge Line," it was also something that was strongly desired by Japanese industrialists who had the bitter experience of a controlled economy during the war. Thus, Japan followed a path different from that of France, which nationalized banks right after the war, or that of Great Britain, which placed the coal mining industry under the government's control. Japan's path was also in line with its traditional economic policy dating back to the Meiji era.

During the Meiji period the government provided industry with incentives for modernization, because the whole nation was underdeveloped. Early in that period, the Meiji government established the state-run Tomioka textile mill in Gunma Prefecture and made it a model plant by importing machines from France. Later the government sold such state-run industrial facilities to the private sector. For example, the Tomioka textile mill and the Miike Coal Mines (reputed to be the best in Japan) were sold to the Mitsui *zaibatsu*, while the Mitsubishi *zaibatsu* took over Nagasaki Shipbuilding. Milton Friedman, Nobel-prize-winning professor emeritus of economics at Chicago University, states that such emphasis placed on the private sector by the Meiji government played a major role in the modernization of Japan. Viewed differently, this meant that *zaibatsu* were already mature enough to take over those industries from the government.

The separation of capital and management was a characteristic unique to Japan in the *zaibatsu* management. The Mitsubishi *zaibatsu* was an exception, in that the Iwasaki families who ran it had outstanding business skills and expertise inherited from their ancestors, who were successful marine merchants toward the end of the Tokugawa Shogunate period. The owners of the other *zaibatsu*, such as Mitsui and Sumitomo, which came into being in the seventeenth century, had little skill in management, and indeed refrained from getting involved in this area at all. The Sumitomo family "Constitution" states that the head of the family must not directly take command of any business. Those owners unconditionally hired managers recommended by influential people, and never fired them. Any dispute between the owner and the manager was to be settled through the mediation of the man who recommended him to the owner. This was the method by which the *zaibatsu* recruited capable business executives.

After World War II, the *zaibatsu* were dismantled, and GHQ

purged prewar corporate managers for their collaboration with the military. As a result, young people who were inexperienced but filled with new ideas suddenly took over the top corporate executive posts and adopted a path of collective management. In Japanese society, this way of corporate management was most suitable to the people's disposition and gave private enterprise a high degree of vitality.

In April 1951, the Japan Development Bank was established as a government-owned agency for the purpose of strengthening Japan's basic industries, and Ataru Kobayashi was named its first president. A powerful business leader before the war, Kobayashi had always avoided publicity and was a rather mysterious figure, even in government and business circles. However, Prime Minister Yoshida recognized his strong leadership qualities, and the collaboration between these men played an important role in determining the postwar direction of Japan.

Yoshida was a career diplomat during the prewar period and understood the vital importance of Japan's relationship with the United States. Convinced that these two countries should never wage war against each other, he was often persecuted by the military for his liberal views. In 1946, he was named prime minister in recognition of his political leadership and strongly held ideals. Except for a short period between 1947 and 1948, Yoshida remained in office until 1954. This unusually long stay in power allowed him to successfully consolidate the nation's political, social, and economic framework. At the same time, his administration allowed the bureaucrats to have an important voice in government policy-making, a system which continues in Japan today.

Kobayashi, unlike the young business leaders who insisted on modified capitalism, believed that the accumulation of capital was the first step in creating a strong and independent nation. As president of the Japan Development Bank, Kobayashi was in a unique position to serve as a "bridge" between government and business for the purpose of achieving economic development. In this sense, his appointment as the head of the newly created bank was a significant event for the business world.

The Japan Development Bank was a major pipeline supplying government money and foreign capital to certain industries. This government money was initially a domestic counterpart to aid given by the United States, and it can be said that Japan used American assistance effectively for strengthening the industrial base. The Development Bank provided long-term financing for capital expenditures in production facilities, which commercial banks were reluctant to support. Because the commercial banks were still weak, the president of the Japan Development Bank was in a very powerful position. To strengthen the core of the Japanese economy, the bank channeled a major portion of its funds to such basic industries as electric power, steel, and maritime transportation. As a result, the business world in Japan, such as the Federation of Economic Organizations (Keidanren), became a gathering of the leaders of those key industries, which were guided and protected by the government and the bureaucracy.

Commercial banks, meanwhile, were short of funds and therefore had to rely heavily on borrowing from the Bank of Japan. Some of these banks loaned sums in excess of their current deposits. Moreover, commercial banks stepped outside of their traditional function of providing short-term operating money and started making long-term loans for production facilities. Though perhaps an unsound banking practice by Western standards, it was Japan's unique way of providing money for industrial development. The Bank of Japan closely monitored the loans by commercial banks and encouraged them to divert more money to basic rather than consumer goods industries. The method proved successful, and "over loans" disappeared in the process of economic development. But, as a result of this policy, Japan's basic industries today are still heavily indebted to the banks.

In contrast, such industries as automobiles, home electrical appliances, and distribution were not favored by the business and financial leaders. These industries were viewed simply as part of the domestic consumer goods market and of little importance in re-establishing a strong Japanese economy. The companies in these areas therefore had to face stiff competition. Those who survived were the ones with well-developed infrastructures.

By the autumn of 1951, Honda Motor was successfully marketing the Type E but needed all the capital it could get. So the company asked a long-term credit bank for a loan of 5 million yen, mortgaging all its facilities, including the Tokyo plant. "Let's entertain them the best we can tonight," agreed Honda and Fujisawa, and they invited the bankers to a party. Half-intoxicated, the two put on an impromptu comic show. In the wilder days of his youth, Honda had learned songs, dances, and stories from his *geisha* friends. Fujisawa, a great fan of classical music, was also well versed in traditional Japanese *tokiwazu* music. The show these two put on was, by all accounts, hilarious. Their comic cross-talk, interspersed with erotic stories, allowed the bankers and *geisha* alike to feel completely relaxed.

The next day, Fujisawa went to the bank, confident that the loan would be granted. The bankers, however, told him that they could hardly consider such a large request, "because we cannot trust a company run by a couple of clowns." Fujisawa was only able to get 2 million yen. When it was reported that a competitor of Honda Motor was given a loan for 5 million yen, Honda and Fujisawa laughed and agreed that, "We probably clowned too much." In the early 1950s, there were more than two hundred motorcycle manufacturers in Japan. Almost all of them went bankrupt because they could not develop innovative engines. Eventually, the Honda Type E drove them out of business and now there are only four motorcycle manufacturing companies in Japan. Ironically, the same bank that provided the mere 2 million yen loan was to lend Honda Motor 100 million yen five years later.

Obviously, Honda and Fujisawa could not rely on banks and the maximum they could expect from shareholders in terms of increased equity would be 10 million yen. Honda Motor could not offer its stocks for public subscription because they were held by a very small group, including the two founders and the other directors of the company, and thus were not listed on any stock exchange. In November 1952, Honda Motor increased its paid-up capital by 9 million yen to a total of 15 million yen. It was an agonizing job for Fujisawa to assemble the funds that were needed. Honda Motor was then building a small number of 50cc engines which were mounted on bicycles. The engines were wrapped in straw mats before delivery, but they looked ugly because the carburetor and exhaust pipe stuck out of the wrapping. Mrs.

Fujisawa said to Honda, "It looks so ugly that I'm reminded of the guts coming out of a chicken. Can't you do anything about it?" "But, madam, that's a machine and I think it's attractive," replied Honda. "But I don't like it," she countered. Overhearing this conversation, Fujisawa had the idea of making these engines more compact. His strategy was not only to make a smaller engine, but also to pack it in a cardboard box for shipment. Transporting any machine in a cardboard box was unheard of at the time. Honda started work immediately on just such a compact design.

This attraction to new ideas went back to Honda's childhood days. When he was in the third or fourth grade, his mother gave him a new sash to go with his kimono on the occasion of the emperor's birthday. At school, his classmates started teasing him, saying, "Hey, how come you wear a girl's sash?"

"I still remember that very well," recalls Honda. "What I was wearing was my mother's blue sash. I was angry because I could not understand why there had to be different colors for men and for women." Even after World War II, he was regarded as a strange person because he used to wear gaudy red shirts instead of the usual white shirt and dark business suit. Honda believed that, "As long as you don't cause trouble or make other people feel unpleasant, you should be permitted to wear clothes of any color you want. This way of thinking is important for inventors and artists. Unless they have the courage and determination to break with established ideas, they cannot expect to do a good job."

Honda thought about product design constantly. When a good idea came to him in his sleep, he would wake up and take notes in the middle of the night. And if the horn blown by the evening noodle vendor distracted him, he would send his wife to buy all the vendor's noodles so he would no longer be bothered by the noise.

What emerged from these struggles and dreams was the Cub Type F. The prototype was completed in March 1952. This engine displaced 50cc, the same as the early model Type A that clipped onto bicycles; but the output had been increased from 0.5 hp to 1.2 hp. Attached to a bicycle, the Type F engine ran well, and its design was quite fancy for the time, with a red casing and white gas tank. Fujisawa lost no time sending a letter to bicycle dealers all over Japan, saying, "After the Russo-Japanese War, when virtually no one in our country knew anything about bicycles or was able to repair even a flat tire, your ancestors had the courage to undertake the retail business of imported bicycles. And their courage is the source of your prosperity today. But your customers in this postwar period are longing for vehicles with engines. Honda Motor has just developed such engines. If you are interested in our products, we hope to hear from you."

Japan at that time had less than 400 motorcycle distributors, and the various manufacturers all competed for their patronage. What caught Fujisawa's attention were the 55,000 bicycle retail outlets located throughout the country. Japan was beginning to look for something new, and Fujisawa's letter provided it. His feelings were a mixture of expectation and unease as he waited for replies. He did not have to wait long. Soon he was swamped with 30,000 letters. The company was able to establish a distribution network of some 13,000 dealers virtually overnight. This was a revolution in the distribution of two-wheeled vehicles.

The prototype engine was completed in March, and by April money from the bicycle dealers was already pouring into the bank in the form of advance payments. This was a big gamble, because although Honda Motor had established trust among its dealers with the Dream, it had yet to start mass-producing the Cub. At the Hamamatsu plant, every effort was made to step up production, and by June Honda Motor was able to make an initial delivery of 1,500 units. The Cub was an immediate success. Some of the dealers came to Honda Motor with large sums of money—2 or 3 million yen—asking to buy out the remaining stock.

The Cub opened a new market among low-income groups and generated good business. But Fujisawa's real aim was to create separate networks for different models, for distributors wholesaled any type of motorcycle manufactured by a certain company. Thus, if a new product was given to an established dealer, the manufacturer could not expect to receive advance payments, because the dealers were busy trying to sell previous products. This led Fujisawa to the idea of setting up one dealer network for each model, a novel idea at the time. It was only much later that major automakers like Toyota and Nissan set up similar schemes of franchising separate products to separate networks. Fujisawa was trying to set up many small pipelines to customers through the distributors. However, some of the more powerful distributors of the Dream Type E soon got together and demanded access to the Cub as well, and a bitter confrontation with Fujisawa ensued.

Production of the Dream was switched from the Tokyo plant to the Shirako plant, located in what is now Wako City, Saitama Prefecture. The plant had been abandoned when Honda Motor bought it in March 1952, but it was quickly remodeled and already in operation by May of the same year. The new plant was ten times the size of the Tokyo factory, and the production volume of the Type E increased dramatically. The old Tokyo plant was made into an engine training school for bicycle dealers, and this in turn served to popularize knowledge about motorcycles throughout Japan.

After successfully establishing separate dealer networks for different models, Fujisawa adopted the strategy of creating modernized factories out of small, outdated plants. He thought that by building modern factories and turning out new models, the networks for all models would be strengthened, thus promoting the rapid growth of the company. And he was convinced that Honda's technologies would live up to that expectation So, in January 1953, the company purchased 100,000 square meters of land, ten times larger than the Shirako plant, in the town of Yamato (now Wako City) and began construction of the Yamato plant (which is now called the Wako plant). In December of the same year, Honda Motor purchased 66,000 square meters of government-owned land in Hamamatsu City and started building the Aoi plant.

The manufacturing industries in Japan were now getting back on their feet, but plant equipment was old-fashioned. Honda Motor decided to import the most modern high-precision machines and equipment from advanced countries in the West. In November 1952, Honda went to the United States for the dual purpose of seeing American industry and purchasing machine tools. The tools started arriving in Japan the following summer, and were installed at the Yamato, Aoi, and Shirako plants. The price of these imported tools totaled 450 million yen. Between the spring of 1952 and the spring of 1954, Honda Motor's total capital expenditure for building the three plants and buying machines from abroad came to a colossal 1.5 billion yen before depreciation. As a result, the net increase in Honda's fixed assets after depreciation was slightly more than 1 billion yen. In order to appreciate what this figure means, one would have to make a comparison with firms like Toyota and Nissan. According to Toyota Motor Company's official report on securities, the net increase in its fixed assets between September 1951 and November 1953 was less than 1 billion yen after depreciation. The comparable figure for Nissan Motor Company between September 1951 and September 1953 was a shade over 300 million yen. It can be seen from these figures that it was quite unprecedented for a motorcycle manufacturer like Honda Motor to make such an enormous expenditure during a similar time frame. An automobile plant naturally requires far greater investment than a motorcycle factory. In other words, Honda Motor was emerging as a company with modernized production facilities long before Toyota and Nissan launched full-scale investment in comparable plants and equipment.

Where did the money come from that enabled the small postwar firm of Honda Motor to carry out capital expenditures far exceeding those of Toyota and Nissan—both companies with a much longer history? The secret was Fujisawa's unusual strategy of setting up separate dealer networks for different models. The Dream was originally sold to distributors with cash payments in advance, but later the consignment sale system was adopted. Honda Motor received promissory notes, which were deposited with the Mitsubishi Bank. With the Cub, the advance payment system was maintained. The Benly was a high performance motorcycle, which first went on sale in August 1953. And the Juno was the world's first scooter utilizing polyester resin. Introduced in January 1954, it had revolutionary performance and design. Those who wished to become exclusive distributors of the Juno had to put up guarantee money, sometimes as much as 10 million yen. It was through these four pipelines that money flowed to Honda Motor to cover capital expenditures.

In 1954, Fujisawa was aiming for a monthly turnover of 1 billion yen, comparable to that of Nissan and Toyota at the time. Here is what he had in mind: "If sales grow rapidly, we will be able to collect money quickly. And if we use promissory notes for payment of what we purchase, we will have operating capital at least on a temporary basis and improve our cash position. Assuming that we sell 1 billion yen's worth per month and our payment is deferred for five months, our income during that time would come to 5 billion yen. And assuming that it takes 1.4 months to collect money for our sales, our accounts receivable would be 1.4 billion yen. When the expenses of 800 million yen are subtracted, the balance will come to around 2.8 billion yen. Even if we spend 1.5 billion yen for capital equipment, the risk will not be great, and we will be all right." Indeed, during the latter half of 1952, when Cub production was increasing rapidly, Honda Motor's cash situation was such that it always had 200 to 300 million yen deposited with the Kyobashi Branch Office of the Mitsubishi Bank. Honda Motor started doing business with the branch office when it moved to Tokyo in 1950. The company had borrowed nothing from the bank, but was rather a depositor of large sums of money. In 1953, the Mitsubishi Bank invited Honda and Fujisawa to their corporate headquarters for lunch, saying that they wanted to have a talk. Fujisawa went dressed in a suit, but Honda wore a jacket and a workman's cap, much to the astonishment of the executives of this prestigious financial institution. They were taken to an exquisite Victorian-style reception room in the bank's headquarters. Representing the bank were Executive Vice President Mitsuo Ogasawara, Executive Director Fukuzo Kawahara (who later joined Honda Motor and is now its special advisor), and Kyobashi Branch Office General Manager Koichi Kataoka.

At lunch Honda and Fujisawa put on their usual clown show, but this time without any risqué jokes. The bankers laughed, but they also asked some tough questions. As far as the motor business was concerned, Honda and Fujisawa seemed to have all the right answers. The bankers were swayed more by their enthusiasm than by their sense of humor. One banker said, "I think you have an outstanding business going for you. I presume, of course, that you will eventually hand over the company to your sons." The two replied, much to his surprise, "We have no such thought whatsoever." This philosophy greatly impressed the bankers, and became instrumental in Honda Motor's gaining the unequivocal trust of the bank.

From the very beginning, Honda and Fujisawa had been telling their employees that Honda Motor did not belong to the Honda family. "This is only natural, because Honda Motor is a public company and is operating with stockholders' money. If the company belonged to the Honda or the Fujisawa family, who would have the motivation to work for the company!" said Honda. This philosophy was heartily welcomed by the employees. It was true that both Honda and Fujisawa would shout and force them to do difficult tasks. Yet, because of this declaration, the employees were motivated to work hard for the prosperity of their own organization, not for the founders' families. Honda and Fujisawa were of the same mind in administering the corporation, and they were categorically against a hereditary system of management. These factors served to eliminate any suspicion that these two men were working solely for the good of their families. Because of the high intellectual standard of the employees and a strong sense of equality within Japanese corporations, to exclude the opportunity of promotion to top executive positions would often lead to a weakening of corporate vitality. One of the key factors in maintaining the energetic spirit of a company is to let the employees know that anyone, if they have ability, can be promoted—even to the chief executive post. It was in this sense that Honda Motor, from the start, chose a path of corporate youthfulness and vitality.

Sales and profits

(in millions of yen)

	Mar., 1950, through Feb., 1951	Mar., 1951, through Feb., 1952	Mar., 1952, through Feb., 1953	Mar., 1953, through Feb., 1954
Net sales	82	330	2,438	7,729
Ordinary profits	4	13	100	514

Fujisawa's dream of monthly sales totaling 1 billion yen was materializing. During the year ending in February 1952, net sales stood at 330 million yen, increasing to 2,438 million yen the following year, and to 7,729 million yen in the year that ended in February 1954. Honda Motor's stock began to be traded over the counter in January 1954, making it a true modern enterprise.

When he first met Honda, Fujisawa promised that he would

come up with the money to finance Honda's technologies. And now he felt totally satisfied—the dream had come true. What he did not know at the time was that a major crisis was about to devastate the company, a crisis that would push Honda Motor near bankruptcy.

4

The Union Cometh . . .

In late May 1953, leaders from Honda Motor's Shirako plant met at a nearby community hall to form an in-company union; also in attendance were organizers from outside labor organizations. Heated discussions took place. Some favored immediate action, saying that if the management found out what they were doing, they would all be fired. Others advised a more cautious approach. Late that night, they finally agreed to take immediate action. The next day, a vote was taken among all the workers, and a general meeting for establishing the union was held on June 27. Many outside sympathizers, waving red flags, converged near the Shirako plant, but the Honda Motor workers asked them to stay away. Fujisawa was invited to the inaugural meeting of the new union, where he told the workers, "I will work hard, and I expect you to work hard also. Let us move forward, following our own judgment."

Until that time, Soichiro Honda had never really thought about labor problems, nor was he experienced in dealing with unions—so the idea came at first as a great shock. And Fujisawa had to ask those with experience, "What *is* a union like?" He recalls that after talking to them, "I came to understand that it is better to have a union. Yet, essentially, the relationship between a company and the union is one of confrontation. They cannot basically be made into one. At the same time, we must also understand that confrontation can take many different forms. I then decided that the most important thing at Honda Motor is for the company to seek to come as close to the workers as possible, and thus to create a human relationship of mutual trust."

The labor movement started in Japan following the solidification of capitalism in the wake of the 1894–95 Sino-Japanese War. There were many labor disputes during the Russo-Japanese War of 1904–05, World War I, and also during the recessions that followed these conflicts. Unions were not protected by law, and some of the labor movements were harshly suppressed by the government.

Starting in 1938, each company and factory began to establish a government-sponsored *Sangyo Hokoku-kai* (meaning "Patriotic Labor Organization" and abbreviated to *Sanpo*). In November 1940, a nationwide federation of *Sanpo* was formed under the banner of the Great Japan Patriotic Labor Organization. This marked the complete dissolution of all labor unions for the duration of the war period.

The first labor demonstration held in April 1901 was heckled by police and rightists.

A demonstration organized by *Sodomei* in Tokyo, October, 1921.

Communist Party members being led off to prison for violating the Peace Preservation Law in the mid-1930s.

The Occupation forces strongly encouraged the establishment of unions, and as a result they were organized at almost every company and plant starting in the very early days of the postwar era. In October 1945, all political prisoners were freed, the Communist Party was legalized for the first time in Japan's history, and in November the Japan Socialist Party was re-established. The government then enacted measures to protect unions and the right to organize. With this new freedom, the labor movement flourished, and by the end of 1946 there were 17,266 unions with a combined membership of 4,925,000, representing an estimated 41.5 percent of Japan's total work force.

In August 1946, two major nationwide labor federations were established: the 850,000 member *Sodomei* (the Japan Federation of Labor) and the 1,630,000 member *Sanbetsu* (the Congress of Industrial Labor Organizations). *Sodomei* was a moderate group which usually cooperated with management and was supported by the Socialist Party, while *Sanbetsu* was a militant organization strongly influenced by the communists. Just as before the war, the labor movement in Japan was thus divided into two factions, with some neutral unions caught in between.

As the cold war between the United States and the Soviet Union intensified, criticism against militant action mounted even within *Sanbetsu*, and in February 1948 *Mindo* (the Democratization League) was formed with the aim of opposing Communist Party control and of democratizing labor movements. Following a major recession in 1949, Japan was plagued by labor unrest and strikes as the government and private enterprises started firing workers. In virtually every labor dispute, unions were the losers. Moreover, in the summer of 1950, the Occupation authorities purged the Communist leaders, dismissing more than 12,000 Communist Party members and activists. The Communist influence over the Japanese labor movement was thus dramatically reduced.

Generally speaking, the labor situation in the 1950s was characterized by a strong confrontation between labor and management. This confrontation was not the classic class struggle between capital and labor. The "capitalist" (in the Marxist sense of the term) was no longer in existence after the dissolution of the *zaibatsu*. And corporate executives, except for a handful of entrepreneurs, were usually no more than former wage earners and representatives of their employees. These corporate managers worked to promote capital accumulation with a view to furthering their companies, while the leaders of the inner circles of business were engaged in expanding what is known in Marxism as "total capital formation" to develop the economy as a whole. This caused discontent and labor disputes among the work force, who feared a revitalization of the prewar financial cliques and monopolistic capital that had led Japan into the war. (It should be noted that even today, "capitalists" in the true sense of the word have not returned to the Japanese scene. Even entrepreneurs who founded their own companies no longer hold large portions of the equity, and have thus become "managers" rather than "owners" of the enterprises.)

In July 1950, *Sohyo* (the General Council of Japanese Labor Unions) was formed with 2,760,000 members, which included many unions that had broken away from *Sodomei* and *Sanbetsu* as well as some belonging to *Mindo*. Unlike *Sodomei*, *Sohyo* emphasized political struggle, but was basically geared to cooperating with management and supported the Japan Socialist Party. After the peace treaty took effect in April 1952, the labor movements in Japan began to take an increasingly anti-American stand, claiming that Japan had regained independence in name only and that in fact the nation was totally subordinate to the United States. Under the slogan of "true independence for the Japanese people," labor organizations launched a series of sometimes violent demonstrations against American military bases in Japan. A postwar recession spread throughout the nation at the end of the Korean War in 1953, and there were many labor disputes for wage increases in such industries as steel, coal, pulp and paper, automobiles, and textiles.

The greatest problem facing Honda Motor at the time was not the union, but its customers. By 1954, consumers were no longer satisfied with the type of transportation provided by the Cub's auxiliary clip-on engine. The Benly motorbike was unpopular because of irritating noises from the gears and tappets. And to make matters worse, the Juno scooter developed problems that resulted in many complaints from purchasers. The smart-looking body, made from polyester resin, was the Juno's major selling point, but was also its weakness. Because the engine was enclosed, serious overheating occurred. The customers were also complaining about the Dream Type E, which was the mainstay of the company's product line. The cylinder capacity had recently been increased from 200cc (already raised from the original 146cc) to 225cc in the hope that sales would improve in the spring, but this improvement in performance only caused new headaches.

Soichiro Honda literally turned pale when he saw the large unsold stockpiles of products that he loved so much. His young engineers maintained that the root of the Type E's problem was increasing the cylinder capacity of an engine that had originally been designed for 146cc to 225cc. Honda, stubborn as usual, refused to budge from his feeling that something was wrong with the carburetor. Meanwhile, Takeo Fujisawa was at a loss over the problem of money. "This is the type of agony that every corporate executive must face at least once," he told himself. Yet, he often had nightmares about the company's checks bouncing.

Honda Motor, which had started out as little more than a shack, began building modern production facilities during 1952 and 1953. The funds came from temporary manipulations—the early recovery of money for products sold followed by a delay in making outstanding payments. In effect, it was a policy of trying to keep warm next to someone else's fire. The catastrophe which struck the company in 1954 was inevitable. Honda Motor's target for that year was a monthly turnover of 1 billion yen, with capital expenditures to be carried out by temporary manipulations. In fact, the turnover during the twelve months from March 1954 to February 1955 totaled 5,979 million yen, and the monthly sales dipped to 500 million yen. Fujisawa even considered declaring bankruptcy and decided to tell Mitsubishi Bank that the company

Sales and profits

(in millions of yen)

	Mar., 1953, through Feb., 1954	Mar., 1954, through Feb., 1955	Mar., 1955, through Feb., 1956	Mar., 1956, through Feb., 1957	Mar., 1957, through Feb., 1958	Mar., 1958, through Feb., 1959
Net sales	7,729	5,979	5,525	7,882	9,784	14,188
Ordinary profits	514	68	186	395	507	1,157

could be placed in receivership. What he had in mind was to present the bank with all the company shares owned by Honda and Fujisawa, and, if necessary, those owned by others who had become company directors since the founding. Honda Motor's shares, even if it had gone bankrupt, would have been valuable, because the company owned extensive modern production facilities and equipment.

The worst was averted, however. The union, learning of Honda Motor's plight, made an appeal to its members in April, saying, "Let's overcome these problems through the powerful unity of the union members, so that we will be able to demand greater rights for all of us who work at Honda Motor!" In a special statement, the union chairman demanded that "the management seek the union members' cooperation in good faith." The management responded positively, and at the same time sought the union's assistance in this emergency situation. As a result of this agreement, labor and management worked together at the Shirako plant to step up production of the 200cc Dream. This special program to make and sell the old 200cc type engine continued from April 20 to May 8, during which time the workers took no days off and sometimes worked all night. On April 27, a week after the program was launched, Honda phoned Fujisawa in a jovial mood, "I had a dream last night. In that dream, I changed the carburetor, and an engine started running and wouldn't stop. Now I know that the basic problem is in the carburetor." Honda lost no time in visiting Mikuni Kogyo, a carburetor manufacturer in Odawara, where he tested a new carburetor and at last solved the problem with the Dream Type E. As the better-performing 225cc Dream was marketed, sales of the 200cc version started to sag and became a burden to the company. In response to this unforeseen situation, Honda Motor was then forced to launch a "special production curtailment program."

Although the support of Mitsubishi Bank had been obtained, the deadline for settling promissory notes was fast approaching. The company had issued these notes to cover a major portion of their 1.5 billion yen expenditure and for payment of components purchased from subcontractors. Late in May, Fujisawa met with some three hundred subcontractors to explain the difficulties his company was facing and to ask for a deferment of payment. He told them that because of the production curtailment, future orders would be drastically reduced, that the company would pay only 30 percent for the orders that had already been placed and for those to be placed in the future, and that no more promissory notes would be issued. What he was saying, in effect, was that he wanted parts and components to be delivered so production would not come to a halt, but he did not see how Honda Motor could pay for them. When the subcontractors finally agreed to these unreasonable demands, Fujisawa was immensely relieved. Even so, the company was barely able to honor its outstanding promissory notes with the cooperation of the subcontractors and a 200 million yen loan from Mitsubishi Bank.

A major trial for the union came in the course of its negotiations for the year-end bonus in 1954. Although Honda Motor's financial crisis was over, the management was in no position to accede to the union's demand, and offered to pay 5,000 yen per employee across the board. The union leaders demanded a collective bargaining session with Fujisawa, who replied that he would rather have a dialogue with the entire union membership of the Shirako and Yamato plants. The union officials insisted on collective bargaining, claiming that they represented all their members. Through the mediation of Soichiro Honda, the union finally agreed to Fujisawa's formula.

Tension mounted for Fujisawa as he appeared before the 1,600 members of the union, for he thought that failure this time would ruin labor management relations. The union chairman asked him, "What do you think of the 5,000 yen per head offer you are making to us?" Fujisawa replied candidly, "The offer is so low I think it's ridiculous. It is our fault that the situation has become such that we had to make such a low offer. Even if we pay you more now, in the event the company goes bankrupt later as a result, we will be blamed for not working hard enough. I expect that our products will start selling well around next March, and I propose to open a new round of bargaining negotiations at that time." This was greeted with thunderous applause from the floor, and ended the negotiations for the year-end bonus. When Fujisawa met with Honda later, they agreed that they had an obligation to live up to that applause.

A tragic labor dispute had taken place at the Amagasaki Steel

Co. in the spring of that year. While the union was preparing its demand for a wage hike, the company proposed on March 29 that, as a means of coping with mounting deficits, production be curtailed and wages slashed by 15 percent. This "reconstruction" plan was interpreted by the union as a malignant offensive on the part of capital, and the union officially turned it down on April 9. The strike escalated gradually, further aggravating the company's bad performance. On April 16, management came up with a new proposal for further reducing production and firing 381 workers. Supported by other unions and local communities, the union responded with an all-out strike. On June 1, the company's checks started bouncing, and the management hit a total impasse. This forced the union to call off the strike on June 25 and accept the company's proposal. Production was resumed by some 1,400 workers who had not been fired, but the company still went bankrupt. All the workers lost their jobs and the union was dissolved on July 5. This dispute undeniably had a major psychological impact on Honda Motor's union members.

The company was able to overcome the 1954 crisis through the concessions made by the union and subcontractors. The burdens on the subcontractors reached about 2.1 billion yen—around 1.5 billion yen in the form of reduced orders and nearly 600 million yen in unpaid bills. Because of this great sacrifice, the management had no choice but to be stringent with its workers when it came to bonus payments. After 1955, labor–management relations began to worsen. In the negotiations for the summer bonus of 1955, agreement was reached with the corporate head office and Hamamatsu plant workers, but those at the Shirako and Yamato plants resisted strongly. Union leaders issued instructions to the members such as, "Take all the days off you are entitled to," and, "Refuse to work overtime indefinitely." Four members of the union resorted to sit-down tactics on a water tank. Since the formation of the union, rank-and-file members had slowly lost interest in union activities. As a result, union leadership tended to be concentrated among a handful of activists, who were thought to have ties with leftist groups or outside organizations. The confrontation between union and management over the summer bonus of 1955 was bitter and emotional.

Honda stayed away from the labor problem, because he thought, "I have no role to play. If I did anything, that would ruin everything." Until now, Honda had devoted himself solely to technical fields, increasing profits, and making the company bigger. He got angry with workers who played baseball on the plant grounds, saying to himself, "In collective bargaining, they complain about having to work too hard. But when it comes to playing baseball, they do it until they become completely exhausted, even though baseball does not bring a single yen to them. What kind of men are they?" But then he thought, "I must recognize that man achieves the highest degree of efficiency when he plays. If someone says he works out of loyalty to the company, he is a damned liar. Everyone must work for himself. Even I work because I like working. I must create a workshop where everybody will enjoy working."

In the West, the prime mover for social development has long been an individual motivation to work for oneself. As pointed out by psychiatrist Takeo Doi, in a society such as Japan one will quite often come across examples of "dependency relationships."[10] For example, within a corporation an individual may have a desire to work for the sake of his own happiness. If he says that explicitly, his loyalty to the organization may be questioned, and he might be accused of damaging the harmony among his colleagues. Recent college graduates no longer hesitate to say publicly that they will work for their own good, for this "me" generation has acquired a taste for independence. Yet, when they become members of an organization, they will still tend to work hard for the good of the company.

This social reality, which is of overriding importance in any discussion of Japanese work habits, has its roots both in the traditional culture of Japan and in the educational system. The Occupation forces imposed an American system of single-track, co-educational schools on Japan, thus widening the access to higher education for a broad range of the population. In 1947, a new school system was established: six years in primary school, three in junior high school, three in senior high school, and four in university, the first nine years being compulsory. After finishing four years at a university, the students could go to graduate school or after completing three years at a senior high school, they could attend a junior college for several years to gain practical and vocational training.

Under this system, which still exists today, the number of those receiving higher education increased drastically. As of 1981, a total of 94 percent (93 percent male and 95 percent female) of those who finished compulsory education went on to senior high school. Moreover, the percentage of adolescents going on to higher educational institutions such as universities and junior colleges soared from 24 percent in 1970 to 38 percent (42 percent male and 33 percent female) in 1980. This comes close to the 45 percent for the United States (1975), and surpasses the 22 percent for Britain (1977), 26 percent for France (1979), and 23 percent for West Germany (1978). This high ratio in Japan is attributable to a decrease in the number of children per family and to the growing affluence of the Japanese people. Of more fundamental importance is the fact that in Japan unless one graduates from a good university, it is not easy to get a good job. Government agencies and major private corporations hire only new and usually male graduates, and it is virtually impossible to switch to a better organization later, if, upon graduation, employment is begun at a second-class company. Hence the competition to get into a good university is frantic, and this in turn serves to increase the percentage of those going into higher education.

Many Japanese mothers become "education mamas," supervising the education of their children, especially sons, from kindergarten—with the ultimate aim of getting them into good universities. Many pupils are sent to private institutions for supplementary study in addition to regular classroom education, and find themselves in the notorious university "entrance exam hell." Because of this severe competition, Japanese school students outclass most, if not all, of their foreign counterparts in international math and science tests. And while in the United States the results of scholastic aptitude tests began deteriorating in the 1970s, such a phenomenon has yet to appear in Japan.

Professor Ezra F. Vogel, of Harvard University, says that competition to get into good universities has served to promote the self-confidence of the Japanese people.[11] In Japan, however, this phenomenon is regarded as the culmination of all social evils. There is no denying that, because of this "entrance exam hell," children are forced to concentrate on simply memorizing what they learn, resulting in the loss of creative thinking.

According to Professor Chie Nakane of the University of Tokyo, there has also been a decline in Japanese paternal authority, which she relates to a decline in the influence of Confucian ethics, originally imported from China. Confucianism underwent a transformation during the Tokugawa period for political reasons, and emphasis was placed on the predominance of men over women and on master–servant relationships. During those feudal years, this transformation was reflected in female obedience to the males in their family and local feudal lords' loyalty to the Tokugawa shogun. This type of Confucianism was also emphasized during World War II, once again for political reasons, as the moral basis of loyalty to the emperor and the waging of war in his name. Even during the feudal age, however, Confucianism was influential only among the elite samurai class in larger cities. In remote countryside areas, Japan's indigenous culture remained strong, and women had greater position and power than men both in the family and in agriculture and fishery.

Immediately after Japan lost the war, Confucianism was abandoned as "old ethics," and the "female society" started regaining power. According to Professor Nakane, this is indicative of how strong the indigenous culture has been—"not that there has been any change in the male–female relationship in Japan, but it meant a defeat for the elite culture imported from China and a renaissance of the basic indigenous culture."[12] As Geoffrey Barraclough, former professor of modern history at Oxford University, says, "indigenous culture has deep roots while civilization has very weak ones. If there is a struggle between them, indigenous culture will win." Since the Meiji Restoration, the Japanese have been eager to import Western civilization, symbolized by the Western style of fashion, music, housing, automobiles, and so on. Professor Barraclough says, "Ways of dress, for example, are superficial. Many aspects of life-styles are superficial." And he adds, "Traditional reinforcement is sprouting up all over the place like mushrooms in the night. People came to the U.S.—the melting pot—to get away from their past heritage. Today, Spanish-speaking people insist on having Spanish spoken in school."[13]

Viewed from a psychological standpoint, there are two principles that motivate us from within—the paternal and the maternal. The former makes a clear distinction, for example, between the subjective and objective, between good and evil, and between the superior and the inferior. Thus, the paternal principle distinguishes an individual from all other individuals, and strengthens him as a totally independent person. The maternal principle, on the other hand, is a principle of absolute equality that makes all individuals interdependent, just as a mother loves all her children equally, regardless of their character or abilities.

Generally speaking, the paternal principle is strong in Western societies. Christianity, which for centuries was instrumental in forming the Westerner's character, makes a rigid distinction between good and evil and thus is a paternalistic religion with uncompromising ethics. In contrast, the maternal principle occupies a major role in Japanese society. For example, in Japanese mythology, the most important being is the sun goddess, called Amaterasu, whereas in the West the sun is a symbol of power and masculinity. And Buddhism, which has exerted a major influence on the Japanese, is a maternal religion, in that it seeks to save everyone through mercy.

In a maternal society like Japan, emphasis is placed on absolute equality, rather than on distinguishing individuals by their characteristics or ability. In virtually all types of organizations, from the company to the university, a greater degree of importance is attached to preventing individuals from "dropping out" than on enabling certain individuals to exercise strong leadership. A similar way of thinking forms the basis of the importance attached to the academic backgrounds of people in Japan. Those who graduate from universities of similar standing are thought to have similar abilities, and should therefore be treated as equals once they enter an organization. This again is based on the maternal principle. Thus "equality" in Japanese society means the elimination of distinctions within a given group. In the West, where the paternal principle is strong, it means equality among independent individuals who will be trained in a manner commensurate with their individual abilities.

These types of relationships may also be seen in many corporate enterprises in Japan. In the West, the chairman of the board makes decisions, and the president plays the role of implementing them. In contrast, the chairman of a Japanese corporation is a paternalistic figure, personifying the corporate spirit, whereas the president is maternalistic and is a representative of all corporate members. Thus, there exists a mother–son relationship between the president and the employees, with the former trying to treat all of the latter equally.[14] This is the very factor which enables Japanese corporations to demonstrate their organizational strength. At the same time, it often tends to bury in the organization those individuals who are innovators.

Considering this background, it was unprecedented that a top corporate executive like Honda would tell his employees that they should work for their own benefit, and not out of loyalty to the company. His reasoning was that in a relationship of strong dependency, it is difficult to enjoy a sense of satisfaction. Rather, one often feels a victim. A sense of satisfaction, thought Honda, would come only when an independent individual meets a challenge without fear of failure and achieves his goal.

In 1957, when the Japanese economy was entering a recession, the union members at the Shirako and Yamato plants escalated their struggle with a demand for a 10 percent pay raise in the annual spring negotiations. The first strike began on March 29 and six days later the management locked out the machine section, declaring that the strike had been instigated by outsiders. A hunger strike was staged in front of the head office on April 8. Union members belonging to the design section became dissatisfied with the tough strike tactics of the union. Their unity broken, the strikers agreed to a 5.4 percent pay increase on April 14. Previous to this agreement, the Saitama Prefectural Labor Relations Board had come up with a mediation plan, calling for a 5.4 percent pay increase plus 100 yen per person across the board. When this plan was reviewed by the company's board of directors, some favored accepting it because the addition of 100 yen was a small amount. But Fujisawa refused to compromise, saying, "Why can't the union members understand us. We gave them a hard time over the 1954 year-end bonus, but since then, we have accepted all their demands."

This labor dispute had a great influence on Honda's way of thinking. In connection with the wage dispute, the company took disciplinary action against four union leaders on May 9, firing the chairman and three others (one of whom agreed to resign voluntarily). The union appealed the case to the Saitama Prefectural Labor Relations Board and the Tokyo District Court, claiming the action was illegal. On October 16, 1958, the labor board turned down the union's appeal. On receiving this news, some members of the board of directors of Honda Motor started printing leaflets saying, "The company has won!" Seeing this, Honda was furious and shouted, "You damn fools! What do you mean by 'winning' the case? This is no battlefield!" As he said later, "I would not like to have a situation in my company where the winner smiles and the loser cries."

On November 24, the Tokyo District Court ruled that, "Breaking through the company lock-out and occupying the roof of the corporate headquarters represented illegal actions on the part of union members. At the same time, however, dismissal of the union leaders was too severe a form of punishment and, therefore, constituted an illegal action on the part of the company." Deep in his heart, Fujisawa felt relieved by this verdict.

That same year, a bitter labor dispute took place at Oji Seishi, the largest paper manufacturing company in Japan. It started in February, when the union demanded a pay hike, but the situation quickly deteriorated when the management, on May 17, proposed a revision of the labor contract, which was about to expire. They also called for an abolition of the union system and severe restrictions on union activities during working hours. In protest against this proposal, the union started an indefinite strike on July 18, but was split into factions, leading to fistfights among its own members. The strike continued until December 9. Fujisawa thought that Honda Motor must do everything possible to avoid the situation of Oji Seishi, and took immediate steps to amicably settle the labor dispute in his company. Therefore, he immediately announced that all disciplinary actions would be rescinded. With the establishment of a modern and cooperative labor–management relationship, Fujisawa thought the time had come again to make major capital investments. In the negotiations for the year-end bonus in 1959, the union came up with a demand unprecedented in the company's history. Honda was pleased, for he thought the demand for such a large sum was indicative of the growth achieved by his company. The management not only acceded to the union's demand in full, but even paid extra benefits to the employees.

Not all labor–management conflicts in Japan were resolved so easily. One of the most bitter labor disputes since the end of World War II took place from 1959 to 1960 in Fukuoka Prefecture at the Miike Coal Mines, which was owned by the Mitsui Coal Mining Company. The cause of this dispute was a "revolution" in energy sources—the change from coal to petroleum. Faced with abundant and inexpensive oil imported from abroad, the coal mining industry was forced to reduce the number of workers. Mitsui Coal Mining, the leader in the industry, proposed the Second Corporate Reconstruction Plan to its unions on August 28, 1959, asking 4,580 workers to retire voluntarily, including 2,210 at the Miike Mines. This triggered the "Miike Labor Dispute." While sufficient numbers of workers volunteered to retire at the other mines, only a very small number did so at Miike, where the workers resorted to waves of strikes starting on December 1. Alleging that there were 300 workers blocking the company's operations, the management at Miike on December 11 issued a notice of dismissal to 1,297 workers, including those 300. On January 25 of the following year, the union defied the company's lock-out by staging a strike for an indefinite period.

On March 17, internal discord split the union into two factions. The company instructed 4,831 members of the more moderate "second union" to return to work, and on March 28, there was a clash between some 2,200 "second union" members attempting to return to work and the members of the militant "first union" trying to block them. Many were injured. On July 5, the company sent 340 workers to the mine on four large ships, and on July 7, chartered eleven vessels, including seven patrol boats, to transport materials and equipment by sea. They were met by strong resistance from the "first union" members, leading to a ocean battle which caused injury to around 200 workers and policemen.

The hopper was the key battleground in this dispute, because it was the only way to deliver coal from the mines. Some 10,000 members of the militant "first union" picketed the hopper, and they were reinforced by another 10,000 supporters dispatched by

Sohyo. On July 7 the District Court issued a summary judgment ordering the picket line to be removed. In response to this action, the police sent 10,000 officers, who were later reinforced by five armored cars, motorized water-cannons, and tear-gas guns. Altogether, 30,000 unionists and police were ready to clash.

On July 19, Hayato Ikeda became the prime minister. Determined to avert bloodshed, he quickly intervened in the Miike dispute. The matter was subsequently brought to arbitration by the Central Labor Relations Board, and the strike came to an end on November 1 with a virtual defeat for the union. This came 282 days after the company resorted to the lock-out; during that time, *Sohyo* had spent 648 million yen and mobilized a total of 295,000 people in support of the union.

It is said that Japanese unions cooperate with management; but this was not true in the early years. Only after the Miike dispute did bitter confrontations between management and labor diminish, and cooperative labor–management relations gain a foothold. The number of labor disputes in Japan stood at 89 in 1945 and 810 in 1946. With some fluctuation, they reached a peak of 9,581 in 1974. Since that time, labor disputes have been on the wane and decreased to 3,737 in 1980. As these figures indicate, labor movements in Japan have undergone qualitative change since the 1960s. In the course of these changes, cooperative industrial relations have been established, the unions have become less resistant to the introduction of technological innovations, and corporate capital investments have increased. As a result, Japanese industry as a whole has been modernized, the national economy has grown steadily, and the income of workers has increased—all these factors contributing to further improving labor–management relations. It was during the 1960s that the Japanese economy started expanding rapidly. In the course of this fast economic growth, the "revolution" in Japan's energy sources certainly contributed to strengthening industry's competitive power on the world markets. At the same time, however, it made the Japanese economy more and more dependent on imported oil, and thus more vulnerable.

As of June 1981, the Japanese labor map was as follows: *Sohyo* was the strongest labor union in the public sector with 4,568,826 members; *Domei* (the Japanese Confederation of Labor), which grew out of *Sodomei*, was the strongest in the private sector with 2,181,903 members; the Federation of Independent Unions had 1,391,346 members; and the National Federation of Industrial Organizations, which was formed as a result of the democratization of *Sanbetsu*, had 63,997 members. In addition, there is

Two views of the annual "Spring labor offensive" for wage hikes, characterized by negotiations (*top*: private railway management–union meeting, 1982) and mass rallies (*bottom*: Hibiya Park, Tokyo 1981).

IMF-JC (International Metalworkers Federation, Japan Council), covering unions in the automobile, steel, shipbuilding, electrical, and machine industries. This federation serves as a body for promoting international exchange and maintains close ties with the other four labor organizations. Statistics show that of the total work force in Japan, which stood at 12,369,000 in 1980, 30.8 percent was organized.

One of the characteristic features of the labor movement in Japan is that most of the unions are "in-company" unions. While this is due partly to the influence of the immediate postwar period, when the ban on unions was lifted and workers started organizing on a workshop level, it is more deeply rooted in the lifetime employment system.

Usually, an employee stays with the same company until retirement age, and it is very seldom that this employee, as an expert in his field, will move to another firm. Japanese have little experience with the type of professionalism that is common in the West. Therefore, the country did not develop a craft union system in which workers skilled in the same field form a union encompassing a number of corporations. In Japan, workers are loyal to their companies and are also loyal to their unions.

This lifetime employment system makes workers of the company cohesive, and strengthens the corporation's power as a group. For this reason, the system developed from the early days of Japan's industrialization and is now firmly rooted in the society. The lifetime employment system is also supported by the maternal principle. Japanese tend to seek interdependence within a group, rather than seeking to live as strong, independent individuals. Needless to say, interdependence works best within a homogeneous society. At the same time, however, this quality of "sameness" within a group leads to prejudice against outsiders and to isolationism.

This prejudice against outsiders is observed in the relations between Japanese and foreigners and also between men and women. When one talks about Japanese society being maternalistic, it not only means Japanese women are maternal but also implies that Japanese men act in accordance with the maternal principle. In today's social structure in Japan, men play the principal roles because the government and bureaucratic organizations are rooted in the traditions of the feudal age—when male superiority was accepted as a matter of course. The male members in such organizations tend to seek interdependence among fellow males and to regard females as outsiders. In the West, society is far more male-oriented than in Japan, and men are regarded as the symbols of power and justice. For this reason, capable women are more easily accepted in society as professionals, whereas in the maternal culture of Japan, it is very seldom that a woman reaches a managerial post.

Japanese women gained considerable power after World War II, but this was only in comparison with the prewar period. Before the war, the wife had to obey the husband, a manifestation of the same feudal ethics which dictated that citizens obey the emperor. Women were not given the right to vote on the grounds that if the husband and wife had different political opinions, the relationship of the wife obeying the husband would be destroyed. More surprisingly, although a woman could be punished for criminal offenses, she was not given any authority to enter into legally binding contracts, because women were regarded as totally incompetent in such matters. Remnants of these prewar traditions still exist, and Japanese women even today are not as professionally active as their counterparts in the West. True, some women have become ambassadors, members of the Diet, high-ranking government ministry officials, and board members of major corporations. But, generally speaking, Japanese women still tend to manage the home, rather than demanding woman's liberation and equal opportunities with men.

During the 1981 academic year there were 1,339,000 male undergraduate students enrolled in colleges and universities as against a mere 386,000 female students, although in junior colleges, women outnumbered men by 329,000 to 38,000. Female employees numbered 21,420,000 in 1980, accounting for 38.7 percent of the total workforce. The leading professions for women were kindergarten and primary school teaching, clerical work at banks, securities firms, and insurance companies, and in manufacturing industries, principally foodstuffs, textiles, electrical instruments, and precision machinery. The Japanese automobile industry is thus still predominantly a man's world.

5

You Meet the Nicest People . . .

Soichiro Honda once observed that, "The Japanese seem to prefer spending their lives on small pieces of land, because they are an agrarian race. The Tokugawa Shogunate adopted an isolationist policy, and tried to turn people's attention to the country's internal affairs. And that was an agrarian way of thinking. But those races that were accustomed to riding horses are different. For example, more than a century before Japan closed its doors to the outside world, Vasco da Gama of Portugal had already sailed past the Cape of Good Hope, which allowed Western Europeans to open their eyes to the entire world and began a new chapter in history."

Such thoughts and a belief in high-speed transportation led Honda to seriously consider testing his products on the world racing circuit. Early in 1954, he entered a machine in an international race held in São Paulo, Brazil, where it placed thirteenth in a field of twenty-two. While this was not a very important race, the result was nonetheless disappointing. Three months later, a public declaration was made in the name of President Honda, stating that his company would take part in the prestigious Isle of Man Tourist Trophy race—the mecca of every serious motorcycle racer.

This was also a year of crisis at Honda Motor. Because of the company's rapid growth following the success of the Dream Type E, over two thousand new workers had been hired. They differed greatly both in terms of ability and salaries, which caused some confusion in the internal organization of the factory. Honda appeared almost every day to supervise his engineers, and his behavior was often abrasive and sometimes violent when he was not satisfied with their work. For their part, some of the workers were disappointed in the "management style" of their boss and began to have doubts about the future of the company. The morale at Honda Motor was plummeting and incidents of sabotage were reported. Coming at such a time, the commitment to take part in this race seemed to raise everyone's spirits. "Most of the workers were so young that they were quite attracted to the idea of winning races," Honda recalls. "Particularly because we had just lost the war, the idea of hoisting the Japanese flag on the Isle of Man gave them much excitement. It really stirred their blood." Fujisawa meanwhile worked behind the scenes, his strategy being, "I'll solve the problem of money, which caused the crisis, and you people work on winning the race."

In June of that year, Honda went to Britain for an on-the-spot study of the Isle of Man. On arriving in England he discovered that British sentiment toward the Japanese was not at all favorable—and he especially disliked being called a "Jap." Honda received another unpleasant surprise when he visited the Isle of Man, which is located between England and Ireland. The Tourist Trophy races are held every June, with several hundred thousand tourists from all over the world in attendance. During the races the main roads on the island form the track, which is 61 kilometers (about 38 miles) long. There, he saw the world's top-ranking racers compete on motorcycles from such famous manufacturers as NSU of West Germany and Gilera of Italy. These motorcycles ran at unbelievable speeds, and their motors were three times more powerful than Honda Motor engines of comparable displacement. To make matters worse, components such as tires and chains were also far superior to those produced in Japan. "How little I know about the outside world! I may have been too audacious in making that declaration," Honda thought to himself.

The greatest problem facing the company was how to increase engine speed without destroying the motor. Honda had succeeded in revving up the Dream Type E engine to 7,000 rpm, but was astonished that the bikes raced at the Isle of Man were revving at over 10,000 rpm. Around that time, some customers complained that when the Sports Cub was revved to its limit, the flywheel would crack. This claim was substantiated by tests at the plant that resulted in fragments of the flywheel breaking the engine housing and hitting the ceiling. Fujisawa, who headed the sales division of the company, was terrified at the possibility of customers being injured by such an accident. Further tests conducted by a components manufacturer showed that the flywheel would crack at 7,500 rpm and fragment at 8,000 rpm.

One day Honda carefully examined a flywheel and instantly saw the cause of the problem because he knew about casting. Due to a design fault, the flywheel was too large, and a slight grinding of its surface was required. He reasoned that an egg stays in one piece because it is covered with a hard shell; but if you crack this shell and start swinging the egg, the yolk and white will come gushing out. Likewise, the surface of the flywheel was hardened by a heat treatment to form a "shell," but if the shell was scraped, the material inside would fragment at a high revolution speed, breaking the flywheel into pieces. The company quickly made new flywheels, which were sent through distributors to replace the old ones. Much to Fujisawa's relief, this prevented accidents, and Honda's racing program had benefited as well.

The blueprints for the engine to be used in the Tourist Trophy races were drawn up by two young engineers, Tadashi Kume and Kimio Shimmura. Honda respected the flexible ideas of the younger generation, who were free from established ways of thinking, but entrusting such an important responsibility to these young engineers was quite a gamble. Their success or failure to develop a winning racing engine could determine the entire future of the company. In most Japanese firms, where seniority is strictly observed, major projects usually go to senior members of the company—Honda usually paid no attention to such traditions. Both Kume and Shimmura remember those days fondly, "We were told to start designing racing engines right after we joined the company. Nothing could have been more interesting, and we were both very excited. If we had gone to another company, we never would have been given such challenging jobs." When the blueprints were completed, the engine was assembled by Honda and Design Section Chief Kiyoshi Kawashima.

The first racing engine encountered many problems when running at high speed, especially with the rod connecting the piston to the crankshaft. At a high revolution speed, a connecting rod is subjected to great stress, and the young engineers thought it was necessary to make this rod heavier and stronger. But it would still collapse no matter how sturdily it was made. Honda asked them, "Why do you have to make it so sturdy? Make it smaller and lighter." He also told them to reduce the size, weight, and number of balls in the bearings. The engineers were afraid that such a fragile connecting rod and light bearings would break at a high revolution speed, but Honda was proved right. Perhaps inspired by an old Japanese saying whose meaning is, "A large tree cannot stand against powerful winds, while the slender and more flexible bamboo can," a major technical breakthrough had been scored.

Following this innovation, Honda asked one of his engineers to describe the motion of a chain. "It goes round and round," was the reply, at which he shouted, "You idiot! A chain makes a reciprocating motion. When its left side goes up, the right side goes down." Honda thought that weight reduction was important for anything that moves in a reciprocating fashion and tried to make the motorcycle chains both thinner and lighter. Chains produced in Japan at the time could not be used for racing purposes, because they would break at high speeds, with a good chance that their fragments would injure the rider. This led Honda to search for improvements, first on his own, and later with the help of Kumakichi Araya, president of a firm called Daido and a close personal friend. Araya adopted Honda's ideas, but applying them was no easy task. In fact, he almost gave up, saying, "This is absolutely impossible!" Honda's persistence finally resulted in the first Japanese-made motorcycle chain which could withstand grueling race conditions, although not in time for the company's initial entry in the Tourist Trophy events.

"Nearly two years after we declared our intention to take part in the Isle of Man races, as the technical levels of components and mechanical features of the engine improved, we were able to come up with an engine powerful enough to compete with foreign motorcycles. The young engineers did a very good job," says Honda. "But that alone was not enough to assure us victory in the Tourist Trophy races. The rider is as important as the machine.

Even if we had a machine with the same level of performance as those of our competitors, we still couldn't win the race without a top-notch rider. We had to develop a racing machine with a superior performance that would win even without a superior rider."

At the R & D laboratories, a study was launched to examine the question of whether the energy generated by fuel combustion in the new engine was being utilized to the fullest extent. An analysis of the exhaust gases showed the emission of large quantities of unburned hydrocarbons and carbon monoxide. Honda firmly believed that there must be ways of generating more power through research into combustion. "In those days, no studies were being made of combustion, not even at university laboratories or by the 'Big Three' automakers in the United States," says Honda. "That was because nobody questioned combustion, which was taken for granted as a natural result of igniting the air–fuel mixture. With our research into combustion, we erased that blind spot."

The research work at the laboratories began with the making of precision measuring instruments. Every phase of the combustion process was scrupulously examined, especially how the flame and power are propagated following ignition of the air–fuel mixture by the spark plug. As the study progressed, they discovered that the configuration of the combustion chamber influenced combustion more than any other factor, and modified the engine design accordingly.

After deciding to take part in the Isle of Man Tourist Trophy race, Honda Motor started to compete in domestic races. In the first All-Japan Motorcycle Endurance Road Race (the "Mt. Asama Race") in November 1955, the Honda Motor racing team won both in the 350cc and 500cc class, but lost in the 125cc and 250cc division. In the second All-Japan Race in October 1957, Honda Motor again lost in both the 125cc and 250cc class, but took first place in the 350cc class. Acknowledging these defeats, Honda conceded that "We should never imitate foreign technology, though a certain manufacturer imitated it and won the race. We must win the Isle of Man Tourist Trophy Race through our own technology, however hard it is to develop."

Honda Motor's long-cherished ambition to participate in the

Tourist Trophy races was realized in June 1959. The culmination of years of research, Honda Motor's racing machines had twice the power of the foreign bikes which Honda had first seen on the Isle of Man. Called the "RC-142," this twin-cylinder, 125cc engine developed 16 horsepower at an astonishing 14,000 rpm. Entered in the fiercely contested 125cc category and manned by Japanese riders, Honda Motor placed 6th, 7th, and 8th, winning the manufacturer team prize.

In 1960, Honda Motor's machines were entered in two categories, finishing 4th through 6th in the 250cc category and 6th through 10th in the 125cc class. Victory was finally achieved in 1961, when Honda Motor won the first five positions in both the 250cc and 125cc categories. Britain's *Daily Mirror* reported that the machines were built like "fine watches," and Honda was overjoyed, saying, "Only by winning at the Isle of Man can we open the way to becoming a world enterprise and selling our products internationally." These races not only served to improve Honda Motor's motorcycle engine technology, but also dramatically elevated the technological standards of the Japanese motorcycle industry as a whole.

The winning machines were ridden by foreigners. Says Honda, "To race at the Isle of Man, we paid foreign riders five or six million yen each, which was a lot of money at the time. When we entered the Formula I automotive Grand Prix races, we paid foreign drivers ten times that amount. Those foreign riders and drivers were so eager to win that they made many demands, telling us, for example, that the machine wobbled or the brakes were not effective enough. And such demands raised our own technical standards. Japanese racers were not like that. They wouldn't tell us anything. Some of them would even damage the machines. Today, of course, there are many good Japanese riders and drivers. Japan has been an underdeveloped country in terms of motorization. In other countries, people have been used to riding at 100 kph (around 63 mph) since they were babies. The Japanese certainly didn't get accustomed to such speed in their childhood."

Toward the end of 1956, Honda and Fujisawa went on a "shopping trip" to West Germany. This was a period when Japan was enjoying an unprecedented economic boom, which the people called—out of both hope and cynicism—the "Jimmu Boom,"

The 1960 TT Race on the Isle of Man.

The 1960 Honda Motor racing team with Kiyoshi Kawashima in front.

after the first emperor of Japan. For the first time since the end of the war, many Japanese began to emerge from poverty and even have some feeling of affluence. Although Christians constituted a small minority of the population, huge crowds celebrated

Christmas Eve with shopping sprees and rounds of parties. Even the government entered into the spirit of things, declaring in an Economic White Paper, "The postwar days are gone!"

In the motorcycle industry, the predominant view was that the days of small motorbikes were gone. Many of the manufacturers were trying to cash in on the "Jimmu Boom" by marketing large, powerful motorcycles. Fujisawa thought differently, and instead of trying to make a quick killing in the marketplace, he was busy formulating a long-term strategy for Honda Motor. The first priority was to develop a lightweight, high-performance motorbike which no other manufacturer could match.

On their way to Europe, Fujisawa spoke enthusiastically about the lightweight motorbikes he wanted his partner to develop. Traveling via the southern route, it took them seventy-two hours to reach their destination, and Fujisawa kept repeating his ideas during the entire flight, stopping only when either he or Honda fell asleep. Honda was totally preoccupied with his plans for racing on the Isle of Man, dreamed only of winning trophies, had little interest in lightweight bikes, and was fed up with Fujisawa's constant chattering.

In Europe, there was a huge market for mopeds and other lightweight motorcycles, and Fujisawa was convinced that the same boom would come to Japan sooner or later. But the one he envisioned was to have a graceful and attractive design, as well as a high performance from a powerful 50cc engine. Arriving in West Germany, they wandered through the streets of Frankfurt, Hamburg, and Munich like two young motor enthusiasts, visiting showrooms filled with motorcycles by such big names as Kleidler and Lambretta. Fujisawa's persistence gradually aroused Honda's interest. At each showroom Honda thought he saw the exact one his partner was asking for.

"Is that the type you mean?"

"No, not those. There's no future for them."

"How about this one?"

"That won't sell."

"What are you asking for, then?"

"I don't know exactly either. But my general idea is a bike powered by a 50cc engine, on which a young couple would start whistling happy melodies."

"Have you seen anything like that?"

"I haven't. That's why we must build one."

A year later Honda asked Fujisawa to drop by the research and development laboratories. There, he was shown a full-size mock-up of a new motorbike. At first glance, Fujisawa was quite impressed with Honda's unique design. "This is going to sell well, at least thirty thousand units a month," said Fujisawa. "What? Thirty thousand a month!" Honda exclaimed. Considering the fact that the total number of two-wheelers sold in Japan at the time was around twenty thousand units a month, Honda's surprise was quite understandable.

This new motorbike was called the Super Cub. Considered by many to be Soichiro Honda's masterpiece, the Super Cub has often been compared to the Model T Ford and the Volkswagen Beetle. The design was revolutionary: rather than the powerful, mechanical appeal of conventional motorcycles designed for speed maniacs, it had a light, carefree image. The "step through" configuration made it easier for women to ride. Indeed, the Super Cub was to become the standard for lightweight bikes throughout the world.

Production of the Juno, the first scooter in the world to have polyester resin components, had been suspended following the 1954 crisis. Every time Fujisawa visited the plant, he would consult with the polyester resin specialists, asking them not to stop their research in this field, regardless of the circumstances. The development of resin casting had therefore continued, and no one was more pleased than these specialists when it was announced that the Super Cub would have a polyester resin body. The first engine which Honda produced after the war displaced 50cc and had an output of 0.5 horsepower. The Super Cub also had a 50cc engine, but developed 4.5 horsepower. It was because of the research efforts for the Isle of Man that the power from the same size engine had now increased nine times. The Super Cub was introduced in the summer of 1958 and became an immediate success. With a graceful design, high performance, easy handling, a centrifugal clutch, electric starter, and low maintenance cost, the bike was a very attractive means of transportation for the public.

Honda Motor soon began construction of a large factory in Suzuka City, Mie Prefecture, to mass-produce the Super Cub.

Until this time, even the company's best-selling model sold no more than 2,000 to 3,000 units per month. The new plant was designed to manufacture 30,000 motorcycles per month from the onset. To many outsiders, the company's plan to invest nearly 10 billion yen in one plant was completely reckless. (At the time, their paid-in capital was only 1.4 billion yen.) Later events proved, however, that Honda Motor was simply ahead of its time.

Many new procedures were adopted in the construction of the Suzuka factory. The board of directors did not impose any restrictions on the amount of money allocated to build the plant, but insisted that the project meet three conditions: (1) the investment had to be recouped within a given period of time; (2) the plant had to be capable of serving as a model for other mass-production facilities; and (3) harmony with the local communities had to be maintained. All other details, including the plant layout, were left in the hands of young employees, who were greatly excited by the idea of designing their own facility. When completed in the spring of 1960—the start of a worldwide economic boom— the Suzuka factory was the largest motorcycle plant in the world.

The 1951 Dream E had been equipped with a revolutionary overhead valve (OHV) engine. The advantage of this system, compared to a conventional side valve arrangement, was that the configuration of the combustion chamber could be modified freely, making it possible to increase the compression ratio and thus improve combustion efficiency. Some imported cars had OHV engines, but no one in Japan had dared to adapt this system to mass production. An overhead valve also made it easier to increase engine speed, but higher rpms created new problems for the intake and exhaust valves, which could not keep up with such high speeds. Honda's idea was to move the position of the camshaft to the top of the engine, close to where the valves were located, thus enabling the valves to open and close without lagging behind the engine. For the first time in Japan, the overhead camshaft (OHC) system was adopted for a small motorcycle engine, when virtually none of the much larger automobile engines had such a mechanism. The 1955 Dream S was Honda Motor's first motorcycle to be powered by an OHC engine, and the Super Cub was later to incorporate a similar design.

Now that both the Benly and the Dream were popular and selling well, Fujisawa started thinking about exporting these bikes. Until then, the company had little experience in full-scale exports. At first, Honda Motor tried to rely on the overseas sales networks of Japanese trading firms, but these channels did little to expand their foreign markets. Unlike present-day Japan, which has accumulated vast foreign exchange holdings, the Japanese economy in the 1950s faced a difficult task in promoting exports and earning foreign currency. Many companies attempted to step up exports, but very few had the resources and know-how to develop overseas markets independently. Most manufacturers relied on trading firms or overseas distributors, with automobile manufacturers preferring to export through trading firms. Now that Japan was recovering from the postwar economic chaos, the country could no longer continue to protect itself behind trade barriers, and there was a mounting pressure toward trade liberalization. Under such circumstances, the Japanese automakers relied heavily on protective tariffs in order to compete with imports.

Fujisawa considered it absolutely necessary to establish an overseas subsidiary that could operate under the direct control of corporate headquarters. Motorcycles that were trouble-free in a small country like Japan could run into unexpected problems, beyond the service capability of the distributors, in a huge country like the United States. Moreover, it would be very costly if spare parts had to be shipped directly to numerous distributors. In Fujisawa's mind, it was important to establish a subsidiary which could both act as the center of sales activities and also assume complete responsibility for servicing.

In addition to the establishment of overseas subsidiaries, another major issue in the company's basic export strategy was the question of which foreign market should be tapped first. A group of Honda Motor's representatives, headed by Kihachiro Kawashima, toured Europe, Southeast Asia, and the United States to conduct market surveys. They came to the conclusion that Europe and Southeast Asia represented the most promising markets. In Europe there was a heavy demand for motorcycles, which were seen as a convenient and practical means of transportation, and lightweight motorbikes were especially popular. In Southeast Asia, people were also beginning to recognize the importance of motorcycles as an inexpensive means of transportation, and many European manufacturers were already exploring markets there. Based on this analysis, the team concluded that the most attractive market for Honda Motor was Southeast Asia, which is geographically close to Japan and where the demand was growing.

Fujisawa disagreed, insisting that the American market must be explored first. His fundamental reasoning was that the world's consumer economy originated in the United States, and goods which were not accepted there would not find markets elsewhere. The United States was the most affluent country in the world, and automobiles were by far the most popular form of transportation. Only around 60,000 motorcycles were being sold there each year, and both Japanese trading firms and American distributors were of the opinion that this market would not grow. If Honda Motor began selling its products in the United States, they argued, this would only reduce the number of motorcycles sold by other manufacturers.

The *sogo-shosha*, a particular type of trading firm not found outside of Japan, was the traditional channel for Japanese manufacturers wanting to penetrate overseas markets. Generally speaking, they have contributed enormously to expanding Japan's export trade. *Sogo-shosha* are, however, much more diversified and perform far more functions than simply exporting and importing goods. They have global networks for collecting information that is vital for commercial activities, ranging from data on weather patterns that will affect crop conditions to in-depth analysis of political situations in other countries. They also engage in transactions of goods and commodities within Japan, between Japan and other countries, and even between third countries. The goods they handle include anything from Christmas tree lights to nuclear reactors. Moreover, *sogo-shosha* often make high-risk loans to small businesses in Japan, loans which ordinary banks would not even consider. In some cases, these small businesses are placed under the direct control of a *sogo-shosha*, which in turn sells their products. The *sogo-shosha*'s influence sometimes extends even to large corporations, whereby they will help these companies obtain funds and will arrange business collaborations. One example of this function is the capital tie-up arrangement between General Motors and Isuzu Motors of Japan, in which C. Itoh & Co., one of the major *sogo-shosha*, played a central role. The most important function of the *sogo-shosha* is the role they play as international systems organizers. For example, a *sogo-shosha* can and often does coordinate large-scale projects aimed at the industrialization of a developing country. Specifically, its work starts with the construction of huge capital projects such as railways, port facilities, and production plants, then goes on to secure the necessary operating capital. Later, it will purchase and finally export the goods manufactured under the project—all under the leadership of just one *sogo-shosha*.

Because of their multifunctional operations, the *sogo-shosha* occupy an extremely important position in the Japanese business world. In Japan, there are powerful groups of companies, such as Mitsui, Mitsubishi, and Sumitomo. These groups are similar to each other in structure, each being made up of companies engaged in diversified industries from light to heavy. At the core of each group is a *sogo-shosha* and a bank, who together play a major role in promoting communication among member companies of the group and achieving unity among them. The member companies of a group are thus bound together by relationships of dependency.

The *sogo-shosha* have evolved in a distinctly Japanese atmosphere and tradition. The root of their eagerness (and sometimes over-eagerness) to collect information from all parts of the world can be traced back to Japan's history of selectively importing foreign cultures and civilizations. Companies in the West normally specialize in the fields of their expertise and try to expand by entering markets with unique products. The *sogo-shosha*, on the other hand, do not specialize in anything, which is probably why this type of enterprise never developed in Europe or America.

The major source of the *sogo-shosha*'s strength lies in information, knowledge, and human relations. Recently there have been moves in Canada and the United States to learn the secret of increasing exports from the *sogo-shosha*. In the United States, during the Carter administration, the Department of Commerce was especially eager to introduce a *sogo-shosha* type system. But it would be difficult, to say the least, for European and American societies, with a culture so different from Japan's, to "Westernize" *sogo-shosha*.

The *sogo-shosha* are not only very powerful, but relying on them for export, in a sense, also means receiving their protection. Therefore, when Honda Motor decided to explore the export market without such help, many people thought that the company was taking a great risk.

With the idea of setting up a subsidiary in the United States, Fujisawa went to see officials of the Ministry of Finance and the Ministry of International Trade and Industry. He was not warmly received and one of the MITI officials told him, "Honda Motor has spent large sums of foreign currency to import many machines from overseas, but you have not done any exporting." The Finance Ministry thus refused to permit an allocation of dollars for Honda Motor to set up the projected subsidiary, as the company had not earned its share of foreign exchange.

Fujisawa then asked Naganori Koyama, a member of the Japanese House of Representatives, to help him obtain the necessary allocations. "I am absolutely dedicated to developing the American market on our own," he told Representative Koyama. "This is going to be for the good of Japan. So let us spend foreign currency just once more." Through Representative Koyama, Fujisawa was able to obtain the Ministry of Finance's blessing. In June 1959, American Honda Motor Co., Inc. was established in Los Angeles, with a paid-in capital of $250,000 (although the original application had asked for $500,000), and a total of $1 million was poured into that company within the next two years.

Fujisawa wanted to make American Honda the base for exploring the market in the United States, using the newly introduced Super Cub as his major weapon. At first, these efforts encountered one problem after another, and neither the Benly nor the Dream, to say nothing of the Super Cub, sold in any significant volume. Following the old maxim, "When in Rome, do as the Romans do," American Honda let the existing motorcycle shops handle the Super Cub. At sales conventions they noticed that most of their dealers wore soiled overalls and had dirty, grease-covered hands. Kihachiro Kawashima, executive vice president of American Honda, began to see why his products were not selling.

In the 1920s, the U.S. economy was booming and many Americans thought they were living in a time of "permanent prosperity." Automobiles had become a popular means of transportation during that decade, and movies were the most popular form of mass entertainment. Film actors and actresses were the new American aristocracy. Italian-born Rudolph Valentino's Latin sex appeal created a sensation among women, while Gloria Swanson, in her black evening dress, was the ultimate symbol of feminine beauty. People longed for the white convertibles driven by their favorite movie stars, and this strengthened their desire for automobiles of their own. Forty years later, the stars had changed, but this image still remained powerful.

The same can be said about the movie industry's influence on motorcycles—only in reverse. Some movie stars gave the impression that motorcycles were for delinquents, and this had a very detrimental effect on the marketing of two-wheeled vehicles. In most American families, mothers frowned upon motorcycles and would not permit their sons to own them. American Honda, working jointly with Grey Advertising, Inc., in Los Angeles decided to launch a major campaign to change this image.

The advertisment that radically altered the image of motorcycles in the U.S.A.

Numerous advertisements were run in such influential magazines as *Life*, *Look*, *Saturday Evening Post*, and *Playboy*, featuring people from all walks of life enjoying the Super Cub under the slogan, "You Meet the Nicest People on a Honda!" This campaign was a great hit, and was followed by the ripely suggestive classic, "The Nicest Things Happen on a Honda!" Both were subsequently used with great success on television as well. Through such advertising, American Honda successfully reversed the image of motorcycles.

Along with this campaign, American Honda established new dealerships to sell the Super Cub. They were chosen not from the established motorcycle dealers, but rather from sporting goods stores and hobby shops. Through this new strategy, the Super Cub gained popularity not as a vehicle for delinquents but as a smart means of transportation for the general public. This in turn marked the beginning of the huge motorcycle market in the United States.

Another noteworthy event during this period was the establishment in 1962 of Honda Benelux N.V. in Belgium as a wholly owned Honda Motor subsidiary. This marked the first time since the end of the war that a Japanese manufacturing firm had set up a production facility in an advanced industrial nation of the West. The plant manufactured a newly developed moped, known as the C-310, which was based on the Super Cub. This moped failed to appeal to European tastes, however, and Honda Benelux had a difficult time selling it, remaining in the red for the first ten years of its existence. But Fujisawa refused to withdraw from Belgium, reasoning that "We shouldn't depend on exporting finished products alone. Accumulating experience overseas is important for our future growth."

Among the Japanese motor manufacturers, Toyota Motor Company and Toyota Motor Sales Company jointly established an American subsidiary in October 1958, but it was soon closed; it was not until 1964 that the subsidiary was reactivated. Thus, American Honda was the first subsidiary of the Japanese motor industry to be successful in the United States. Japan's motorcycle exports to the United States, which were approximately 6,300 units in 1959 when American Honda was founded, increased to 148,000 units in 1963, due primarily to Honda Motor.

Although today the *sogo-shosha* are very active worldwide, the manufacturers of such high-technology products as cars, color televisions, cameras, and computers choose to export their products independently for sale through their own networks. There is little room left for *sogo-shosha* to engage in exporting those types of products that require after-sales servicing, for in these areas there are strong bonds connecting the manufacturers and consumers directly. In this sense, Honda Motor's strategy of cultivating its overseas markets through its own subsidiaries not only represented the frontier spirit of the company but also was well ahead of its competitors. The Super Cub served to create a huge market in the United States, and this opened the way for Honda Motor's expansion into Europe, Southeast Asia, and other areas.

Later, Fujisawa felt a cold chill run down his back when a leading American business figure told him, "You know, if you had chosen any other country, you wouldn't have gotten approval for setting up your subsidiary so easily. You were able to do it only because you chose the United States." Fujisawa thought to himself, "In our country, companies always seek protection from the government and want to have the entry of foreign competitors blocked. The Americans, on the other hand, are quite open-minded about accepting foreign companies. What great self-confidence they have!" Given the current trade friction problems between Japan and the West, Fujisawa's remarks are not without irony.

A country's dependence on foreign trade is often defined as the proportion of foreign trade to the GNP, in which case Japan has shown a slight increase since the end of World War II. The rate of dependence on imports and exports for 1979 were 14 percent and 13 percent, respectively. These figures, compared to other countries for the same year, are much lower than Great Britain (rate of dependence on imports, 29 percent, and on exports, 25 percent), West Germany (23 percent, 25 percent), France (21 percent, 19 percent), and the Netherlands (50 percent, 48 percent), though they are higher than the figures for the United States (10 percent, 8 percent). This means that most of the economic activities of Japan are supported by the domestic market. It should also be noted that the Japanese postwar economy has been more dependent on production for the domestic market than during the prewar period, the rate of dependence on both imports and exports in 1938, for example, having been 23 percent.

Japan does, however, depend greatly on imports for many goods that are indispensable to the population and to industrial activities. According to the statistics for 1980, Japan relies on imports for 100 percent of the cotton, wool, natural rubber, maize, phosphate, bauxite, and nickel ore used in the country. It depends on imports for 85 percent of its energy requirements, and for 99.8 percent of the crude oil consumed, which accounts for about 70 percent of its primary energy supply. Likewise, Japan imports 99.6 percent of the iron ore needed domestically, 98.3 percent of the copper concentrate, 96.2 percent of the soybeans, 90.7 percent of the wheat, and 79.1 percent of the coal. Food and raw materials account for about three-quarters of Japan's total import amount.

Japan is often said to be a "catalyst nation." The Japanese archipelago, viewed as a whole, is somewhat like a giant chemical complex, and when raw materials are added, with an excellent labor force acting as the catalytic agent, it produces industrial goods quite efficiently. Japan has imported the necessary raw materials with foreign exchange earned through the export of these industrial goods. Consequently, the interdependence between Japan and other countries has become much intensified.

Because the Japanese economy was vulnerable in the early years of the postwar period, the Japanese government set up an exchange rate of 360 yen to the U.S. dollar in 1949, and at the same time enacted the Foreign Exchange and Foreign Trade Control Act. Aimed at achieving an equilibrium in the balance of payments, stabilizing Japanese currency, and effectively utilizing scarce foreign exchange, this act contained some very restrictive clauses such as the prohibition of free foreign exchange transactions, a centralized control over foreign exchange by the government, the introduction of a quota system on imports, and the liberalization of exports.

In the early 1950s, the deficiency in foreign currency was offset by special procurements by the U.S. military, which was then fighting in the Korean War. In the latter half of the decade, the Japanese economy moved toward a new growth strategy, an economic development based on capital investment for modern plants and equipment, rather than in the area of arms production as in the prewar period. In the early 1960s, the government began to consciously implement high-growth economic policies. Japanese imports began to increase rapidly in line with this overall economic growth, for as Japan lacked natural resources, it was essential to import massive quantities of raw materials in order to expand the economy. Increases in imports from the United States were especially significant; these imports accounted for about one-third of the total, and during the 1950s the annual average trade deficit with the United States was as much as $470 million. This trend continued during the early part of the 1960s. Thus, Japanese foreign trade showed a consistent deficit before 1964, and it was not until 1967 that Japan's gold and foreign currency reserves exceeded $2 billion. The goods essential to the growth of the Japanese economy were supplied primarily by the United States, resulting in a large trade imbalance. Furthermore, because of its poor accumulation of capital and technology, Japan was obliged to introduce foreign capital and technology from the advanced industrial nations of the West, and especially from the United States. Under these circumstances, the liberalization of foreign trade and foreign exchange transactions became an issue in the late 1950s, and in 1960 the government decided to institute some fundamental changes.

The business community feared that through trade liberalization, Japanese industries would no longer be able to compete with advanced countries in the West and might be destroyed. Taizo Ishizaka, chairman of the Federation of Economic Organizations, had a strong belief in liberalism, and insisted on the importance of U.S.–Japan cooperation. He was convinced that the Japanese economy would survive and prosper in the open market. As the top leader of the Japanese business world, he chided the industrialists who were reluctant to follow a course of liberalization, and Ishizaka thus played a very important role in the government's new programs.

At the time, however, there were few business leaders with Taizo Ishizaka's confidence. Interestingly, the leftists were the most pessimistic of all about liberalization. These groups, which included opposition parties in the Diet, labor unions, and intellectuals, thought that the United States would dominate the Japanese market through aggressive export drives and rule over Japanese industries by extending long-term loans, and that the working class would consequently become victims of U.S. imperialism. Thus, one of the reasons Japanese leftists so fiercely opposed the signing of a new U.S.–Japan Security Treaty was the fear that Japanese military subordination to the United States would be then combined with Japan's economic subordination.

In 1963, Japan accepted Article 11 of the General Agreement on Tariffs and Trade (GATT) and agreed not to put quantitative restrictions on imports. The following year, Japan became an "Article 8" nation of the International Monetary Fund (IMF), and the yen regained its convertibility. Japan could no longer restrict external payments or the international flow of funds for current transactions; the Japanese economy was now in an open market economic system. Japan also joined the Organization for Economic Cooperation and Development (OECD) in the same year, thus achieving the status of an "advanced nation." The liberalization of foreign trade and foreign exchange transactions continued, and in 1967 the Japanese government decided on a basic policy regarding the liberalization of capital transactions.

The cabinet, led by Prime Minister Ikeda, launched a "national income-doubling program" in 1960. The basic concept of this program was to double Japan's GNP by the target year 1970, and to increase the per capita income to the level achieved by the advanced countries in the West during the late 1950s. Japanese exports were the key to the success of this program, and the government expected them to increase by 10 percent annually, while overall world trade was anticipated to increase by only 4.5 percent a year. Many economists thought that the economic policies of the Ikeda cabinet would fail, because it seemed impossible to achieve such a high increase in exports while at the same time carrying out trade liberalization. The program did, in fact, run into many problems, especially with regard to deficits in the international balance of payments. But the result was far beyond most observers' expectations—the average annual substantive growth rate for the decade was nearly 11 percent.

The liberalization of trade resulted in exposing Japanese industries to severe international competition and in strengthening the competitive power of the Japanese economy. The trade balance, both overall and specifically with the United States, showed a surplus in the mid-1960s. This pattern has become even more pronounced since the early 1970s, when Japan started to export capital and the multinationalization of Japanese corporations began in earnest. Only after the oil crises of 1973 and 1979 did Japan suffer from a sharp increase in the cost of imported crude oil (the import bills for crude oil in 1980 increased by $49 billion over the cost in 1972), but it was able to overcome this difficulty through the competitive advantage of Japanese industrial technology and production. This means that although there was a substantial transfer of income from Japan to the OPEC countries, this was offset by the transfer of income to Japan, mainly from the advanced countries in the West.

Japan has been conscientiously promoting the restructuring of its economy, with the basic recognition that a free and unrestricted trade system would contribute to development of world trade. At the beginning of 1982, Japan had twenty-seven "General Agreement on Tariffs and Trade" residual quota items. Five items were in the area of mining and manufacturing products such as coal, leather, and leather products. The remaining items were agricultural products, including such major items as beef, milk and cream, processed cheese, processed beef and pork, oranges, fruit juice, wheat flour, and rice. As for tariffs, after participating in the negotiations for a linear tariff reduction during the 1960s, the so-called Kennedy Round, Japan advocated the Multilateral Trade Negotiation (MTN) of GATT, the so-called Tokyo Round, in the 1970s. Ninety-nine countries participated in MTN, and they concluded the six-year negotiations in April 1979, having reached a substantial agreement on the reduction or abolition of non-tariff barriers, and the creation of international regulations as well as the reduction of tariffs. According to this agreement, the tariffs of the major countries are to be reduced equally every year over a period of eight years, starting in 1980. Japan allowed tariff concessions on approximately 2,400 mining and manufacturing industrial products and 200 items in the agricultural area. These reductions were implemented in 1978, far in advance of the original schedule. The average tariff on mining and manufacturing industrial products in Japan will have fallen to about 3 percent after the eight years' tariff concession, which will be much lower than the 4 percent in the United States and 5 percent for the European Economic Community.

Japan enforced the new Foreign Exchange and Foreign Trade Control Act in December 1980. The basic policy of the old act was to prohibit manufactured imports and foreign exchange transactions. Through the new act, substantial liberalization of capital transactions and direct investment in-flows have advanced greatly and trade procedures have become simpler. As for capital transactions and payments abroad, the government has retained the power to control them in the case of an emergency, which may create some problems in the future.

In spite of these efforts, Japan has created trade friction with the advanced countries. During the late 1950s, trade friction with Western countries occurred in the fields of textiles, such as cotton products, and light industrial products. In the latter half of the 1960s, trade friction was common in the area of manufactured products, mainly steel, and Japan voluntarily restricted such exports to the United States and the European Economic Community. The greatest issue of this period, however, was the negotiation covering the textile trade between Japan and the United States. These negotiations started in June 1969 when President Nixon demanded that Japan voluntarily restrict the export of woolen textiles and synthetic fiber products, which Japan rejected. The Japanese textile industry resisted this demand, insisting on the principle of free trade. But in March 1971 the manufacturers declared a voluntary self-restriction unilaterally, with a view to breaking the deadlock over negotiations. This move was rejected by President Nixon and the negotiations reached a new low. This problem, set against the backdrop of an increasing Japanese trade surplus with the United States (which reached $4.1 billion in 1972), had become a political issue tied to the return of Okinawa to Japan by the U.S. government. Finally an agreement on the voluntary restriction of exports to the United States was reached in January 1972.

In the 1970s, trade friction between Japan and the United States occurred in the fields of color television sets and steel. In 1977, the Orderly Marketing Agreement (OMA), the agreement to restrict the export of color television sets to the United States, was concluded between both governments. In the latter half of the 1970s, trade friction became a problem between Japan and the Western countries in the field of machinery such as automobiles, and Japan voluntarily restricted such exports to the United States, Canada, and the EEC. Trade friction is now also an issue in the fields of advanced technology, and will be an important "battleground" in the 1980s.

According to the White Paper on International Trade (1981 edition) of the Japanese government, setting the labor productivity in the United States in 1979 as 100, Japan had a rating of 208 for blast furnace output, basic steel products, and the iron and steel foundries industry, 111 for machinery except in the electrical industry, 119 for the electrical machinery industry, 124 for the transportation equipment industry, 100 for motor vehicle equipment and the motorcycle industry, and 134 for the instruments industry. In some manufacturing industries, Japan thus ranks with or exceeds the United States. This White Paper stresses, however, that the overall average productivity for all manufacturing industries of the United States exceeds that of Japan by approximately 20 percent, and that the U.S. still enjoys high labor productivity.

The trade friction between Japan and the West is occurring in the fields of industrial production where Japan has a distinct competitive advantage. The issue has become not only an economic problem but a political one, because the areas of friction have now expanded to the basic industries of other countries such as steel and automobiles. Moreover, the long recession and high unemployment in Western countries since the oil crisis in 1973 makes the political issue even more serious. In this situation, the United States is demanding that Japan liberalize the import of beef and oranges, which are residual quota items. Recent trade friction is seen not only in these fields but also in such services as banking, insurance, and distribution, which are now also under strong pressure for liberalization. The report on Japan–U.S. trade by the Subcommittee on Trade of the Committee of Ways and Means, U.S. House of Representatives, was published in September 1980. This report recognizes that Japan's domestic product market is open in principle, but that non-tariff trade barriers (NTB) have not yet disappeared. In the United States, many feel that the closed characteristics of the Japanese market are undoubtedly due to NTB, and that Japan's market should be as open as that of the United States.

The systems and the customs of a nation state develop their roots through indigenous culture. Therefore, the Japanese recognize Western society as something very different from their own, and it must certainly be true that Westerners find much that is strange in Japanese society. A clear understanding of the differences in each culture is important to any kind of international understanding; but stressing only the differences does not make for meaningful international relationships. Many of the arguments in the United States, such as identifying the difference in Japanese business customs as a sign of unfair competition in Japan, are both emotional and one-sided. On the other hand, it is vitally important for Japan to further change the closed characteristics of its society. Approaching these issues emotionally will only lead to further misunderstandings on the part of both countries. Fujisawa's high regard for American open-mindedness and self-confidence in the 1960s seems sadly dated in today's complex international scene.

6

Automobiles, Racers, and Research

Honda Motor Company was scoring one success after another with its motorcycles, and Soichiro Honda now wanted to expand into the automobile field. In a 1961 policy statement, MITI had come up with what was later known as the "three-group system," which called for a division of the existing passenger car manufacturers into a mass-production car group, a minicar group, and a special-purpose vehicle group. The plan also stipulated that no newcomers would be allowed to enter passenger car production. Hearing of this scheme, Honda was enraged, shouting, "Are the bureaucrats trying to block our plans to build cars?" Honda fought back, his strategy being to attack the government through the mass media. The crux of his argument was that, "Democracy is meant to make individuals happy. I have fostered my own business, made profits, and paid taxes, thus contributing to the nation. Under these circumstances, why is it that a private enterprise such as mine has to be sacrificed for the sake of the nation?" Although MITI had the "three-group system" worked out on paper, actually prohibiting newcomers from entering automobile production would have run contrary to the principles of free enterprise—and was illegal as well. But Japanese bureaucrats had great authority and were able to take such steps as establishing import quotas and directly controlling inward investments of foreign capital. The ministry's tactics also included making "suggestions" to certain industries that they form joint-planning groups and, during periods of recession, even establish production cartels. This was accomplished through the direct funding of private enterprises and by indirectly asking banks to provide financing for these companies. Although some of these suggestions could have been interpreted as a violation of the anti-monopoly law, the question never came up because these steps were taken within the realm of "administrative guidance." By combining these various kinds of authority, the ministry was thus able to lead an industry in a direction that was in line with government policy.

What made this system so effective at the time was the existence of an unofficial consensus among government agencies and industry. Traditionally, Japan has been a communal society where an atmosphere of mutual trust and cooperation takes priority over legal and contractual obligations. This is especially true when the parties are working together toward a single goal. If there had been an unofficial consensus between MITI and the automobile industry when the "three-group system" was first announced, the ministry's administrative guidance might have worked, and opponents to the scheme within the industry could have been persuaded to fall in line. In reality, the industry as a whole opposed any such plan.

Although the two largest members of the group, Toyota and Nissan, did not take active steps to fight the plan, they also realized that the ministry's scheme would eventually strengthen government control over the auto industry, which was obviously not to their advantage. Their strategy was to delay trade and capital liberalization until they became internationally competitive as private, free enterprises. Until such time, they naturally wanted to receive protection and financing from the government. Because of this lack of support from the auto industry, MITI was forced to shelve its scheme.

Japan had been in political turmoil during the year prior to the ministry's announcement. In January 1960, the new security treaty between Japan and the United States was signed, and ratification by the National Diet was needed. Leftist forces were opposed to maintaining close ties with the United States, insisting that Japan must become a neutral nation. Opposition to the ratification was led by the Japan Socialist Party, the largest opposition group in the National Diet, and by *Sohyo*, who sought to mobilize the public in general, and especially workers and students.

On May 20, the ruling Liberal Democratic Party forced a vote on the treaty ratification, over the strong opposition of the other political parties. Demonstrators opposing the treaty started marching around the National Diet building every day, and on May 26 their number reached an unprecedented 170,000. Under such mounting tension, U.S. Press Secretary James C. Hagerty arrived in Tokyo on June 10 in preparation for President Dwight D. Eisenhower's official visit to Japan, the first such visit by an American president while in office. Hagerty's car was immediately surrounded by demonstrators on his arrival at Tokyo International Airport, and he had to be evacuated to the American Embassy by helicopter.

On June 15, militant *zengakuren* student demonstrators forced their way into the National Diet building compound, clashing head-on with police and resulting in the death of a young woman from the University of Tokyo. The Diet all but stopped functioning, and in the midst of these violent demonstrations, the new Japan–U.S. Security Treaty came into force. Prime Minister Nobusuke Kishi, a hard-line conservative who had staked his political life on this treaty, resigned shortly afterwards. He was succeeded by Hayato Ikeda, who, unlike his predecessor, took a "soft" approach to governing the country by emphasizing economic development, under the slogan of "tolerance and patience."

As the nation's attention shifted from politics to economics, conservative tendencies gained strength and so also did the bureaucrats. In order to realize Ikeda's "national income-doubling program," automobiles had to be fostered as an important strategic export industry, and the government wanted to exercise as much control as possible over its development. After 1955, such firms as Mitsubishi Heavy Industries, Fuji Heavy Industries, Toyo Kogyo, and Suzuki Motor joined Toyota and Nissan in producing passenger cars. This unregulated expansion was of great concern to MITI, who believed that a large number of competing auto firms could only result in disaster. The ministry also reasoned that excessive competition among the manufacturers would be detrimental to bringing the Japanese auto industry into a competitive position with the American "Big Three."

Within MITI, Enterprise Director Shigeru Sahashi played a leading role in drafting the "Law for the Promotion of Specified Industries," which was aimed at giving various privileges to such strategic industries as steel, automobiles, heavy and electrical machinery, and petrochemicals—with a view to strengthening their international competitive power. For all practical purposes, this represented a reincarnation of the "three-group system" for the auto industry. Strong criticism was voiced from many quarters against this bill, on the grounds that the possibility of government control over the economy would re-emerge. In spite of such opposition, the bill was formally presented to the National Diet for deliberation during the 1963 session.

Because of these moves on the part of the government, Honda Motor had to accelerate its schedule for starting car production, so that the company's entry into the automobile field would be a fait accompli. Until then, Fujisawa had thought it was necessary for the company to acquire sufficient technical know-how first. He recalls, "I felt like a man who was being pushed into the ring before he had learned how to box." At the 1962 Tokyo Motor Show, Honda Motor exhibited a light-duty truck and a prototype sports car. The company sponsored a contest in which the public was invited to guess the price of the new sports car. A total of 5,730,000 postcards were received in response to this promotion. "If that law passes the Diet, we will stage a huge protest demonstration against MITI on the strength of these postcards," Fujisawa said angrily.

During the 1962–63 period, Honda Motor's export earnings surpassed those of both Toyota and Nissan. MITI ignored this fact and, under a policy of promoting the nation's exports, still tried to prevent Honda Motor from entering the automotive field. It was this contradiction that infuriated Fujisawa, who realized that the company's plan to mass-produce cars would have to proceed cautiously.

There is a pervasive belief in the West that great harmony must exist between Japanese industry and the government—the so-called Japan, Inc. theory. Such is hardly the case. Government and business in Japan are, in fact, frequently in a state of bitter confrontation with one another. The type of harmonious relationship imagined in the West would be extremely difficult to cultivate in postwar Japan, for even today the Japanese people have not forgotten the nightmare of World War II, when the entire national economy was controlled by the government for the furtherance of the war effort. Japanese businesses now want to maintain a strong spirit of independence. Milton Friedman emphasizes that government intervention in private affairs serves to weaken corporate vitality. In this sense, the basic factor behind the major recovery and development of the Japanese postwar economy has been the sustained energy of private business. Although they have indeed been subjected to administrative guidance in the past, with the liberalization of trade, foreign exchange regulations, and capital transactions, the government's control over the private sector is now very limited.

By the mid-1960s, the war in Vietnam had escalated to the point that even some of the major Japanese steelmakers decided to halt all shipments to that country. At the same time, scores of vessels from the Mitsui O.S.K. Line headed toward Saigon loaded with Super Cub motorcycles. Arriving at the mouth of the Saigon River, these ships had to wait their turn to sail upriver to the main port facilities. This usually took around three days, and the insurance companies would not accept any liability, for there was a high risk of the ships being attacked. Honda Motor faced a difficult decision. If even one ship was sunk, the company might go into the red, but if the shipments to Vietnam were stopped, Honda Motor would be stuck with a large unsold inventory of Super Cubs. The matter was left entirely in the hands of a group of young section chiefs.

One day, Takeo Fujisawa came to see them and casually asked, "Are we still receiving letters of credit from Vietnam?" "Yes, sir, we are," was the reply. "Well," said Fujisawa, "I guess economic activities must be under control." Having made this rather oblique pronouncement, he left without further comment.

Fujisawa is said to be a contemplative businessman. When a problem occurred, he would enter the tea ceremony room of his house and meditate to arrive at a solution. To him, the most important aspect of corporate management is that the fundamental philosophy be understood and accepted by everyone.

In the early days of the company, Fujisawa not only found solutions, but also personally translated his thoughts into action, often in the role of a dictator. Later his methods changed, and he would usually go no further than dropping hints about his theories. Fujisawa came to believe that true leadership meant not making all the corporate decisions, but rather doing nothing at all. He was, of course, quite anxious to teach the employees, but at the same time Fujisawa tried to stay away from specific corporate decision-making as much as possible. This was his own style of Japanese management, and it was aimed at delegating authority so that employees would take their own initiative in making judgments and carrying out specific actions—all based on the theories they had learned from Fujisawa.

This strategy was not always easy on his subordinates. To them, it was like being told the first half of a poem, with instructions to complete the verse. The first half of the "poem" he gave to the young section chiefs was "economic activities must be under control." The section chiefs interpreted the second half of this poem to be, "So go ahead with the shipments to Vietnam." Yet they were to spend many sleepless nights, haunted by the fear of a ship loaded with their motorcycles going to the bottom of the river in Saigon. The bikes were manufactured at Honda Motor's Suzuka plant and shipped from the port of Nagoya. At the peak period, vessels carrying 7,000 to 12,000 motorcycles left the port at the rate of one every other day. The section chiefs even visited the ship captains with bottles of *sake*, to wish them a safe voyage. Fortunately, the ships with the big "HONDA" insignias were spared from attack, and in an eighteen-month period from 1967 to 1968, Honda Motor shipped a total of 600,000 Super Cubs to Vietnam.

In 1966, there was a sharp and sudden drop in the sales of all Honda motorcycle models in the United States, including the Super Cub, which had long enjoyed unmatched popularity. The motorcycle sales by American Honda, which had averaged more than 20,000 units per month, were expected to dip to 8,000 in September, and 2,000 in November, creating an acute fund shortage of $44 million. The sum represented 2.4 percent of Japan's total foreign exchange reserves, which stood at $1.8 billion at the time. Nor could American Honda borrow dollars in the United

States from Japanese banks, because the Japanese government had imposed a ban on the overseas lending of dollars in order to centralize foreign currency holdings and use them efficiently. Faced with a huge stock of unsold motorcycles, American Honda was at a loss as to the best direction to take.

The local representatives attributed the sales drop to the war in Vietnam, which had sent many young Americans to Southeast Asia. But as Fujisawa surveyed the city of Los Angeles from his hotel room window, he saw a healthy, prosperous consumer society and was unconvinced.

The Super Cub had been an instant success in the United States. Honda Motor continued to sell this model by simply increasing the engine power, but the basic styling had not changed. Volkswagen's stubborn refusal to alter the design of its "Beetle" had served as a model for Honda Motor. Fujisawa now realized this strategy was all wrong. He noted a distinct lack of effort to develop new models because the Super Cub had enjoyed such long popularity. And an atmosphere of neglect had been created in the factories as well, because producing the same model year after year was no longer a challenge. "The sales people must have forgotten the basic theory that vehicles are fashions," thought Fujisawa.

Returning to Tokyo, he took steps that were completely contradictory to what common sense would dictate. Fujisawa's plan was not to make any drastic effort to reduce the unsold inventories until the company could start full-scale shipments of motorcycles with a totally new design image. Shipments of all models to the United States, including the Super Cub, were suspended, and American Honda adopted a policy of reducing prices within the limits permitted by the anti-dumping laws whenever dealers placed new orders. Fujisawa knew that by the following spring, the unsold bikes would become outdated models, so that further price reductions would be legally permissible. By that time, new models would be introduced to boost sales again, resulting in a drop in the inventory to a reasonable level by August.

He sought loans from Mitsubishi Bank and the Bank of Tokyo to finance the inventories. The Bank of Tokyo obtained the necessary foreign exchange, and the two banks jointly provided

Honda Motor with a total of $47 million to finance both the inventories in the United States and a shortage of funds in Europe. Fujisawa told the banks, "We will repay you the entire sum by August next year, but we will not try to make repayment by installments before then." The reason for this provision was to ensure that American Honda would not be forced to sell off their inventories at a great sacrifice.

Fujisawa had an almost animal-like intuition for delicate changes in the social condition. When he thought about his recent visit to the United States, he could almost feel the rhythm of a fast-beating electric guitar. He then went to the R & D Center, and asked that a "different-looking" model be developed, even if it used the same basic framework and engine as the current one. "Do it quickly, because I want to start shipping it to America by the end of the year," he said. With that request, Fujisawa went to the summer resort area of Karuizawa, north of Tokyo. This was a psychological tactic on his part, for both inside and outside the company, everyone regarded Fujisawa's vacation as an indication of his confidence in solving the problem.

At American Honda, the Super Cubs were painted in gaudy colors to make them as appealing as rock music. And at the R & D Center, staid Japanese designers worked in the style of counter-culture artists to create bold psychedelic markings. These "different-looking" motorcycles were produced and shipped to the United States in large quantities before the year ended—a stop-gap measure while full-scale model changes were being developed. Fujisawa's unusual maneuver worked and sales in the United States picked up around the spring of 1967. By July the company had repaid all the loans from Mitsubishi Bank and the Bank of Tokyo.

Three years earlier, Honda Motor had announced that it would take part in the Formula I Grand Prix races. Ever since the company's victories at the Isle of Man motorcycle races, the R & D Center had wanted to develop racing cars. When this plan was finally approved, Honda Motor was already manufacturing a limited number of four-wheeled vehicles. One model was the light-duty T-360 truck, which had a maximum engine rating of 30 horsepower and a top speed of 100 kph (63 mph). The T-360 had the performance of a sports car, and became the first truck of its class to make high-speed transportation possible. Honda Motor's other entry into the automotive field was the model S-500 sports car. With an engine displacement of only 500cc, it developed 44 horsepower at 8,000 rpm and had a top speed of 140 kph (88 mph), a performance record surpassing the 1 liter cars of those days. The company's next sports car, the S-600, had 57 horsepower and improved acceleration and maneuverability. Emphasis was placed on the export of this model, which gained considerable popularity overseas.

These cars and trucks were engineered to produce high rpms, high horsepower, and good combustion—technologies that the company had perfected at the Isle of Man motorcycle Tourist Trophy races. Since the introduction of these vehicles had to be moved up due to the threat of the "three-group system," Honda Motor was in a position to offer only a small number of sports cars, for they were not yet ready to mass-produce passenger cars for the general public. This led the company to develop passenger car technologies through the grueling Formula I races.

The Formula I project began to take shape early in 1963, when the first drawings for the engines were completed. In the summer of that year a prototype engine was tested, and toward the end of the year test runs were being conducted with the newly completed body. Even during the design stage, the engineers were determined to reach a top speed of 270 kph (170 mph), and the first prototype racer was thus named RA-270. This car was strictly for testing purposes; the engineers were at the same time working on the RA-271, which was aimed at actually competing in the Formula I races.

Winning a Formula I Grand Prix was, and still is, the greatest honor that can be achieved in automobile racing. The rules at the time stipulated that until 1965 the cylinder capacity of a Formula I racer must not exceed 1,500cc, but that the limit would be raised to 3,000cc the following year. This meant Honda Motor had only two years left in which to compete with the smaller displacement machines. The company therefore decided to begin its racing program with the Monaco Grand Prix, the first event of the 1964 season, which is held in May.

Because of this tight schedule, Honda Motor opted to develop the engine alone for the RA-271, and asked Lotus of Britain to produce the body. The company thought that by so doing Lotus would also help out in areas where Honda Motor lacked experience, such as in the selection of a driver. A serious problem occurred just three months before the Monaco Grand Prix, when Lotus made the shocking announcement that they could not provide a Formula I body after all. At the time, Jaguar of Britain had complete control over the racing division of Climax Company. Because Lotus was receiving financial aid from Jaguar, it was forced to sever its ties with Honda Motor and team up with Climax. Honda Motor was infuriated by this "breach of promise," but had no choice but to do everything itself.

At the same time, the company faced the difficult problem of selecting a driver. Yoshio Nakamura, then manager of the Honda Formula I racing team, says, "From the beginning, we never thought of hiring Japanese drivers, because they lacked the experience and skills. We considered some of the Isle of Man motorcycle riders, but we noted that the gap was too great between 'riding' a motorcycle and 'controlling' a racing car. Nor did we find anyone suitable among the then active Grand Prix drivers. We had to select a new face."

A young American by the name of Ronnie Bucknam was the chosen face. Although he had proved himself invincible in local races on the U.S. West Coast, he had no experience in Formula I. In July, the first RA-271 was air-freighted to Europe. Any racing machine must be tuned so that it will perform to its maximum capacity in the actual race. This process is called "developing" the racer. The driver tests the car a number of times, points out any shortcomings, and thus develops the machine in close cooperation with the members of his team. This is perhaps analogous to the relationship between an athlete and a coach, and is a decisive factor in maturing the machine.

Bucknam tested the 12-cylinder RA-271 and found problems in the linkage of the twelve carburetors. Otherwise, the car appeared to be ready for the race. The RA-271 missed the Monaco Grand Prix and made its debut on August 2, 1964, in the German Grand Prix, a fifteen-lap race on the long 22.8 km (14.2 mile) Nürburgring circuit. On the first day of the official practice, the RA-271 was forced to return to the pit after scraping the underside of the body against the racetrack surface. On the second day, the pistons seized up due to engine overheating. The machine was entered into the final race after stop-gap repairs, but was badly damaged when it hit an embankment after twelve and a half laps. Fortunately, Bucknam escaped injury. Honda Motor's debut on the Grand Prix circuit had been unimpressive, yet the RA-271 did keep improving its position in the actual race, even though it was not able to finish. This encouraged Nakamura, who thought, "On the straight-line home stretch, Bucknam was running at speeds no worse than Ferrari or Lotus. We can hope to win Grand Prix races if we continue improving the RA-271."

The second RA-271 was air-freighted from Tokyo in time for the Italian Grand Prix, held in Monza on September 6. It was fitted with a newly devised fuel injection system, replacing the carburetors which had caused problems at Nürburgring. In the final race, in which the cars ran for seventy-eight laps on a 5.75 km (3.6 mile) track, Bucknam's machine developed trouble on the thirteenth lap, and limped back to the pit billowing white smoke. The engine had badly overheated and was gushing boiling oil. The car was obviously in no condition to continue racing, and had to be withdrawn. The final event of that year was the U.S. Grand Prix on October 4. During the official practice, the RA-271 again had its front end badly damaged. In the hundred-and-ten-lap race held on the 3.7 km (2.3 mile) Watkins Glen course, the engine quit at the end of the fiftieth lap. The coolant had completely evaporated, and the motor was nearly burned out. The 1964 Grand Prix season had been filled with problems for Honda Motor. The company demanded that Bucknam push the racer hard to test the limitations of the RA-271, and although the car was more powerful than its foreign counterparts, a poor service record kept it from being in top condition for the actual races. A lack of endurance is fatal to any Formula I machine, and Honda realized that this problem had to be solved before there could be any hope of winning races.

For the 1965 Grand Prix season, Honda Motor also contracted with Richie Ginther, an American driver with extensive Formula I experience. Bucknam was said to be capable of driving a winning car, but of not being able to refine a car to win. Ginther, on the other hand, was well-versed in all aspects of racing cars and was regarded as an expert in "developing" machines. His contract with Honda Motor made him the number one driver of a racing team for the first time in his career.

Honda Motor developed the new RA-272, with improved potential, for the 1965 season. These machines were entered in the second event, the Monaco Grand Prix. Although considerable improvements were made through the efforts of both Ginther and Bucknam, continuing mechanical problems prevented either of the machines from winning. Soichiro Honda went in person to watch the U.S. Grand Prix at Watkins Glen on October 3. Although he had long been a motor racing enthusiast, with much experience of being in the driver's seat himself, this was the first time for him to watch his company's machines competing on the Grand Prix circuit. It was also to be his last. Ginther was able to finish, but two laps behind the winner and in the seventh position. The Honda Motor team had done badly, and Honda recalls, "I could hardly keep my eyes on the race because I felt as though my entire system was turning upside down when I watched our machines."

With only one race left in the season, the Mexican Grand Prix, a defeatist atmosphere surrounded the team. They were afraid of developing the reputation that, "Although Honda Motor has powerful engines, it just can't win; it did well with motorcycles, but is no good with racing cars." Nakamura made a major decision, and asked corporate headquarters in Tokyo for total control over the handling of the Mexican Grand Prix. His request was granted, and after arriving in Mexico City he completely reorganized the team. Nakamura thought that in Mexico City, with an altitude of 2,400 meters (around 8,000 feet) and where the air is thin, the key to winning the race lay in proper engine combustion and air-fuel ratio. His aim in reshuffling the team was to make certain this theory actually worked. In complete disregard of the intra-company seniority system, he therefore adopted a rigid policy of "the right man in the right position."

The Mexican Grand Prix was held on October 24. The cars were to race sixty-five laps on the 5 km (3.1 mile) track. In private tests, the two drivers did extremely well. Ginther was bent on winning, and his growing confidence served to lift the spirits of the entire team. Nervous, he demanded that Bucknam switch cars when the latter's machine seemed faster in the official practice. In the final race, Ginther ran in first position from the start. As he was going through the final turn, his machine started drifting, and he found himself blocked by another racer. Struggling to control the car without reducing speed, he crossed the finish line 2.89 seconds ahead of the runner-up. This marked the first Formula I Grand Prix victory for Honda Motor; Bucknam had finished fifth. Returning to the pit, Ginther hugged Nakamura, saying, "We did it!" He was swamped by enthusiastic Mexican fans as he

The first Grand Prix victory for Honda at Mexico City in 1965, with (*left*) Yoshio Nakamura and the driver, Richie Ginter, on the winner's platform.

made his way to the honor platform. And from the racing circuit, Nakamura cabled Tokyo, *"Veni, Vidi, Vici"*—"I came, I saw, I conquered"—a message Julius Caesar sent to Rome after another famous victory.

That same year, Honda Motor also took part in the Formula II races with its 1,000cc, 4-cylinder engines. The driver contracted in this category was Jack Brabham, an Australian-born Britisher, who as a one-time world champion was regarded as a top Formula I driver. He had also played the part of a Grand Prix race driver in a movie, and given advice to Honda Motor on matters related to racing. On the Formula II circuit, however, he and his machine lost every race.

This came as a great disappointment to Tadashi Kume, who designed the Formula I and Formula II engines and headed the Formula II racing team. Around this time, he was visited at his hotel in London by Kiyoshi Kawashima. "I feel like hanging myself," mumbled Kume. "There's a pine tree over there. Go ahead," joked Kawashima, who then told Kume of the many hardships he himself had experienced at the Isle of Man. "At the beginning I, too, was disgusted for not being able to win at the Isle of Man. Our rider, Kenjiro Tanaka, was injured and hospitalized. Foreign riders staged a hunger strike, saying our machines were too dangerous. I really felt like hanging myself when I went to see Kenjiro at the hospital. And sure enough, I saw a pine tree," Kawashima remembered with a laugh. With the laughter, Kawashima also tried to give some encouragement, saying, "It's important to make decisions on the spot, without asking for instructions from headquarters. That's what I did."

The Brabham–Honda Formula II racing combination was to win an unprecedented eleven straight victories during the following year. Formula II racing does not receive as much publicity as Formula I races, in which the world's top drivers compete. Yet, the series of victories won in Formula II races was very important to the management of Honda Motor. The 4-cylinder, water-cooled, 1,000cc engine which Honda R & D developed for these races had an extremely high output of 160 horsepower and withstood the most grueling racing conditions. The technology thus gained could be readily transferred to the mass production of compact passenger cars.

In 1966, the cylinder capacity of the Formula I Grand Prix racers was raised to 3,000cc, and Honda Motor came up with the new RA-273. Although the engine output of 400 horsepower was second to none, the car weighed 740 kilograms, far exceeding the minimum weight requirement of 500 kilograms. The heaviness of this new machine more than offset the engine's formidable power. Because of delays in the development, the RA-273 was only entered in the Italian Grand Prix, which took place on September 4. Apparently due to the excessive weight, a tire burst and the car jumped over a guard rail. It smashed into a tree and was badly damaged. Ginther suffered broken bones, but was not seriously injured. During the remainder of the season, the Honda Motor team competed in the U.S. and the Mexican Grand Prix, but won neither race. Ginther and Bucknam's contracts expired, and both left the team at the end of the season.

For the 1967 Grand Prix races, Honda Motor contracted John Surtees, a top-ranking British driver. The son of a motorcycle racer, Surtees had grown up around engines and racing. He first became famous as a motorcycle rider, and then as a race car driver; in 1963 he was hired as Ferrari's ace driver. During a sports car race in Canada in 1965 he was seriously injured, and his comeback was described by many as a miracle. He was by far the best and the most powerful driver ever contracted by Honda Motor.

In his initial appearance at the South African Grand Prix on January 2, this "reliable man" as he was called by his teammates, managed to finish third. Yet the improved RA-273 remained excessively heavy and failed to win any of the subsequent races, even with the skill of Surtees. The company then entered the new RA-300 in the Italian Grand Prix at Monza on September 10, competing on the 5.75 km (3.6 mile) track for sixty-eight laps. This car was not only more powerful than its predecessors, but was 130 kilograms lighter. In this race, Surtees was competing against such big names as Jack Brabham and Jim Clark. The car driven by Clark was the front-runner until the twelfth lap, when a flat tire put it one lap behind. Clark made a furious effort to catch up, and in the final lap the trio was engaged in a fierce neck-and-neck battle. Because of his earlier efforts to catch up, Clark's machine ran out of gas, allowing Brabham to take the lead. The spectators were on their feet and breathless, as Brabham and

Surtees neared the finish line. Just then Brabham noticed an oil slick in front of him, and his split-second hesitation enabled Surtees to grab the front position. He received the checkered flag a scant 0.2 seconds ahead of Brabham.

In early summer of that year, Kume had been elaborating on a plan for a new engine in London. At the time, the RA-301 was under development as the successor to the RA-300 at the Honda R & D Center near Tokyo. The engine that Kume had been working on was to become the successor to the RA-301. After completing the drawings of the newest engine, he returned home in the late summer. All of the Formula I and Formula II engines until that time had been water-cooled, and so was the engine designed by Kume in London. Soichiro Honda was meanwhile trying to develop an air-cooled engine, which was contrary to both established theories and common sense, for almost all automobile engines were water-cooled. Honda ordered Kume to scrap his drawings and start designing an air-cooled engine.

At the R & D Center, the engineers favored water-cooled engines, because they thought the cooling problems of Grand Prix engines could be solved only in this way. They also felt strongly that water-cooled engines were preferable to air-cooled engines in the field of mass-produced cars. Compared to an air-cooled engine, a water-cooled power plant gave off less noise and vibration, and was more effective in heating the interior of a car. There was, however, a much more fundamental reason that led the engineers to favor water-cooling—the problem of controlling exhaust emissions. Smog had been identified as a serious problem in Los Angeles as early as 1940. In 1955, Dr. Haagen Schmidt, of the California Institute of Technology, discovered that specific smog results from a photochemical reaction of nitrogen oxides and hydrocarbons, sometimes called "photochemical smog." This prompted enactment of the Clean Air Act in the United States in 1963, which was amended in 1970 to impose rigid control on automobile exhaust emissions.

At the Honda R & D Center, an air pollution research laboratory had already been established to study the problem of reducing the emission of noxious gases, the leader in the field being Tasuku Date. The engineers began to think that in order to quickly clean up exhaust gases, a water-cooled engine was preferable, for it was easier to maintain a constant engine temperature. A bitter dispute between Honda and his engineers ensued. He was fond of telling them a story: "During World War II, General Erwin Rommel defeated the British Army in the North African deserts. The reason was simple. There was no water in the desert. So the Germans adapted air-cooled Volkswagen engines to their military vehicles." Historians might take issue with Honda's interpretation of the North African campaigns, but his technical analysis was sound: "A so-called water-cooled engine is actually an air-cooled engine using water as an intermediary. So let's do away with the water-cooling system, which is complicated and causes trouble."

Takeo Fujisawa once said, "Since I am given the total responsibility for the management of the company, if someone asks who manages it, I would answer that I do. But Mr. Honda is the president of the company. He is like the sun; he is bright and magnanimous." In the past, the engineers had followed Honda as though he were a god; but now their opinions began to clash. At the R & D Center, Kume had designed what he felt was the strongest of all the Honda Motor racing engines, the water-cooled RA-300 that had powered the car that won the Italian Grand Prix. He agreed to work on the development of air-cooled engines, but was all the while suspicious of his boss's thinking. A dedicated engineer, he was soon committed to developing the best and most perfect air-cooled engine in the world. The result was the air-cooled RA-302 Formula I engine, which was mounted on a magnesium alloy body, the weight of which had been reduced so that it barely met the minimum requirement of 500 kilograms.

The RA-302 made its debut in the 1968 Grand Prix season. The occasion was the French Grand Prix held in Rouen on July 7. The car was air-freighted from Tokyo and was subjected to rigorous testing. There was no doubt that the RA-302 had terrific acceleration; but there was also a serious defect—the engine would easily overheat. Nakamura feared that excessively high engine temperature might not only reduce the acceleration, but could also cause the loss of lubricant and ultimately the destruction of the engine. He therefore asked French driver Jo Schlesser to take it easy and not go too fast. Schlesser, who was hired on a spot contract, promised to heed that advice.

The RA-302, the last racing car that Honda Motor made, with engineer Tadashi Kume (extreme left), before the fatal French Grand Prix, 1968, in which the driver, Jo Schlesser (second from right), was killed.

Surtees was given the assignment of driving the new water-cooled RA-301. The French Grand Prix was held in heavy rains. Surtees's car was in the lead group, while Schlesser was running at the tail end. "Jo is cautious. He must be trying to finish," thought Nakamura, and he was grateful to the driver for keeping his promise. But disaster came on the third lap, when Schlesser suddenly lost control of his machine and smashed into an embankment. Almost fully loaded with fuel, the car immediately burst into flames. Schlesser had no chance of escaping. This came as a horrible shock to Kume, who was managing the team at Rouen. Surtees's second place finish meant nothing to him now. Kume and Nakamura did everything they could to comfort the bereaved family, then returned to Japan.

What was waiting for them back at the Honda R & D Center was yet another air-cooled engine. Honda was throwing all his energy into the development of the air-cooled Honda 1300 mass-production passenger car. This vehicle was to incorporate many new innovations, and Kume was told to join the development program. He was flabbergasted, saying to himself, "This company doesn't learn anything."

7

The Great Engine Dispute

During the latter half of the 1960s, Japan was enjoying the greatest and most sustained period of prosperity in the nation's postwar history. The country was now in the final stage of its rapid economic expansion, and most Japanese were beginning to feel genuinely affluent. With more than half the population comprising people born after the end of the war, the nation as a whole could more easily forget the hardships, poverty, and hunger of the 1940s. In 1968, Japan's gross national product (GNP) surpassed that of West Germany and became the second largest among the capitalist countries, exceeded only by the United States. The per capita national income still lagged far behind that of the advanced nations of Western Europe and North America, yet Japan was approaching an objective it had held since the Meiji Restoration, that of catching up with the West. However, the Japanese economy was expanding much more rapidly than the economies of Western European countries, bringing about great improvements in the income of its citizens, although the accumulation of social overhead capital, such as housing and public facilities, lagged conspicuously behind.

Having studied changes in prices, interest rates, wages, commercial activities, and the production of coal and steel in Europe and America from the eighteenth century, Russian economist Nikolai D. Kondratieff, director of the Conjuncture Institute, reached the conclusion in his essay, "The Long Wave in Economic Life," that there was a long-term fluctuation around every fifty years in the capitalist economy. This theory is known as "Kondratieff's long wave." This economic fluctuation, or "wave motion," is normally characterized by twenty years or more of continuous economic expansion, followed by another twenty-odd years of contraction. During the growth period, there is a strong and sustained prosperity, as both prices and interest rates go up. Toward the end of this cycle, an acute supply shortage of primary products appears, ushering in steep inflation. Socially, people become increasingly active during these periods of economic expansion, giving impetus to liberation movements, and toward the end of such periods, social contradictions become more apparent, increasing the chance of revolutions and wars. The case is reversed during periods of economic contraction, although near the end of these periods, crises sometimes reach such a critical stage that wars can also flare up. With respect to the cause of this long-term wave motion, American economist Joseph Schumpeter came up with a theory of technological innovation—when industry starts adopting a large number of technological innovations, a period of economic expansion begins.

The first wave motion of "Kondratieff's long wave" started in the late 1780s, and the second began around the middle of the nineteenth century. When the third wave motion started in the early 1890s, Japan had already passed through the period of confusion resulting from the Meiji Restoration. The Constitution of the Great Japan Empire (the so-called Meiji Constitution) was promulgated in 1889 and the first election of the House of Representatives took place in 1890, thus consolidating Japan's domestic political structure. Japan's economy was ready to make a great leap forward at a time when the world was entering a period of major economic expansion.

The third long wave motion entered a phase of economic contraction around 1920, following the end of World War I, just as the fully expanded world economy was beginning to shrink. During this period of contraction major disorders characterized world politics and economics, contributing to the outbreak of World War II.

The economic expansion of the fourth long wave motion started immediately after the end of the war. Overcoming the chaos of occupation, Japan took positive measures to promote heavy and chemical industries, as opposed to the light industries that had previously formed the core of the nation's economic activities, and sought to increase the capitalization of Japanese industry as a whole. The success of this policy of promoting heavy and chemical industries can be attributed to several factors.

The first was active investment in the production facilities of heavy and chemical industries. After the war, the Occupation forces purged the family members of the *zaibatsu* and the corporate executives who had served the *zaibatsu*. They were replaced by young and relatively inexperienced managers in their forties and fifties. Although criticized as being "third-class executives," they were also "reckless" managers, and engaged in stiff competition for the expansion of production facilities by actively channeling money from third parties and borrowing from banks. This was done in an effort to make up for the loss of the individually owned prewar corporations. In a homogeneous society such as Japan, the best way for these "third-class executives" to show their capabilities was through quantitative expansion of production facilities. In this sense, they were very different from their predecessors, who usually chose the cautious path of building up a corporation's capital assets. These new executives began to introduce the most up-to-date technology, so their production facilities would become modernized as they continued to work on overall expansion. And because Japan had not yet accumulated sufficient scientific and technological know-how, they actively sought new technologies from the industrially advanced nations of Europe and North America.

Private enterprise thus served as the "locomotive," pulling the entire Japanese economy along the path of growth, and a new prosperity was ushered in as private investments and capital expenditures multiplied. Between 1955 and 1961 major industries, including the capital-intensive steel and electrical power industries, launched extensive programs to expand their facilities, which led to rapid economic growth. Now that private enterprise had become sufficiently strong through investment efforts, the next task was to achieve competitive strength for Japan's principal heavy and chemical industrial products on the international markets. Capital expenditures thus increased dramatically between 1965 and 1970, especially in such industries as steel, automobiles, and chemicals. During this boom, the capital expenditures for private enterprise accounted for more than 20 percent of the gross national product, in sharp contrast to the unusually low 55 percent or less accounted for by private individual spending. Leftist theoreticians argued that such capital expenditures were excessive and unhealthy, that the living standard of the working class was being victimized, and that a depression arising from excessive production was inevitable.

Until today, however, Japan has not experienced any serious recession such as existed before the war. One major reason has been the government's control over the fiscal and monetary system, under which the government would increase public spending during times of economic contraction to boost the economy. As a result, the domestic gross capital formation (public spending, private expenditures for facilities and inventories, and spending on housing) accounted for an unusually large proportion of the domestic national product (DNP) in Japan. In 1963, for example, the proportion in Japan was 36 percent as compared with 18 percent for the United States, 17 percent for Britain, 26 percent for West Germany, and 25 percent for France. The comparable figures for 1973 were 40 percent for Japan, 19 percent for the United States, 21 percent for Britain, 26 percent for West Germany, and 26 percent for France. As Japan was behind other advanced nations of Europe and North America in its modernization programs, it gave priority to the accumulation of capital in an effort to "catch up with the West."

Japan has been able to avert a depression caused by excessive production because the accumulation of gross capital served to create new domestic employment opportunities, to increase private income, and to rapidly expand the domestic market, especially for durable consumer goods. Initially, this took the form of popularizing electric washing machines and refrigerators, which liberated housewives from many chores. Having thus gained more leisure time, the housewives started wanting black-and-white televisions, the sale of which grew by leaps and bounds starting in the late 1950s. The diffusion of consumer durables gradually spread to more expensive items; automobiles became increasingly popular among the young, while many families bought color TVs and air conditioners. The diffusion of color televisions formed the basis of today's electronics industry in Japan. Japan's mining and manufacturing industries grew very rapidly after World War II. Their production index in 1970 reached 4,200 as compared with the base figure of 100 for 1946, when production in Japan was at rock bottom, and it rose to 6,500 in 1980. Production of crude steel increased from less than 2 million tons in 1945 to 111,400,000 tons in 1980, the latter figure being comparable to that of the United States.

The labor force which supported this rapid production increase was supplied mainly from farm villages. In 1950, about 50 percent of the total working force was engaged in primary industry (farming, fishing, etc.), and about 30 percent in tertiary industry (service), while those in secondary industry (manufacturing) accounted for only 20 percent. Beginning around that time, however, an increasing migration from farms and villages to industrial plants and large cities took place. As a result, the 1980 statistics showed that those in primary industry accounted for 11 percent, in secondary industry 35 percent, and in tertiary industry 54 percent. Those farmer-turned-factory workers at first formed a strong labor offensive against the "third-class executives." This "nuisance," however, also served to make the new management understand the importance of recognizing the basic rights of the workers, which in turn contributed greatly to fostering their growth as true leaders of business circles. Although these labor offensives usually ended in failure, without the confrontation between labor and management at the time Japan probably would not have achieved the cooperative labor–management relations and the resultant high economic growth that started in the 1960s.

The government periodically conducts surveys on the people's living standards, primarily to see how they regard their living conditions. The surveys showed that those who think their living standard is middle class (not necessarily that they consider themselves as belonging to the middle class) increased from 77 percent of the population in 1960 to 90 percent in 1970, and the percentage has remained virtually unchanged to date. This eloquently attests to the character of a homogeneous society such as Japan.

By the end of the 1960s, Japan had achieved affluence and

social stability, and the world economy had also reached the final stage of economic expansion as explained by "Kondratieff's long wave." This prosperity gave rise to new and unforeseen problems. Depressed minorities demanded their rights. Sensitive young people became "angry youths." "Student power" rampaged the world over, and Japan was no exception.

For Honda Motor, whose rapid growth was closely linked to this great expansion of the Japanese economy, the year 1969 represented a turning point. The company's switch at that time from air-cooled to water-cooled engines did not just represent a change in technology. Soichiro Honda had been strongly convinced that the automobile engines of the future would be and should be air-cooled and he had ordered that all research and development pertaining to water-cooled engines be suspended.

The company's first mass-produced, air-cooled automobile, the N-360 minicar, was introduced to the Japanese market in the spring of 1967. Incorporating technology developed for the Formula I and Formula II Grand Prix racing machines, the N-360 had a high-performance, twin-cylinder engine, with an output of 31 horsepower and a top speed of 115 kph (72 mph). Reversing the conventional thinking that an automobile engine should power the rear wheels, this car had a front-wheel drive (FWD) system. Honda reasoned that, "An FWD car does not require a long drive shaft to transmit power from the engine to the rear wheels, an advantage for a small car, as a lot of space can be saved. Furthermore, a car of this type, being pulled from the front rather than pushed from behind, has greater running stability."

Until that time in Japan, no one had produced a FWD automobile. Even in Europe, where compact cars were the mainstay of the industry, the front-wheel drive system was in its infancy. Beginning with the N-360, all of Honda Motor's passenger cars to date have adopted the FWD system, thus setting the pace for the entire Japanese automobile industry. Only in recent years have the major American car manufacturers started producing FWD automobiles, this development running parallel with their attempt to improve fuel economy by "downsizing" most product lines.

The N-360 was an immediate success, and soon became the top seller among the minicars. The minicar boom, which had started shortly after 1965, was instrumental in the motorization of Japan. In 1966, the nation's total production of minicars was 260,000 units; three years later production had more than doubled. Always restless for a new challenge, Soichiro Honda started work on an even more innovative air-cooled engine. However, many of the engineers at the R & D Center did not share Honda's enthusiasm; indeed, some even considered his ideas dangerous. These dissenting engineers had to sneak away from their boss and hide in a secluded room on the second floor to make drawings of water-cooled engines. They often heard Honda shouting from below, "You guys upstairs, come down!" Such resistance on the part of his engineers worried him, for Honda was trying to marshal the energy of the entire department in the creation of an air-cooled engine that would be both a masterpiece and long-remembered in automotive history.

Tadashi Kume was to play an important role in this project. Though still favoring a water-cooled system, Kume tried to hide his displeasure and cooperated with Soichiro Honda on the development of air-cooled engines. The result of these efforts was the Honda 1300, which was introduced in May 1969. Reflecting Honda's philosophy of "revving up to get more power out of the engine," the Honda 1300 was powered by a 1,300cc air-cooled engine packing 100 horsepower and with a top speed of 175 kph (110 mph) and 7,200 rpm—a performance level comparable to the 2,000cc cars at the time. The car also featured front-wheel disc brakes and a front-wheel drive system. The engine incorporated what was called the DDAC (Duo-Dyna Air Cooling) mechanism, which not only prevented overheating but also solved the noise problem that had plagued air-cooled engines in the past.

Honda wanted to come up with new, even higher-performance air-cooled engines. While Takeo Fujisawa appreciated the Honda 1300 as an innovative automobile, its high production cost was a great financial burden. The engine had several unique features reflecting Honda's brilliance as an engineer, but it also required the use of many expensive aluminum parts. Because of the engine's high performance the body had to be very sturdy, and as a result the target weight of the car, 800 kilograms, was exceeded by 130 kilograms. Though the car appealed to driving enthusiasts, in fact the company lost money on every Honda 1300 sold.

The U.S. Congress had amended the Clean Air Act, setting forth stringent automobile exhaust emission standards. The new law called for a 90 percent reduction in the emission of hydrocarbons and carbon monoxide by 1975 and a 90 percent reduction in the emission of nitrogen oxides by 1976. Carbon monoxide control, though less strict than the U.S. standards, was already in effect in Japan. Emission control was about to become a major task for the entire automobile industry. This was of great concern to Kiyoshi Kawashima, the senior managing director of Honda Motor. He asked not Honda, but Fujisawa, to meet with the company's engineers. Until then, Fujisawa had kept away from all technical issues, but he was prepared to listen. The meeting was held late in the summer of 1969 at the resort town of Atami.

"In order to reduce hydrocarbons, carbon monoxide, and nitrogen oxides contained in the exhaust gases, the engine must be revving slowly, and the fuel must be burned slowly at low temperatures," said one of the engineers.

Said another, "This is completely opposed to our past efforts at obtaining high output from a high-revving engine. Yet, without our thorough knowledge of combustion at high revolutions, we would not be able to theorize about emission control."

"The boss says this can be done with an air-cooled engine, but that's impossible. We may be able to do it with a water-cooled engine. Unless we stop working on air-cooled engines now, it will be too late. If we continue to stick to air-cooled engines, we won't be able to sell any of our cars because of the emission control regulations," was the third opinion.

This led Fujisawa to think, "I must respect the results of their work, and their conviction and enthusiasm." Yet, in consideration of Honda's position, Fujisawa went no further than to say, "I now understand that water-cooled engines have their merits."

Shortly after this meeting, Fujisawa had dinner with Honda. They had not seen each other for quite some time and Fujisawa's mind was made up: "If Mr. Honda refuses a water-cooled engine, this would mean he is following a path different from mine. If the two of us cannot go in the same direction, our teamwork will not function." At the dinner, Honda told Fujisawa, "The same thing can be achieved with an air-cooled engine, but I guess that's difficult for a man like you to understand."

Fujisawa replied, "You can do one of two things. You can continue to serve as the president of our company, or you can join the engineers at Honda Motor. I think you should choose now."

Honda looked unhappy to have to make such a decision but replied, "I'm sure I should continue to be the president."

"Then," said Fujisawa, "you will permit your engineers to work on water-cooled engines, too, won't you?"

"I will," Honda agreed.

Their conversation had lasted no more than a few minutes, after which the meeting turned into a party with both of them drinking *sake* and singing old folk songs together. The next day Honda went to the R & D Center and told the engineers, "Okay, now you can work on water-cooled engines." His true feelings were quite another matter, and it was noted that Honda never smiled when anyone talked about water-cooling. The engineers were especially careful to avoid discussions with Honda on emission control when it came to the choice between water-cooling and air-cooling, because that would have started yet another heated, theoretical debate. Instead, they explained their preference for water-cooled engines with respect to noise, vibration, and heating.

A prototype car mounting a water-cooled engine was ready for testing one cold, rainy day toward the end of November. Honda personally tested the new automobile, and after bringing the car to a stop, stayed inside for a while after turning off the ignition. When he finally got out, he remarked, "It's warm inside." Even Honda had to admit this was quite different from an air-cooled car, which becomes cold inside as soon as the engine stops. Since then, all of Honda Motor's automobiles have been powered by water-cooled engines. Looking back, a melancholy smile appears on Honda's face as he says, "Air-cooling was the limit of my technology."

The dispute over cooling systems showed that even Honda's outstanding technological instincts could not overpower the organizational structure of the engineers at the R & D Center. He was pleased that the engineers he had been educating were now grown-up, which was why he did not take any disciplinary measures against the resistance staged by Kume and the others. "Naturally I was chagrined many times," Honda said after his retirement. "But oblivion is a wonderful thing. As I liked machines more than anything else, every time I felt low, I was able to forget things by tinkering with machines. That has been a great blessing to me."

At Honda Motor, a great deal of authority is delegated to the lower ranks, reflecting the corporate confidence in the enthusiasm and abilities of the employees, as well as the company's desire to encourage their hopes for the future. For example, when new university graduates take competitive examinations for employment with Honda Motor, they are interviewed by middle-management people. Since the retirement of the two founders in 1973, the members of the board of directors have not been involved in the hiring of new graduates at all, the company's philosophy being that the middle-management staff is younger, more sensitive, and has better foresight in judging the applicants. Moreover, it is thought that the applicants would also feel much more at home with these members of the company. Honda often told his employees, "If you hire only those people whom you understand, the company will never get better people than you are. Don't try to hire people just because you like them. Always remember that you often find outstanding people among those whom you don't particularly like."

At most Japanese companies, the hiring of new college graduates is regarded as an important event, one that determines the future of the organization. The applicants are therefore interviewed by members of the board of directors, sometimes including the president, and will be evaluated not only in terms of their overall competence, but also in regard to their ability to cooperate with their colleagues. An applicant with a strong personality is rarely hired without the specific approval of the president of the company. Except during the very early days of the company, neither Honda nor Fujisawa ever gave an interview, even when other members of the board used to participate in such hiring.

Never once has Honda claimed ownership of the company he founded. He always thought that exercising his power and authority to force his ideas on the employees would have a destructive impact on their innate sense of egalitarianism. Honda believed that this was not the way to perpetuate the enterprise, and Fujisawa completely agreed with him. This philosophy is best expressed by Soichiro Honda himself, who said shortly after founding the company, "Honda Motor does not belong to the Honda family." This declaration was not just lip service to the employees, as exemplified by two facts.

When Honda resigned as representative director and president of the company, he assumed the near-honorary role of "supreme advisor," with no authority to represent the company. Fujisawa, who resigned from the post of representative director and executive vice president, assumed a similar honorary position. In most Japanese corporations, the representative director/president is promoted to representative director/chairman of the board, where he retains a strong voice in the corporate management. This is especially true in a company headed by the founder, who very seldom loses his "representative" rights unless he makes major blunders. In this respect, the case of Honda Motor is a very rare exception.

It is also significant that Honda Motor's founders refused to let their sons run the company, and even barred them from entering as low-ranking employees. This rule has now been extended to every member of the board of directors. At Honda Motor, there is a basic philosophy that every member of the company is equal, the only difference between the president and ordinary employees being the role they play within the company. Long before his retirement, Honda said "No matter how outstanding the founder of a company may be, there is no guarantee that his son is equally capable. The corporate presidency must be handed over to a person possessing the most distinguished qualities of leadership."

In 1969, the *New York Times* reported that Toyota and Nissan had secretly recalled some 27,000 of their passenger cars sold in the United States. The story was carried in the Japanese press on May 28, first bringing to the public's attention the so-called defective car problem. Several weeks later, it was reported at a meeting of the House of Representatives Judiciary Committee of the Japanese National Diet that some of Honda Motor's cars were suspected of defects. Some critics claimed that the steering system of the N-360 and its derivatives at Honda Motor was defective, and a few went so far as to attribute certain accidents involving the N-360 to these defects. Refuting such charges was to be a great test of the collective leadership of Honda Motor Company.

Japanese automakers made public the names of all defective cars in June 1969. This was followed by the establishment in September of a system for recalling such cars in Japan, under which the manufacturers were to announce the model names and the specific nature of the defects, and to immediately recall the automobiles. A similar system had already been established in the United States, which had a much stronger consumer movement. In April 1970, the Japan Automobile Users' Union was established, which demanded huge indemnities from manufacturers, claiming that some of the accidents involving their vehicles were due to defects. These charges caused serious repercussions throughout the industry.

Honda Motor was especially hard hit by this group. In June 1970, the union demanded that the company pay 80 million yen ($222,000) to the family of a man who died while driving his N-360 in Nara Prefecture. According to a verdict handed down later by the Tokyo District Court, "By giving due consideration to possible loss of trust and decline in sales resulting from criticisms of and attacks on the N-360, and in order to minimize the damage to the company, Honda Motor in August 1971 acceded to the demand in the form of payment of a solatium." The union also demanded additional large sums in connection with other accidents involving the N-360.

The defective car problem assumed such magnitude that it was taken up by the Japanese National Diet in September 1970, and representatives of the automakers were called upon to testify. The public also began to take a critical attitude toward defects in automobiles. All of the cases in which the Automobile Users' Union blamed accidents on automobile defects have now been resolved—either the manufacturers were not indicted for lack of evidence or the courts rejected the union's demand for re-examination of certain cases.

In November 1971, the Tokyo Prosecutor's Office arrested and indicted Haruo Abe, counsel to the Japan Automobile Users' Union, and Fumio Matsuda, executive director of the union, for attempting to blackmail Honda Motor for 1.6 billion yen (about $5 million). According to the charges, the two blackmailed or attempted to blackmail a total of nearly 2 billion yen from such companies as Toyota Sales Co., Nissan, and Hino Motors, including 80 million yen they successfully collected and another 1.6 billion yen they attempted to collect from Honda Motor.

In a verdict handed down on August 12, 1977, Judge Taro Okubo of the Tokyo District Court was in almost complete agreement with the prosecutor's accusations, and sentenced Abe to three years imprisonment and Matsuda to two years. The verdict revealed that from its very beginning the Automobile Users' Union was receiving funds from car dealers who had switched from Honda Motor to another manufacturer. It also showed that the union was in serious financial trouble, because its publications did not sell well. For that reason it tried to collect huge sums of compensation money from the manufacturers.

On June 28, 1982, Judge Masao Niizeki of the Tokyo High Court reduced the terms the lower court had given. In the ruling, Niizeki sentenced Abe to two years and Matsuda to eighteen months in prison, suspending both sentences for four years. He also declared the two defendants not guilty on the charge of extorting 80 million yen from Honda Motor. In his ruling, the judge said that although the two had deviated from the normal practice of consumer movements by actively engaging in claims negotiations involving money, they had also made a significant contribution by drawing the attention of the public to the problem of defective cars.

The concept of a "defective car" is somewhat at odds with the Japanese legal system. Following the end of World War II, this system was democratized under the influence of American and British law, and tends to provide for the strong protection of individual rights. Yet, there remained cultural differences with the West, where conflicts over individual rights are resolved by reference to contracts, whereas in Japan people tend to place more importance on intra-society harmony than on legally binding documents. For this reason, there are fewer contractual disputes and a smaller number of lawyers in Japan than in the West. Many business corporations educate their own legal experts internally. Roughly speaking, in the United States there is one lawyer for every 500 people, whereas the comparable figure for Japan is one for every 10,000.

In Japan, one can claim damages if damage is caused by an illegal act. Except in the case of default regarding obligation, the plaintiff must prove that the damage was the result of an intentional act or fault on the part of the defendant. Recently, however, the principle of strict liability, which started in the United States, has entered the Japanese legal system. One example of an area where this principle is applied is that of product liability. In Japan, where massive quantities of consumer durables are mass-produced, it is difficult for a consumer who suffers from a defective product to prove the manufacturer is at fault. Under the principle of strict liability, the consumer is freed from this obligation and if a product is objectively recognized as being defective, it is assumed that the manufacturer was at fault. This way of thinking is likely to become stronger, in the West as well as in Japan.

It was Ralph Nader who first attacked car defects in the United States and became instrumental in establishing the recall system. In January 1971, Nader came to Japan and conferred with Soichiro Honda. No other leader in the Japanese auto industry cared to meet with him, for they felt that Nader was not working for the good of the industry. The two discussed such areas as motorcycle safety and the difference in specifications between cars for export and those for the domestic market. It is said that Nader was quite impressed with Honda's way of thinking.

Although the Japan Automobile Users' Union lost the court battle in its attack on Honda Motor, it still succeeded in causing great damage to the company. The N-360 minicar and other variations in its series had been best sellers and the mainstay of the company's product range, their cumulative sales total exceeding 1 million units in September 1970 for the forty-four months following the car's debut. After the union's charges were made public, sales began to decline drastically. In June of the following year, the company launched a new minicar named Life, incorporating a totally new product image and powered by a water-cooled engine. However, the new model could not quite make up for the drop in sales of the N-360. The company suffered large losses from the N-360 that were compounded by the deficits resulting from the Honda 1300, and was now forced to make up for these losses with the profits from motorcycles.

The defective car incident was Honda Motor's third major

crisis, following the management crisis of 1954 and American Honda's crisis in 1966. Fujisawa recalls, "I thought the company would be forced into bankruptcy by some outside forces. The earlier crises were all due to mistakes made within, and we were able to rectify those situations through our own efforts because we were at fault. But this time we could not do anything, because the cause of the crisis did not exist in the company. We had no choice but to wait and see. But there was something else, and that was that the collective leadership functioned very well. Neither Mr. Honda nor I said anything to the four senior managing directors about their handling of the crisis, because we thought they had to be trained and to gain experience to prove themselves as being capable of running the company in the future. They did a very good job, indeed. And it was most gratifying for us to see that they had now matured."

8

The Legacy of the Founders

"All is flux." Implied in this expression is another old Japanese saying, "Those who flourish are destined to fall into decline." An attempt to escape from this destiny lay at the very basis of Fujisawa's management philosophy. He was also influenced by the thinking of Kojiro Yoshikawa, a scholar of Chinese literature, who said that when weaving a cloth, the warp, which does not move, represents principles that do not change. Fujisawa believed that managing an enterprise is like weaving a cloth, in which the "warp" of corporate management philosophy must not move.

The early enthusiasm of the founders was expressed in the March 1954 issue of the house organ, which said, in the name of President Soichiro Honda, "Since technology knows no national boundaries, we must always keep our eyes open to the entire world." This made some of the employees laugh. They said to themselves, "What bold talk by the president of a company which is about to go under!" The company was indeed facing a major crisis, but in the end Honda and Fujisawa were able to make the entire work force understand the "warp" of the company, and thus avoided going into bankruptcy. The employees also began to understand that the goal of making the company a global operation was a guideline for the organizational "warp."

Overcoming the crisis of 1954, Fujisawa started setting up a modern organizational structure. During the preceding decade, the company had been under the dictatorial leadership of Honda and Fujisawa, and was filled with the frantic energy of a rapidly

growing concern. Fujisawa thought this energy should be channeled into a modern organizational structure, and asked ranking
officials of the firm, "Now that we have become a company of
medium size, what do you think we ought to do in order to
become a company with global operations?" The answer was
pessimistic, "Large enterprises have advantages over smaller
firms like ourselves in every respect: financial resources, capability of employees, technical standards, and the ability to sell." Fujisawa countered, "Then we will never be able to become a global
company. Yet, the fact is that we started out as a very small outfit
after the war, and have triumphed over larger corporations in the
production of motorcycles. How do you explain that?" After
lengthy discussions, the officials began to understand that large
companies also have weaknesses and blind spots that prevent the
fullest utilization of individual skills. Fujisawa left no stone un-
turned in his study of these "blind spots" in large corporations,
and took on the task of creating an organizational structure in
which every human resource and skill would be utilized to the
fullest extent. He thought that the weaknesses of large corporations could be best summed up in the phrase, "Those who flourish
are destined to fall into decline." He also knew that Honda Motor
would sooner or later be governed by the same law.

In 1949, Sir Winston Churchill's *The Second World War* was
published in Japanese translation, which Fujisawa read thorough-
ly. He was very impressed with the British leader's foresight and
tough spirit, and he followed these principles in his corporate
management. Fujisawa recalls that, "Churchill complained about
overly detailed radio reporting concerning the war, when in fact
little was happening, because he thought such coverage would
only make the British people nervous. He also criticized the insuf-
ficient supply of meat, and ordered some of the ships borrowed
from the United States to transport meat to Britain, even at the ex-
pense of badly needed weapons. His idea was that the people
must be fed sufficiently if they were to persevere in a long war. In
Japan, Prime Minister Tojo toured the city on horseback, and
when he opened a garbage can, complained because he found
things that were edible. This shows the fundamental difference in
thought between the leaders of the two countries."

From Churchill, Fujisawa learned how important it is for a

leader to have foresight. "But," he says, "I just couldn't read the final chapters of Churchill's book, because they dealt with Japan's defeat and made me miserable." Fujisawa came to feel that it was imperative to avoid corporate crises triggered by grandiose ideas implemented with little regard for the long-range future of the company. From that point of view, the most dangerous situation was Honda Motor without Soichiro Honda. Fujisawa realized that, "We must not continue relying on Soichiro Honda forever. We cannot be assured of continued corporate activity unless we have not just one but many Soichiro Hondas. We must foster experts in various fields. And we must establish an organizational structure in which such experts can fully exercise their skills." The first concrete result of this thinking was the establishment of an expert system, and the second was the autonomous status given to Honda R & D Center.

"The offensive move in our corporate management strategy is to take the first step to create the expert system. But we must not move too fast. If we do, we will end up with form but no substance. The system will be completed only after a large number of experts have been made part of the company and are accepted by everyone. This should be a 'defensive' move. But the R & D Center, which is the vanguard of the company, must be given autonomy right away," thought Fujisawa.

As he was crystalizing this idea, Fujisawa thought, "We must foster a second and a third Soichiro Honda. But what would happen if a genius were to be placed in a conventional corporate organizational structure? He certainly would not be able to climb up the ladder to a high position by virtue of his work. If, on the other hand, he were given a managerial job with many subordinates, he would have to keep himself busy with miscellaneous chores, and he would not be able to carry out his research work freely. In either case, he could not exercise his skills and be rewarded properly. Let's assume two people enter our company in the same year. One of them, a non-engineer, gains fancy titles like supervisor or manager with a number of people reporting to him, while the other, an engineer, keeps working on his own project and has nobody below him. How would the engineer feel? Even if he is satisfied with what he is doing, how would his wife feel? She certainly would not be satisfied if she compares her husband's status with that of his friend who has become a manager."

More basically, Fujisawa realized that there were fundamental differences between a research and development department, whose mission was to study advance technologies and be prepared to face many trials and failures, and a production department, whose purpose was to mass-produce goods, accumulate profits, and not make mistakes. These two departments, he thought, cannot and must not be operated under the same financial or organizational structure. His conclusion was that the R & D Center should have an autonomous organizational structure, with no corporate "pyramid," so that each engineer could devote himself to his own specialized field of activity.

When he proposed the idea of making the R & D Center independent, the company was going through a period of strained labor relations. Fujisawa's proposal thus met heavy opposition from union leaders, who thought he was trying to weaken their organization. Company executives met to discuss Fujisawa's proposal, but very few were in favor. Fujisawa remained firmly convinced that unless the R & D Center were made autonomous, there would be little progress made in research and development activities and his future hopes for Honda Motor would be lost.

He was even determined to turn in his resignation if this proposal was rejected, but he waited patiently for his ideas to be understood by everyone concerned. In June 1960, Fujisawa attended a meeting of 150 ranking officials of the company and again made his proposal. The majority view, however, was that research and development could be carried out under the existing system and that an independent R & D Center would not solve the problem. Some officials even said that Fujisawa could not understand the situation because he had never worked in an organizational structure. The following month, he disregarded their opposition and bulldozed his proposal through.

Honda R & D Co., Ltd. was thus set up as an autonomous organization, and Soichiro Honda assumed the presidency of the new company. This was the first time in the Japanese auto industry that the research and development department of a corporation had been given an independent and autonomous status. Fujisawa describes its structure as a "paperweight" type, consisting of "lone wolf" engineers devoted to their respective technical fields. In the more common "pyramid" type structure, there is a limit to the number of managerial posts that can be financially justified. In a "paperweight" type structure, there can be any number of people with such titles as chief engineer or executive engineer. They can be promoted even though they have no subordinates reporting to them, and can be made directors solely because of their technological excellence.

Soichiro Honda emphasized that, "The driving force behind corporate success is ideas. Therefore, even at the R & D Center, priority must be given to the ideas of those who work there, rather than to technology itself. True technology is the crystalization of philosophy."

Today, each of the R & D engineers is entitled to choose and register a research theme, and after proper evaluation can pursue that project alone. The underlying philosophy is to allow the engineers to define the area of their responsibility and to enable them to utilize their ambitions and abilities to the fullest extent. If an engineer with specialized expertise were to be placed in a "pyramid" type organization, he would be bound by the organization, which would make it difficult for him to form a project team consisting of the right people in the right positions, free from the problems of seniority. In a "paperweight" type structure such as at Honda R & D, formation of any type of project team is possible because the individual engineers are lined up "sideways," rather than from top to bottom. The general manager of the R & D Center, while performing administrative duties, does not issue orders from the top of a pyramid, but rather serves as a "lubricant" to facilitate the smooth operation of various project teams. At Honda R & D, even within a project team researching a single theme, more than one type of work is started from the outset, so that the results can be compared and the best finally chosen.

Honda Motor's first corporate organizational structure was established in 1953. The in-company union was formed the same year, and a bureaucratic "pyramid" structure was implemented as a stopgap response. "I was not satisfied with that structure," recalls Fujisawa. "Neither Mr. Honda nor I had any academic background to speak of. But each of us was an expert in our respective fields. We were not the type of managers who would look after our subordinates. Nor were we the type, ourselves, to feel comfortable in a 'pyramid' type structure. If we had been placed in such a structure, we would have only gained reputations as incapable managers. Our talent would have been wasted. Unless we made the most of experts, Honda Motor would not be able to grow as a unique company."

Behind this thinking was Fujisawa's own experience in his one-year military career. Of the ninety-five men, including Fujisawa, who joined the army at the same time, ninety-two became officers, but he left the army without advancing higher than corporal. In a "pyramid" type organization like the army, a soldier is evaluated by his immediate superior. Even a cadet, who could become a military leader in the future, gets no promotion unless he is lucky enough to have a good superior.

In developing Honda Motor's organizational structure, Fujisawa often thought back to the military organization he had experienced. If the system is such that each employee is evaluated only by his immediate superior, it is highly likely that some of them will fare poorly. Fujisawa's aim was to make experts out of as many company employees as possible. Honda Motor could not hope to become an international company unless it had many experts such as Soichiro Honda in technology and Takeo Fujisawa in management. But the relationship between an expert and the head of a section or a department may not always be amicable. Fujisawa thought, therefore, that his organizational structure must not bind an expert by a single line to his immediate superior; rather, the organizational lines must run both sideways and vertically, to form something resembling a spider web.

"Drawing up an organization chart can be done in less than an hour, because all that is required is to define responsibilities, create departments and divisions, and name those who head them," says Fujisawa. "I made the R & D Center an autonomous body as an 'offensive' measure. Technology is the driving force for the growth of Honda Motor, and R & D is the vanguard. I did not want to lose any time establishing a system in which the engineers could do their work without hindrance.

"Setting up overseas subsidiaries like American Honda was also an 'offensive' move. For Honda Motor to expand its motorcycle exports and grow to become an international corporation, we could not be on the defensive. By setting up an independent R

& D Center and establishing overseas subsidiaries, I am proud to say that we took the lead in Japanese industrial circles. But we had to avoid undue haste in cultivating experts. We had to wait patiently until a number of experts had emerged who were satisfactory to everyone. Establishing the organizational structures of the head office and factories should be a 'defensive' move, rather than an 'offensive' move. In short, organizations should be matched to individuals, not individuals to organizations."

In 1955, Honda Motor launched a full-scale program for streamlining production processes and clerical work, in order to both cultivate experts and establish a modern organization. Japan was then in the midst of an unprecedented economic boom, and under such circumstances corporate executives would normally try to step up production and boost corporate profits. Fujisawa deliberately avoided such measures. He felt strongly that the company must follow its own path, no matter how difficult that might be, in order to secure the "warp" of the corporate management structure, and thus grow to become an international enterprise. Fujisawa's strategy was to reduce production costs without boosting production and in the process to try to improve production methods and raise the technical level of the employees. "For a modern enterprise, the price of its products is extremely important," he says. "In order to be viable in international competition, the product must be priced competitively throughout the world. Increasing production is the easiest method of reducing costs. But, if you seek to achieve simultaneously the three goals of streamlining production, elevating technical standards, and increasing production, you will end up not fully achieving any of these goals. That is why I dared to choose the most difficult path of reducing costs without increasing production."

At the time, very few Japanese companies thought of streamlining production methods or clerical work, and virtually no one dreamed of competing in the international market. Japanese industries therefore asked the government to adopt a policy of "economic isolationism" in the form of import restrictions. Under the leadership of Soichiro Honda, the company followed its own path without relying on the government or financial organizations. Fujisawa was firmly convinced that a company that could not face global competition head-on could not escape from the law that "The prosperous must fall into decline."

In late 1956, Fujisawa accompanied Honda on a tour of West Germany, where they visited a Volkswagen plant. What most impressed them was the way cars were assembled without any paper work. At the same time, Fujisawa was surprised to learn that a young man operating a large stamping machine was being paid much more than an elderly man operating a small one, and that the workers generally accepted the system of lower wages as an employee became older and weaker. He thought, "In Japan, we take it for granted that wages increase according to age, partly because of our traditional respect for elders and partly because of the seniority system. The West German system may make more sense than ours, but we cannot adopt it in its present form."

At each factory of Honda Motor, there was an unwritten law that the conveyor line must not be stopped. As a result, each section of the plant tended to stockpile large quantities of semi-finished products. Each time these products were moved, someone with greasy hands had to fill out papers. Remembering what he had seen at the Volkswagen plant, Fujisawa thought that by carefully monitoring components and goods at the entrance and exit of the factory, this paperwork could be eliminated.

The following year, Honda Motor adopted a new filing system, whereby all the documents in each department would be filed in such a way that anyone, even from another department, could look at them and understand the work flow. Fujisawa also installed office desks that only had space for personal belongings, so that no official papers would be kept by individuals. And in 1958 graphs replaced numbers at factories, to allow easy visualization of parts inventories and production volumes.

The process of controlling production and rationalizing clerical work had the byproduct of improving the skills of those operating machine tools. Some of the most up-to-date machines were imported from abroad, but sat in a corner of the plant virtually unused. Honda himself often visited the plant, and when he saw the workers try to operate these machines exactly according to the instructions, his reaction was, "Don't you know these machines were made well before the instruction manuals were printed? Technology makes progress every day. You must try to obtain a better performance than that given in the manual."

Along with these efforts for internal modernization, Fujisawa launched a program to strengthen the distributor network. From his long experience in manufacturing, he was fully aware that distributors or dealers, when they have a strong product, tend to order large quantities, sell them fast, and receive payments as quickly as possible to minimize their accounts receivable. In this sense, the Dream and the Benly were strong products, and the sales people of Honda Motor were anxious to sell them as quickly as possible. One thing that bothered Fujisawa, however, was that some distributors were still slow in making payments. This situation was something to be expected for a new company like Honda Motor, because the good distributors were already associated with larger manufacturers. But he feared that if the company tried to increase production, it would end up with yet more accounts receivable that were hard to collect.

Because Honda Motor refrained from increasing production, its products gained a higher reputation among the distributors scrambling for them, and thus promoted a stronger corporate image. Fujisawa sought to take advantage of this situation by cultivating distributors who were reliable and loyal to Honda Motor. At the same time, he stopped delivering goods to those who were in arrears, even if this meant not being paid at all. This cut down on the number of bad distributors, thus enabling the sales department to conduct business without fear of not collecting money.

The Bank of Japan raised the discount rate in March and again in May of 1957, switching to a tight-money policy as the country's international balance of payments went into the red. In conjunction with the discount rate increases, Honda Motor lowered the prices of its products twice. Altogether, they were dropped by around 20 percent as a result of the efforts to reduce production costs. Fujisawa called the salesmen to a conference and asked them, "The factories are now ready to increase production. Are you ready now?" They were, and the sales department saw a bright future even if a recession occurred. The unprecedented economic boom in Japan came to an end in June of that year. Just as the recession started, Honda Motor moved to increase production. Two and half years of restraint had paid off, and in the midst of the recession the company was able to capture a whopping 80 percent share of the Japanese motorcycle market. A further reduction in production costs stemming from expanded production volume enabled Honda Motor's products to be priced competitively on the international markets. Between March 1953 and February 1954, the company's net sales totaled 7,729 million yen and inventories (mostly parts) 967 million yen; in the twelve months from March 1958, however, sales doubled to 14,188 million yen, while inventories were halved to 454 million yen. During this period, the proportion of inventory to sales was reduced to one-quarter. The equity ratio also improved from a low of 10.5 percent at the end of February 1955 to 43.9 percent at the end of February 1961.

Fujisawa also created a system whereby each employee kept a notebook in which to record details of his work and his own creative activities. When he moved from one workshop to another, he carried the notebook with him, so that whatever he achieved in the previous job was carried to the new workshop. At meetings, the presentation of ideas was made from the notebook by its author; thus a superior could not take credit for what was created by his subordinates. Fujisawa viewed this system as the basis for fostering experts. He once wrote in the company's house organ: "I do not believe the time will ever come when we will be producing those motorcycles of ten years ago again. They are already outmoded and have very little commercial value. Yet we must not forget that they were outstanding products ten years ago. And they served as the foundation of our corporate growth. When we were producing them, we invested the best of our knowledge, ability, and pioneer spirit; it follows that the joy and hardships we experienced at that time must be recorded." These notebooks are still being used today, especially at the factories, and they not only serve to enhance communication between superiors and subordinates but also contribute to tapping various ideas for such purposes as the improvement of production facilities.

Yet there were many problems to overcome before the expert system was completed. For example, an employee must receive proper evaluation before he can qualify as an expert. Generally speaking, however, the labor union tended to resist such an evaluation of individuals. Fujisawa hated to damage the relationship of mutual trust between management and the union, which he had worked so hard to establish. For this reason, he waited until the time was right. In April 1968, the expert system was formally instituted, fifteen years after the temporary system was established in 1953.

Western observers might wonder why Honda Motor waited. In North America and Europe, members of labor unions want to be properly evaluated for their individual abilities in their respective fields of expertise. Unless such an evaluation is made they would think they were regarded as incapable, or that their ability had not received proper assessment. This kind of professionalism has also been the cause for forming union organizations beyond the individual corporate framework and for creating unions by trade, not by corporations. In a maternal society like Japan, most people are strongly group-oriented, and tend to believe that everyone within a given group must be equal. These factors caused labor unions to resent the evaluation of individual members. And management also had to respect such sentiments on the part of the unions, for they were seeking to make this egalitarianism the basis for good labor–management relations, by avoiding large wage disparities among the employees

Honda Motor's fundamental thinking in instituting its organizational structure is that technology plays an extremely important role in modern industry, and that fostering a large number of experts will become the driving force for corporate development. Thus, the company always tries to simplify as much as possible the pyramid-type administration system in order to maximize administrative efficiency. At the same time, the company tries to enhance corporate vitality with a large number of experts trained on the job.

This new expert system was first implemented among technically minded employees directly related to production, and then extended to others, including those in clerical fields. In both areas, qualified experts are classified into four ranks depending on the degree of their expertise, and everyone is given an opportunity to advance to a higher rank. Wages are thus determined by the qualification rank of an employee. While the number of managerial posts is determined by corporate requirements, there is no limit to the number of qualified experts. Fujisawa instituted two promotion systems, one for managerial positions and the other for expert ranks. Managers are given the responsibility for carrying out daily work routines, while experts are responsible for such things as developing new technologies, in-depth studies of new fields of activity, trouble-shooting that cannot be done by the managers alone, and identifying potential problem areas, such as on the production lines.

Honda Motor's expert system has recently been adopted by a number of other Japanese enterprises. Yet, in major companies, managerial posts are still the only way for employees to gain promotion. During the days of rapid economic growth, such companies were able to place virtually all of their capable employees on the paths of promotion by creating new managerial posts by expanding their organizational structure or by setting up subsidiaries. Starting with the first oil crisis of 1973, however, it has become increasingly difficult to enlarge organizational structures, and, moreover, as the average age of the work force has increased, there are no longer a sufficient number of managerial posts. As a result, the "pyramid" type structure can no longer function efficiently. These circumstances have led other Japanese corporations to adopt the expert system, but no small number of their employees feel their hopes for the future are dashed when they are given "expert" positions.

Even after many Japanese corporations started issuing new shares at the current market value, Honda Motor refrained from following suit for quite some time. Selling new shares at current value is an easy way of "raising" funds at a low cost. "But," says Fujisawa, "if we did that, Honda Motor would lose its unique reputation for putting 'technology first' and become a company thinking about 'money first.' If a company fails in its performance after issuing shares at the current value, the stock market price will fall drastically, causing losses to the shareholders. Our shareholders have confidence in the orthodox management of Honda Motor, and we must live up to our tacit promise to them. Moreover, if the stock market price plummeted, uneasiness would be caused among our employees. I do not think we made a mistake by steadfastly following the policy of issuing new shares at face value."

Japanese corporate fund-raising has undergone many changes

since the 1970s. In the past, when a company increased capitalization, new shares were allocated to the existing shareholders in
proportion to their holdings, and were issued at face value. In
other words, the shareholder would receive the premium, namely, the difference between the face value and the current market
value. Thus, receiving an allocation for new shares was regarded
as the shareholder's privilege. This led management to shy away
from the expensive means of raising funds through issuance of
new shares at face value, and to rely more on the less costly means
of borrowing from banks. This is readily understandable, for if
new shares are issued, the company has to pay dividends out of
the profits and also bear approximately the same tax burden,
whereas in the case of borrowing from a bank, interest payments
are all that is required. Moreover, interest payments are legally
considered as business expenses, and are therefore tax-free.
Because of these factors, the management tended to place more
emphasis on expanding the scale of the company than on making
large profits for the shareholders. This way of thinking was instrumental in bringing about a sustained period of high economic
growth.

In 1969, Nippon Gakki, the manufacturer of the Yamaha brand
of musical instruments, issued its new shares at the current
market value, and this practice became common among major
Japanese companies during the 1970s. This was possible because
the Japanese economy as a whole had been strengthened and was
capable of providing funds for new shares at the higher current
value rather than the face value. In issuing new shares at the current value, the premium goes directly to the issuing company,
enabling it to secure funds cheaply. Some Japanese companies
around that time abused this means of securing funds in order to
speculate in land and stocks. These companies were not only bit-
terly criticized for this, but were to suffer severely themselves
from excessive speculation during the recession that followed.
Fujisawa thought that his company should not issue new shares at
the current value until such a method had been well accepted in
the business community. Indeed, since 1955, when Honda Motor
overcame its crisis and started becoming a modern corporation,
the company's financial policy has been most conservative.

Fujisawa, however, did take aggressive measures to sell automobiles. Indeed, before Honda Motor introduced the N-360 minicar in the spring of 1967, it had moved very fast to establish a rather unconventional car dealer network. The dealer networks of the major Japanese automobile makers, such as Toyota and Nissan, had covered the entire country. The automobile market seemed to be closed to Honda Motor, for its dealerships had been selling motorcycles, and were very small in scale. Various steps were taken to enable those small dealers to concentrate on selling. For example, a new company called Honda Sales Research Co., Ltd. was established to provide the dealers with marketing know-how; Honda Used Vehicle Co., Ltd. was set up to take care of trade-ins; and Honda service factories were established in key cities throughout the country to do servicing and repairs.

In February 1971, Honda Motor announced the concept of its newly developed CVCC (Compound Vortex Controlled Combustion) engine system aimed at meeting automobile exhaust emission control regulations. The so-called stoichiometric weight ratio between air and fuel fed to an internal combustion gasoline engine is about 15:1. In conventional engines, however, the air–fuel ratio had been on the richer side, between 10:1 and 15:1, in order to assure smooth engine operation. Reduction in hydrocarbons and carbon monoxide would require the use of leaner air–fuel mixtures of around 17:1 or 18:1. The use of such a lean mixture also serves to lower the maximum temperature inside the engine, resulting in the reduced formation of nitrogen oxides that are generated at high temperatures. The trouble with such a lean mixture, however, is that ignition becomes difficult. At Honda R & D Center, engineers were working on cleaning up the automobile exhaust gases by burning leaner mixtures. The idea was originated by Tasuku Date, senior executive chief engineer. "The reasons why a lean mixture cannot be ignited is that the energy of the sparks generated by the ignition plug is too small," thought Date. "Suppose the ignition is generated by a small conventional engine rather than directly by a plug, and the lean mixture flames from the initial engine. Then we would not have to rely on unknown technology such as computer control. If we follow this path, all we would be doing would be to combine proven technology. In doing so, we may be able to come up with a new low-pollution engine by the 1975 deadline required by the

Clean Air Act." Around 1971, a group of engineers at the R & D Center emerged who were willing to give the "Date concept" a try.

The general tendency within the automobile industry throughout the world at that time was to rely on catalytic converters as an after-treatment device to clean up the three pollutants; hydrocarbons, carbon monoxide, and nitrogen oxides. Resisting this approach, Honda once said, "The human body is made up of mineral water, the composition of which is similar to that of sea water. It does not contain heavy metals. What would happen if catalytic converters were installed in a large number of automobiles, emitting platinum, palladium, and other heavy metals that would then enter human bodies? There are too many unknowns. At our company, let us try to clean up the exhaust gases inside the engine itself without relying on catalytic converters." When the emission control regulations were announced, they felt encouraged. They thought that on the basis of the accumulation of research into combustion, they could become "champions" in emission control and contribute at the same time to the worldwide effort to fight pollution. Many experiments were conducted, which culminated in the new concept of attaching a small auxiliary combustion chamber to the main combustion chamber, supplying a rich (air–fuel ratio of 4:1 or 5:1) mixture to the former and a lean (18:1 or 20:1) mixture to the latter, each through a separate carburetor, with the spark plug located in the auxiliary chamber. This system was called the CVCC engine system. At the time of the combustion, the peak temperature in the auxiliary combustion chamber reaches about 1,600°C, but in the main combustion chamber that is held down to about 1,000°C, which is an effective means of reducing the formation of nitrogen oxides. Moreover, as the lean mixture supplied to the main chamber contains a large proportion of oxygen, it reduces emission of carbon monoxide. Although hydrocarbon emission also decreases with the use of a lean mixture, it turned out that hydrocarbons suddenly increased in the air–fuel ratio range tried by Honda Motor. The company solved this problem by oxidizing hydrocarbons within an improved exhaust manifold system.

In April 1972, the United States Environmental Protection

Agency held a public hearing on the 1975 emission control standards stipulated by the Clean Air Act, at which time the "Big Three" of Detroit insisted on a one-year postponement of the implementation of the standards. In the autumn of that year, Honda Motor's prototype cars mounting CVCC engines were shown to the public. The following year, the National Academy of Sciences of the United States gave top marks to Honda Motor's CVCC engine, which it said was the world's first to meet the 1975 standards set forth by the U.S. Clean Air Act. This announcement by the academy encouraged the Japanese Environment Agency to go ahead with their original schedule to enforce emission standards. In May 1973, the first hearing was held on the Japanese 1975 emission control standards. While a majority of the Japanese manufacturers favored a one-year postponement, Honda Motor and Toyo Kogyo were the only two companies to state unequivocally that they could meet the standards on time. Subsequently, all of the Japanese automobile manufacturers have been able to meet the Japanese 1978 standards, which were regarded as more difficult to achieve as they called for a 90 percent reduction in the emission of nitrogen oxides. In addition to improvements in engines, the development of the three-way catalyst, which serves to reduce all three pollutants—hydrocarbons, carbon monoxide and nitrogen oxides—contributed to the industry's success. As a result, car manufacturers today have a choice between CVCC type systems and after-treatment devices. This choice can now be made not only from the point of view of emission control but also from the standpoint of fuel economy, maintenance, and performance characteristics.

Although Honda Motor's plans for future technology are top secret, it is obvious that the company will push to reduce exhaust emissions and improve fuel economy. At the same time, it will try to achieve better performance characteristics, despite the fact that, at least in the past, there has been an incompatibility between the reduction of emissions and an improvement in fuel economy on the one hand, and achieving better performance on the other. One specific result of the efforts in this direction is a new engine system called CVCC II. Its main feature is that the position of the auxiliary combustion chamber has been moved closer to the center of the main combustion chamber, resulting in quicker combustion speeds and higher combustion efficiency. Another feature is the "Rapid Response Control System." The earlier generation of CVCC engines, which generated power through combustion of lean air–fuel mixtures, had shortcomings in acceleration performance. During acceleration, when the load on the engine is heavy, quick response is difficult to obtain unless the engine is fed with a rich mixture at a ratio close to stoichiometric. In such engines burning rich mixtures, the nitrogen oxide formation is controlled by sending a part of the exhaust gas back into the combustion chamber in order to lower the temperature there. This process is known as exhaust gas recirculation or EGR. In the "Rapid Response Control System" of the CVCC II engine, a lean mixture is fed to the engine during low load conditions such as cruising with a low EGR ratio, while in heavy engine load conditions such as acceleration, a rich mixture is fed with a higher EGR ratio. The CVCC II is also fitted with an improved catalytic converter to control hydrocarbons. Thus, this new generation of engines has been able to achieve low emission levels, high fuel economy, and good performance characteristics, all at the same time.

In June 1971, shortly after the company announced the concept of the CVCC engine system, it introduced the water-cooled minicar Life. Around that time, the automakers in Japan were engaged in a fierce competition over the speed of their products- an area where Honda Motor's vehicles excelled. Its N-360 minicar, introduced in the spring of 1967 with an air-cooled engine, incorporated technology gained in the automobile Grand Prix races, and with its 115 kph (72 mph) performance revolutionized the image of the minicar. Things began to change, however, with the problems stemming from alleged auto defects. Fujisawa was most keen to sense this change. When he read in newspaper articles that some of the American car manufacturers were reducing the top speeds of their products, he realized that the days were gone for the car industry to engage in competition over speed. By that time, however, the high-performance Life was already coming off the assembly lines. Fujisawa telephoned Senior Managing Director Kiyoshi Kawashima to discuss the feasibility of reducing the top speed of that model. As a result, the maximum speed of the Life was dropped to 100 kph (63 mph).

In retrospect, Fujisawa feels that "Not all of the dreams I had at the time of joining the company Mr. Honda founded have come true. Mistakes have been made, and our successors will say to me, 'Even you have made mistakes!' After all, I am human, and could not be expected to do a perfect job. But I can say at least that I did not do anything that would be a burden to our successors." He had great expectations for the CVCC engine system, and also became conscious that his days as an executive were over. September 1973 marked the 25th anniversary of the founding of Honda Motor, and Fujisawa decided that he would retire on that occasion. The circumstances surrounding the Japanese automobile industry were severe, and Fujisawa thought that the top executives must possess youthfulness: "The older one becomes, the hastier one tends to become in decision-making. It is absolutely essential that a person be named the president of a company during his forties." In January 1973, Fujisawa told the board of directors: "I would like to retire on the company's founding anniversary this year. The president is still active, and I think it better if I do not tell him of this, so that he will have time to make his

Soichiro Honda (left) and Takeo Fujisawa (right) at the Idea Contest the year before they retired.

own decision." Upon hearing of Fujisawa's decision, Honda said, "When we retire, the two of us will do so together." In October 1973, the two founders officially retired; Honda was sixty-six and Fujisawa sixty-two.

The secret of the success achieved by Honda Motor lies in the fact that its founders were fully aware of their own limitations. Except in the company's early days, Honda almost never attended the board of directors' meetings. After the establishment of the executive board system in 1964, Fujisawa stopped attending these meetings as well. The entire corporate management was left in the hands of the four senior managing directors, including Kiyoshi Kawashima, who now is the president. "As the vice president and I were the founders of the company," Honda says, "we had much greater power than those who joined us later. Imagine what would have happened if we attended the board meetings with such great power. The other members would have simply listened to us and thought how to please us. Such a meeting would have been like a meeting with predetermined conclusions. If they were left alone, on the other hand, they would do their best to achieve the best management. If the board came up with a wrong decision, all we had to do was to tell them to think it over."

Professor Daniel Bell of Harvard University believes that "Every society has a center—not just in a geographic sense but in a moral sense. It is some image of allegiance, loyalty, faith. In the United States, we used to call it the American Dream—the idea that this society was free, open, mobile, in other words, people of talent would have a chance to go up. This was an element which held the society together."[15] In the paternal society of the West, the mounting demand for more rights often serves as a force which disintegrates the society, heightens social tensions, and in some cases gives rise to nihilism. That is why in the West, so much importance is attached to the "center" as a way of making the society coherent. In a maternal society such as Japan's, which is held together by strong dependency relationships, cohesiveness is a natural function of Japanese culture. These relationships of dependency and obligations have been termed "frames" by Professor Chie Nakane of the University of Tokyo, and Japanese very seldom willingly step outside these "frames."[16] Within a corporate "frame," this tendency is expressed in an allegiance to the company, and within the "frame" of the nation it becomes nationalism.

In the West, the leadership of the corporate management occupies the "center" of the organization, and its unifying force spreads either from the center to the perimeter, or in a pyramid type structure, from the top to the bottom. Top executives and middle management gather their staff together to work out plans, which are handed down to the lower levels through the chain of command, with the workers doing their jobs simply by following the manuals given to them. This type of "top down" system is likely to be resented in Japan, where employees present various ideas of their own in the hope that their opinions will be reflected in corporate activities. This is closely related to the high quality of Japanese products such as automobiles.

Honda and Fujisawa of course have a common hope for the perpetual prosperity of the world-famous company that they built. Yet, since their retirement neither has said anything about the management of Honda Motor. Each man has achieved fame and wealth in just one generation, and they are now walking on new and separate paths. Fujisawa lives surrounded by the works of modern art of which he is so fond. He seldom comes to the company office, and spends time taking care of his garden.

Though satisfied with the years he spent with Honda, Fujisawa says, "Looking back at my many years of experience in managing the company, I can recall incidents in which my decision-making was not perfect and in which I wish I had acted differently. One such incident was when we were competing in the Formula I and Formula II Grand Prix races. We first entered the Formula I races in 1964, and in the second year we had already won the Mexican Grand Prix. And in 1966, we teamed up with the top-notch driver Jack Brabham and scored eleven consecutive victories in Formula II races. This unprecedented feat is worthy of high praise.

"The Formula I machines were powered by 1,500cc water-cooled engines, and the Formula II with 1,000cc, 4-cylinder water-cooled engines. Those engines incorporated technologies that could be readily transferred to mass-production engines. By winning the Formula I and Formula II races, I think the company already possessed sufficiently sophisticated technologies to mass-produce automobile engines. More than that, I think the company had already mastered techniques to build car bodies.

"Despite the fact that we had already made sufficient progress with mass-producible water-cooled engines, I did not make a perfect decision, and that still is a source of regret. When the Honda 1300 was being developed, no discussion was made as to whether the car should be powered by an air-cooled engine or by a water-cooled engine. Some of the engineers wanted to work on a water-cooled engine, but I did not listen to their wishes. That is what I particularly regret.

"The Civic model, which has gained the reputation of being 'the basic car of the world,' has been received most favorably in many parts of the world despite such unfavorable factors as the worldwide recession and the high value of the Japanese yen. Some engineers may say that today's Civic would not have come about without their experience with the air-cooled engine for the Honda 1300. But I feel that on the basis of the achievements with the Formula I and Formula II racing cars, we could have made a car like the Civic at the time we developed the 1300.

"If we had chosen an alternative course at the time of developing the Honda 1300," says Fujisawa, "I feel we would have made a perfect decision. If we had done that, the company probably would have made a much greater leap forward at the time when the Japanese automobile industry was entering into a period of rapid growth that will never be repeated again.

"Honda Motor has been able to grow through the top priority given to technology. But there are times when the management must take priority over technology."

Soichiro Honda opened a private office in the heart of Tokyo shortly after his retirement, and he now keeps himself busy tackling problems related to technology and philosophy through the Honda Foundation, which he himself has created. Former French President Valery Giscard d'Estaing was especially interested in the activities of the Honda Foundation. When Honda met with him in Paris, the French president told him he considered Honda to be an extremely happy person in that he was able to spend his "first" life as an industrialist and is now pursuing his "second" life delving into problems related to technology and philosophy. Technology has always been his dream and his love. "Life is not worth living if one cannot do what one likes most," he says.

"What I fear is that no matter how well things are going now, there is no guarantee that they will continue to go well forever," says Honda. "In this changing world, it is odd to decide everything for the future at this point in time. If a decision is left open, one can be flexible to future changes. In this sense, I do not believe in making a will. Even if one's will is left, the world keeps on changing anyway. I will not make a will, and will die a quiet death, because I believe that the basis for prosperity is not to predetermine what the future of Honda Motor should be."

Japanese religion, philosophy, and the closely related views on life and death are very different from those of Christianity. In the Orient, there is the philosophy of an endless series of rebirths (*samsāra* in Sanskrit), also one of the most basic doctrines of Hinduism. Generally speaking, the Japanese accept this way of thinking, and they believe in the continuity of life. In the West, while death is thought to be compensated for by an afterlife, it still is an enemy that one should try to fight as long as possible.

Robert J. Lifton, a psychiatrist and professor at Yale University, studied the views on life and death of six leading Japanese figures (Maresuke Nogi, a military leader, Ogai Mori, a novelist, Chomin Nakae, a philosopher, all of the Meiji Restoration era; Hakucho Masamune, a novelist active at the beginning of this century; and Hajime Kawakami, a Marxist economist who lived from 1879 to 1946, and Yukio Mishima, a novelist of the post-World War II period), and published the book *Six Lives, Six Deaths*, which was written jointly with Shuichi Kato and Michael Reich. Comparing the views on life and death of the Japanese and Americans, Professor Lifton says, "My colleagues and I, in connection with this book, had to address the paradigm of symbolization of the continuity of life. In Japan, the continuity is one aspect that is enormously important. And another related aspect, we felt, was a certain Japanese sense that the cosmos is there, nature is there, one goes back into it—that is something appropriate, acceptable and inevitable for the Japanese, as opposed to the Western sense of fighting it."[17]

Such philosophical differences between Japan and the West are also reflected in social phenomena. In the West, when rationalism goes to extremes, it gives rise to nihilism, which in itself stems from the denial of rationalism, and this leads to actions destructive to the society. In Japan, on the other hand, the heightening of rationalism gradually melts into profound Oriental philosophy, and leads to an acceptance of human fate. There have lately been moves among American business executives to study the Japanese style of management. And this trend is seen not only in management but also in changing attitudes toward life and death. Says Professor Lifton: "The Americans have a lot to learn from a certain Japanese attitude to death. In the U.S., the measures of suppression of ideas of death went very far—there was a tremendous amount of denial of death. The trend is reversing itself now."[18]

For business executives, and especially for entrepreneurs, philosophy or basic ways of thinking are as important as corporate business strategies. The founder's philosophy tends to live within the corporation for a long time. Soichiro Honda is a rationalist, and has directed his enthusiasm toward scientific and technological development. These days, however, he is attracted to Oriental philosophies, and that was why he did not choose to fight to secure sustained control over the company he had founded. He believes in the continuity of the "corporate life" even after his retirement. In other words, he trusts the younger generations, and is optimistic about the future.

Honda says, "One thing I never say is 'Young people nowadays . . .' After all, the same thing was said about me when I was young. The younger generations are naturally more advanced. Although I have already reached the age of having to think of the 'landing' of my life, a person gets a better feeling when he is pulling back the control stick to lift the airplane. What I am trying to do is to help younger people fly safely. I would say to young people: 'Have your own purpose in life, hold your control stick tight, and fly high.' "

After retirement, Soichiro Honda created two foundations. One is the International Association of Traffic and Safety Sciences, with funds put up jointly, but privately, by Honda and Fujisawa. It holds symposiums to conduct research on traffic safety problems on a worldwide scale. The other is the Honda Foundation, which is funded primarily by Honda himself. Though its endowment of about 1.1 billion yen is small compared with those of the Rockefeller Foundation or the Ford Foundation of the United States, its activities can be considered unique.

The activities of the Honda Foundation are called "DISCOV-ERIES," which represents the initials of "Definition and Identification Studies on Conveyance of Values, Effects, and Risks in Environmental Synthesis." The basic theme is Honda's thought that "science and technology have contributed greatly to the happiness of mankind, but at the same time they have brought about many miseries." Specifically, the DISCOVERIES movement is aimed at discovering problems of human beings in the total environment and at finding means of solving these problems.

The foundation has held several international symposiums, starting with "The 1st DISCOVERIES International Symposium," held in Tokyo in October 1976 on the theme of "An Intelligent Human Approach to Traffic Problems." Attempts were made to discover academic and cultural approaches to the question of what transportation means to modern society and to future generations. The second symposium was held in Rome in 1977. Through discussions on the theme of "Review to Cope with Mega-crisis," it was confirmed that "(1) the interdisciplinary approach adopted by DISCOVERIES is indispensable in resolving the various problems faced by modern society, such as population, food shortage, energy resources, and mutual understanding; and (2) new scientific approaches, and in particular data analysis by computers, should be used together with traditional scientific methods related to mankind."

The principal theme of the third DISCOVERIES International Symposium, held in Paris in 1978, was "Communication in Human Activity." His Majesty the King of Sweden delivered the opening address at the fourth DISCOVERIES International Symposium. Forty specialists from such fields as science, political science, sociology, and philosophy met to discuss "Man and Society—Automated for Information Processing."

Addressing the final day of the first symposium held in Tokyo, Soichiro Honda said, "Until now, I have not had much association with scholars. I have now discovered that the scholars are like kindergarten children because they endlessly ask questions of 'why?' to seemingly obvious matters. This attitude has been so new and fresh to me that I could not help but stay throughout the entire symposium."

In connection with the DISCOVERIES symposiums, Honda often goes overseas, where many people have asked, "Why are you so concerned about such problems as technology and philosophy, when you are the owner of Honda Motor?" When he answers, "I am not the owner of the company," they are invariably caught by surprise, and at the same time are impressed by the fact that he is a self-taught man without a formal educational background. He and Fujisawa left their managerial positions at Honda Motor together, and they both disclaimed ownership of the company. This way of retirement is virtually unthinkable in the West, and is exceptional in Japan as well.

9

Under Kawashima's Leadership

Every corporation has a history, and the characteristics of that organization must be understood within the context of the times. Moreover, these characteristics are deeply rooted in the cultural background of the country where the corporation is established. This is especially true in Japan, where the management system has evolved through trial and error during the entire course of the country's modernization, particularly during the postwar years. Under the leadership of Soichiro Honda and Takeo Fujisawa, Honda Motor has become virtually synonymous with Japan's "economic miracle." But corporations, especially during periods of rapid expansion, do not grow in a uniform way. Sometimes they grow almost explosively, while at other times they tend to gather their forces internally, and to outsiders it might appear that the corporation's growth has nearly come to a halt. Reviewing the history of Honda Motor, one would notice that ever since its founding, the company has undergone such a change almost every ten years.

The first cycle was from the firm's inception to the corporate crisis of 1954. This was a period of great expansion for the company, when it dominated the Japanese motorcycle market with the Dream Type E and the advantage of modernized production facilities. Yet throughout this period, the management system at Honda Motor was no better than what could be found at any small, countryside plant, with Honda and Fujisawa exercising virtually dictatorial control.

The next period was from the management crisis to the creation of a tightly knit board of directors in 1964. Honda Motor had now become a worldwide enterprise by conquering the motorcycle market with the Super Cub. The company's management style was beginning to assume the characteristics of a large, modern corporation, and plans were being made to educate successors to the founders.

The third cycle extended to 1973, when Honda and Fujisawa retired. These years were marked by the company's full-scale entry into the production of cars and trucks, great success in its passenger car range, and the development of the low-pollution CVCC engine system. In the management area, a collective leadership system was gradually being formed.

The fourth cycle began in October 1973, when Kiyoshi Kawashima assumed the presidency, and this cycle is continuing now. During this period, the company has pursued a number of innovative policies, including an active international strategy to make Honda Motor a multinational corporation.

The management system under Kawashima might best be described as one of collective leadership. While it would be premature to pass judgment on the accomplishments of the "collective leadership," it should be noted that Honda Motor's gross turnover, which stood at 366.7 billion yen during fiscal year 1973, exceeded 1 trillion yen in fiscal 1979—an achievement unmatched by any other Japanese company founded after World War II. This turnover increased to a remarkable 1.5 trillion yen ($6,800 million) in fiscal 1980. This figure is equivalent to only one-tenth the turnover of the world's largest automaker, General Motors Corporation, and about one-third that of Japan's two auto giants, Toyota and Nissan. Yet, in terms of actual growth rate, Honda Motor's performance has been a "miracle."

Japanese corporations exist in an environment quite distinct from that of the United States and Europe. Theoretically, under Japanese commercial law the stockholders are the owners of a joint stock company. In fact, these stockholders do not have a strong sense of ownership, and there is a widely held view in Japan that a company exists for the good of its employees. Virtually all members of the board of directors are chosen from among the employees of the company. These directors are of course obliged to improve corporate performance, pay dividends to the stockholders, and increase equity for the benefit of the stockholders. But their primary concern is to increase the company's market share (for which they are often willing to sacrifice short-term profits), to expand the scale of the company, to raise the salaries and improve the welfare of the employees, and to offer them sizable bonuses in addition to their regular salaries. Although this bonus is classified as being part of past wages for accounting purposes, it is in fact a means of sharing profits with the employees.

According to statistics issued by the government, the rates of this biannual bonus against the monthly wages in 1979 were as follows. In the case of male white-collar workers who graduated from four-year universities working for companies with more than a thousand employees, the amount was equivalent to their salary for 5.2 months in the mining industry (¥1,378,900 for a worker who is 37.0 years old), 4.2 in the construction business (¥1,091,600; 35.1 years old), 5.2 in manufacturing (¥1,379,500; 36.1 years old), 5.0 in wholesale and retail (¥1,254,400; 33.9 years old), 4.6 in the financial and insurance areas (¥1,726,000; 34.5 years old), 5.6 in realty (¥1,481,600; 35.2 years old), 4.7 in the transport and communications industry (¥1,080,800; 35.4 years old), and 4.4 in the electric and gas industry (¥1,229,000; 36.2 years old). Male blue-collar graduates from high schools and technical colleges belonging to companies with more than a thousand employees received a 4.5-month bonus in the food industry (¥897,500; 31.4 years old), 3.6 in the textile industry (¥622,200; 31.7 years old), 4.3 in the chemical industry (¥904,800; 32.9 years old), 3.4 in the steel industry (¥727,000; 33.9 years old), 3.6 in the electric appliance industry (¥666,500; 30.1 years old), and 3.3 in the transport equipment industry (¥650,000; 29.9 years old). The rate of biannual bonus against monthly wages usually changes according to business fluctuations.

The labor unions of private corporations in Japan are very careful if they think a large raise in wages might cause inflation or unemployment. Generally speaking, Japanese people are eager to save money, and even blue-collar workers have large savings deposits (according to statistics released by the Bank of Japan, this amount averaged 3,450,000 yen or $16,000 in 1981). This also makes workers and unions very sensitive about inflation. After 1970, when the growth of the economy turned sluggish, labor unions were very concerned about maintaining the lifetime employment system and not so aggressive about getting large wage increases. The number of strikes thus declined. This tendency is certainly to the advantage of the employers. The most serious problem facing labor unions today is how to maintain the lifelong employment system and at the same time extend the retirement age from fifty-five to sixty.

It should be noted that Japanese corporations were quite different before the end of World War II. During that period, *zaibatsu* families controlled holding companies. These companies were the major stockholders of many large corporations and absorbed a large share of their profits. In the prewar days, there were four major *zaibatsu*—Mitsui, Sumitomo, Mitsubishi, and Yasuda—plus a number of smaller ones like Asano, Kawasaki, Furukawa, and Nissan. Almost all major Japanese corporations were under the control of these *zaibatsu*. Although the elite members of these corporations had a strong sense of loyalty, ordinary workers were paid low wages and felt little sense of unity with the company. A dramatic change in this situation came about immediately after the war, when the Occupation forces dismantled the *zaibatsu* in a bid to deprive Japan of its ability to wage another war. They also liberated the farmers, destroying the landlord–tenant relationship that had been so detrimental to Japanese agriculture, and created owner-farmers. One reason for this measure was to further the demilitarization of Japan, for the once formidable Japanese Imperial Army was made up almost entirely of tenant farmers. It was not long before the sons of these farmers, riding the tide of industrialization, moved to big cities en masse, got jobs at factories, and infused industry with a spirit of agrarian cooperation. Thus, after the end of the war, a sense of unity gradually developed between management and blue-collar workers. Great progress was made in formulating the Japanese management system based on this spirit of unity, and the basis for a cooperative labor–management relationship was established. The success of the Japanese economy today, which is rooted in this unique system of management, can be traced back to the liberal postwar democratic reforms instituted by the Occupation forces.

As in Europe and North America, the supreme decision-making body of a corporation in Japan is the stockholders' meeting. In Japan, however, this meeting is no more than a ceremony, an understanding on all major issues having been reached between the company and major stockholders beforehand. Such meetings are usually brief, and very seldom will an individual stockholder express objections to any item on the agenda. This spirit of harmony, in sharp contrast to the melees that sometimes erupt at shareholders' meetings in the West, can be attributed to the system of owning stocks in Japan.

Since 1947, holding companies that control corporations have been illegal; instead, Japanese companies now tend to own each other's stock. For example, two companies that deal with each other in business transactions will also exchange shares as a means of cementing their relationship. As a result, of the total number of shares listed on the stock exchange, more than 70 percent are owned by corporations and less than 30 percent by individual stockholders.

During the postwar era, companies that had belonged to a *zaibatsu* joined together again to establish new groups, such as the Mitsui Group and the Mitsubishi Group. A bank usually forms the core of such a group, within which the member firms will own each other's stocks. Under the Anti-Monopoly Law, however, a financial institution such as a bank, a trust company, an insurance firm, or a securities company is not permitted to own more than 5 percent of the issued shares of another company, the purpose being to prevent a financial institution from dominating an industry. Thus within each "group," companies can establish a close relationship through the mutual ownership of stocks, without running the risk of being dominated by a banking firm. While there are cases where stocks are mutually owned by companies belonging to different "groups," this is more an exception than the rule.

In this system, the major stockholders of one corporation are usually companies within the same "group," and these stockholders are quite familiar with the status of the company in question. Therefore, it is rarely necessary for these stockholders to be briefed at a formal stockholders' meeting. Under this system, the member firms within a group usually agree to keep dividend rates low on a reciprocal basis, which in turn enables them to allocate large portions of their profits to internal reserves for further corporate growth. The stockholders are not in a position to receive generous short-term dividends, but in the long run this is more than offset by the accumulation of sizable capital gains. The system also enables the management of an individual corporation to concentrate on long-range strategies, without being bothered by pressure from stockholders for quick returns.

In a Japanese corporation, the highest decision-making body is the board of directors, and in this sense there is little difference from an ordinary American company. But a Japanese firm is distinct from its American counterpart in several important ways.

The board of directors of a Japanese corporation includes very few non-executive, outside members. As a result, the board members are of the same educational and social background, know each other well, and find it relatively easy to reach a consensus. Moreover, it is rarely the case that board members will enter into a heated discussion on any agenda item or vote to amend or to reject any proposal put to them. These members are classified into "ranks"—the highest (at least in theory) being the chairman, followed by the president, one or more executive vice presidents, senior managing directors, managing directors, and directors. (These are English translations of the titles adopted by Honda Motor; other Japanese corporations have different English titles, such as executive director and senior vice president.)

In reality, the ultimate decision-making function of a Japanese corporation rests in a meeting of the senior members of the board, consisting of either managing directors or senior managing directors and those of higher rank. A plenary meeting of the board usually does little more than approve what has been previously decided by the senior members. One drawback of this system is that decisions are made by a small group of internal executives, as compared to the American system where decisions are made based on the views expressed by representatives from many different outside fields.

The board of directors of a Japanese corporation not only serves as the highest decision- and policy-making body, but each member is also a full-time executive in the company. This is very different from an American corporation, where the chairman of the board has the highest decision-making authority, and below him is an executive organization headed by the president, as the chief executive officer, followed by a number of executive vice presidents. In other words, in the United States there is a clear distinction between policy-makers and executives, whereas in Japan the same people play dual roles.

Another feature unique to Japan is that under commercial law, a corporation must designate one or more members of its board of directors as "representative directors," namely, those who have the right to represent and make major commitments on behalf of the company. In certain Japanese corporations, the chairman is vested with this right, but the chairmanship is usually no more than an honorary position given to a retiring president. Unlike most American companies, where the chairman of the board is totally responsible for the affairs of the company, these responsibilities within a Japanese corporation are generally shared by a group of representative directors. For this collective leadership to function well, there must obviously be a strong sense of unity and mutual trust among the board members.

This type of collective leadership and collective responsibility characterizes the top management of Honda Motor Company. The company has never had a chairman, for when Soichiro Honda retired from the presidency, he chose not to accept such a position. Honda Motor followed a policy of division of responsibility even when it was run by the two founders. Although Honda was the president and Fujisawa the executive vice president, they shared equally in the executive duties and responsibilities of the firm. Fujisawa recalls, "When Mr. Honda ran into an impasse on a technological matter, there was nothing I could do to help him because I was a total amateur in technology. Similarly, when I could not solve a problem related to corporate management, I could not ask Mr. Honda for help because he was totally engaged in technical matters." Except during the first few years of the company's existence, the two seldom met or consulted with one another, each preferring to operate within the area of his respective expertise, a type of management system that was possible only because the Japanese auto industry was in the early stages of development, and international political and economic conditions were stable. Fujisawa was aware of this problem, and decided that rather than having individual offices, all the board members should work together in one room. He reasoned that by doing so the members, through their daily conversations and common information base, would better understand one another and act promptly to changes in the circumstances surrounding the company.

Within Honda Motor's board of directors is a body called the *Senmu-kai* (meaning literally, "a meeting of the senior managing directors"). This group consists of the president, three executive vice presidents, and four senior managing directors, all of whom are representative directors. At this meeting of representative directors, agenda items for a plenary session of the board are adopted. At the plenary sessions the directors actively discuss those items, but almost never reject any of the agenda items proposed by the *Senmu-kai*. Again, this is because the members of the board share the same up-to-date information and develop unified points of view.

For all practical purposes, the *Senmu-kai* is the highest decision-making body within Honda Motor. Yet issues of major importance, such as the appointment of upper management personnel and medium- to long-term corporate planning are always discussed by the president and executive vice presidents. The top management of Honda Motor thus takes the form of collective leadership and collective responsibilities among the president and the three executive vice presidents. "When Mr. Honda and I were active in the company, things were stable. For example, the foreign exchange rate was fixed at 360 yen to the dollar," says Fujisawa. "But today, the exchange rate fluctuates drastically, and as a result the consolidated profit figures turn out to be far different from what one could have anticipated. And this can lead to a false impression of the company's performance. Besides, the oil crisis triggered sharp increases in fuel costs and has led to turmoil on the international scene. In this kind of world, the president cannot be expected to bear the entire burden himself. At Honda Motor, the president and the executive vice presidents share the responsibilities collectively. The company is and must be one entity."

In 1973, Honda Motor created three expert committees under the *Senmu-kai*. One committee dealt with personnel, another with equipment, and the third with finance. They were given the task of evaluating corporate affairs from the standpoint of these major areas and of identifying problems within the organization. The work flow in a company is usually divided in a vertical manner, leading to poor communication among the various divisions and a lack of organizational flexibility. The expert committees at Honda Motor were created to promote flexibility in corporate activities and a structure that was free from this vertical sectionalism. All managing directors and ordinary directors belonged to one of these three committees.

The committees came into being shortly before Kiyoshi Kawashima assumed the presidency of the company, apparently in preparation for the changeover at the top management level. At the time, Honda Motor was in such a favorable position that some cynics even suggested that the company could survive under Kawashima's management by simply eating up the interest accruing from the huge assets left behind by his predecessors. Initially, Kawashima did indeed refrain from adopting drastic or flamboyant new strategies. He concentrated instead on a careful review of the system established under Honda and Fujisawa and on strengthening the company's infrastructure. Specific ways to implement the new president's strategy were assigned to the expert committee.

The new management system under Kawashima almost coincided with the oil crisis, which brought about sharp increases in the cost of oil products and caused run-away inflation in Japan. In the fall of 1973, all Japanese auto manufacturers raised their car prices by 7 to 8 percent, mainly due to the additional cost of controlling exhaust emissions. Almost immediately, car makers raised their prices again by approximately another 10 percent because of the sharp increases in oil prices. Honda Motor was the only exception, a decision that was most welcomed by the general public and applauded by the mass media. Kawashima's strategy was twofold: to promote Honda Motor's corporate image as "an honest, sincere company" and, perhaps more importantly, to give added impetus to his program of reinforcing the corporate infrastructure. By refraining from raising car prices, he was thus urging the workers to reduce production costs as a means of strengthening the company's competitive position.

Several years later, Kawashima declared, "Now is the time to take action!" This signalled the beginning of an aggressive strategy by Honda Motor, consisting of three major elements. One was to increase car and truck production to 1 million units per year, which upper management recognized as the minimum condition for the company to survive as an automaker and at the same time maintain an acceptable growth rate. This target was met in 1981. The second strategy was to boost motorcycle production both at home and abroad. Honda Motor's motorcycle production today has exceeded 3 million units per year. The total sales show an excellent balance—one-third of the bikes are made and sold in Japan, another third are manufactured in Japan for export, and the remainder are manufactured and sold overseas. The final step was to increase production and sales, mainly outside of Japan, of what the company calls "power products," which include multipurpose power units, generators, tillers, lawnmowers, outboard motors, and water pumps.

All of Honda Motor's products are based on compact, high-performance engines, which have been the company's heritage since the early days of Soichiro Honda. Honda Motor has made no plans to diversify into fields unrelated to engines or to become a conglomerate by taking over other companies. Some corporations enter unrelated fields as a means of protecting themselves against risks, but Soichiro Honda said long ago that this kind of diversification would be dangerous, for it could lead the management to think lightly of the main business of the company.

Among the many aggressive strategies launched by Kawashima, the most important may prove to be the construction of an automobile plant in the United States. A feasibility study of the project dates back to 1971, and a full-scale study was initiated during the early days of his presidency, shortly after the first oil crisis. In 1975, a formal project team was established, consisting of representatives from the production engineering division, the research and development division, and American Honda Motor Co., Inc. The following year, their study on specific aspects of car production in the United States had narrowed the number of candidate sites to around thirty and a detailed investigation by two American consulting firms was commissioned. At a meeting in August 1977, the *Senmu-kai* agreed to pick the final site from two choices in Ohio. After a series of negotiations with the state government, it was decided to build a motorcycle plant near Marysville. The establishment of an automobile plant in the United States was based on the company's experience in building a motorcycle plant in Kumamoto, on the southernmost large Japanese island of Kyushu, and on the successful management of motorcycle production in Ohio starting in September 1979.

The project to construct the Kumamoto factory was headed by Shigeru Shinomiya, executive vice president of Honda Motor, and construction work got underway in June 1974. Primary emphasis was placed on designing the Kumamoto factory to produce motorcycles for export at an internationally competitive level, on producing not only complete motorcycles but also major components for assembly abroad, and on the plant achieving a break-even point even if it had to operate at 50 percent capacity in reaction to dramatic changes on the international scene. Experts in their thirties were appointed to serve as the leaders of various design groups for the project, and their ideas and suggestions were taken seriously. If these responsibilities had been handed over to more mature people in their forties, they would have built a plant well suited for today's circumstances. It was hoped that the younger generation would build a plant for the future.

Since the Kumamoto factory had to be profitable at a 50 percent working capacity, much thought was given to lowering the transportation costs for components, which is usually a large portion of the cost of manufacturing motorcycles. This involved cost reduction not only in the factory, regarding the stocking and transport of components to be assembled abroad, but also in the supply of goods from outside vendors to the plant, transportation from the factory to the ports of Hakata and Moji in northern Kyushu, and even transportation to the final assembly plants overseas. In building the Kumamoto factory, the company also gave high priority to harmonizing with the local resident communities. This was important, because the cooperation of local residents was indispensable in locating suppliers at convenient sites and assuring the efficient transportation of components to the plant.

The so-called free-flow line was adopted at the Kumamoto factory on a major scale. Under this system, those working on the assembly line can change the speed of the conveyor at any time. An individual worker stops the line to perform his job and, when finished, steps on a pedal to send the product to the next stage. In order that the entire line should not come to a halt, there are three or four idle positions before and after each station. This free-flow line has been very efficient in relieving workers of the pressure of chasing a constantly running conveyor.

The drawbacks of the system are that it is far more expensive to build than a conventional conveyor line and that it is more difficult to improve production efficiency. Despite the cooperation of the workers at the Kumamoto factory, there was a considerable delay in achieving the factory's target of increasing the daily production volume from 300 engines in February 1976 to 1,000 engines within six months. To improve this situation, the factory adopted ideas from members of its quality control circles. These groups, known as NH (standing for "Now, Next, New Honda") circles at Honda Motor, are voluntary and not only research given themes but are also concerned with employees' welfare and recreation. The factory executives also strongly supported the NH circle activities and initiated a number of measures to boost employee morale. Eventually, it was realized that the problem of efficiency on the free-flow line was one of mastery. As the executives and workers became better acquainted with the system, production efficiency improved greatly, more than making up for the high cost of installation. And since the workers operated with the line standing still, better quality standards were achieved. By early 1981, the Kumamoto factory was producing 60,000 engines and 30,000 motorcycles per month, and had attained the target of breaking even at 50 percent capacity.

Honda Motor has a rather flexible system for introducing new products to the market, called the SED (Sales, Engineering, and Development) system. On developing a new product, a small project team is selected from among these three departments to evaluate the needs of consumers, to develop the product, and to build or operate the mass-production lines effectively. The first product based on this system was the Accord, which was introduced in 1976. The Accord was a model developed to meet the needs of users more affluent and older than those buying the Civic, Honda Motor's "basic car." The Accord won a high reputation for Honda Motor as a manufacturer of high-class small cars, and it is this model that is to be produced in Ohio.

The 1.2 liter City, introduced in 1981, was also a product of the SED system. The main theme of the City's development was to improve both combustion efficiency and performance. To achieve this goal, the body was made as lightweight as possible by reducing the amount of sheet steel used. To produce the maximum interior space and solidity with the minimum materials, the ideal form is a sphere. The City was thus designed as close as possible to this shape, while at the same time striving for minimum air resistance. The City is unusually high (58 in) in comparison to the length (133 in) and with the nickname "tall boy" is very popular among young motor fans. It was also the first 1.2 liter gasoline-powered car in Japan to achieve 20 kilometers per liter (47 miles per gallon). The first two-wheeled vehicle produced through the SED system was called the Honda Express (Roadpal NC-50 in Japan), a family bike first marketed in 1976. It was a "bicycle-type" motorcycle with a 50cc engine and had pipe construction. Sophia Loren appeared in the Roadpal TV commercials and the bike found an eager market in Japan. Prior to the mid-1970s, the annual sales of motorcycles was 1,150,000 units; today it is two and a half times that number.

Industrial wages in Japan have already surpassed those of Western European countries and now rank with those of the United States, except in the auto and steel areas. The Japanese wage system differs from that of the West in several important ways. One is the relationship between seniority and ability. When an employee reaches an advanced age and his working ability begins to decline, his wages are not decreased. Generally speaking, this means that older employees receive higher wages. This is one of the reasons Japanese employees prefer to stay at the same enterprises for their entire working lives. Another difference is that up to around forty years of age, employees who entered the company at the same time receive almost the same wages. Even those who come from top-ranking universities as future management staff are not given any special salary increases. Employers will observe them over a long period of time to see if they have the ability to assume important positions.

The wage system at Honda Motor is essentially based on these fundamental points. The same structure applies equally to office workers and factory workers, whether they be men or women. Total wages are divided into three parts: monthly wage, biannual bonus, and a retirement grant.

Monthly wages consist of the basic wage (the total of the regular wage and additional regular wages) and an allowance. There are seven ranks in the basic wage system: 1st rank, junior common; 2nd, common; 3rd, senior common; 4th, foreman; 5th, assistant manager; 6th, manager; and 7th, general manager. The evaluation and promotion of these ranks is carried out every year in April. There are four categories of additional wages, which are determined according to the employee's achievement during the previous year, whether they are a specialist, whether they supervise others, and in regard to the business achievement of the company as a whole. Allowances are given for non-absent or semi-non-absent service, overtime, holiday work, night work, dependents, housing, and transportation. Employees who live in the colder regions of Japan even receive a special allowance to help with their high heating costs.

The average salary level at Honda Motor as of February 28, 1982 was as follows ($1 = about ¥220): total number of employees, 24,964; average age, 30.3; average length of service, 9.3 years; basic wage, ¥177,708; allowance, ¥34,282; total monthly wage, ¥211,990. Male workers numbered 23,099; average age, 30.8; average length of service, 9.7 years; basic wage, ¥182,432; allowance, ¥35,567; total, ¥217,999. Women workers numbered 1,865; average age, 24.8; average length of service, 4 years; basic wage, ¥119,214; allowance, ¥18,346; total, ¥137,560.

The starting wage as of April 1982 was as follows: university graduates, ¥131,200; with an M.A., ¥145,000; with a Ph.D., ¥157,700; and technical college graduates, ¥119,400. There is no distinction made between those from top-ranking universities and lower-ranking universities. Bonuses are paid in July and December; and the average in 1981 was ¥1,060,000, a total of 4.9 months' wages.

The retirement age at Honda is fifty-five, but if an employee wants to continue working, he can stay at the company for other five years at a lower salary and bonus. But he is deprived of his managerial title. On retirement, each employee receives a lump-sum retirement grant. In case he leaves spontaneously, the grant is paid according to the contemporary wage.

Although there is little wage difference among those who enter the company at the same time, at retirement age the wage and retirement grants differ to some extent according to the employee's ability and contribution to the company.

Data regarding retirement grants are not released by Japanese companies, but according to statistics published for 1980 by the Association of Managers of the Kanto district, the average amount paid to those who graduated from universities and retired at 55 with an average of 32 years of service was 39 months of basic wages (about 18 million yen) for enterprises with more than 500 employees.

Honda Motor manufacturing plants adopted a five-day working system on alternate weeks in 1965, and in 1972 this was expanded to cover every week. The production lines now shut down each Saturday and Sunday. In the Sayama manufacturing plant, they work in three shifts of eight hours; the first group from 7:00 A.M. to 3:45 P.M., the second from 3:35 P.M. to 12:00 A.M., and the third from 11:55 P.M. to 8:10 A.M. Each group takes a 45-minute rest; the second group also takes two 15-minute coffee breaks, and the third two 10-minute coffee breaks.

Honda Motor gives their employees 117 days of paid holidays (including Saturdays and Sundays). Those with more than five years of continuous service receive 5 days vacation time, and those with more than ten years of service receive 9 days. (These paid vacations can be converted into short-term sick leave.) For marriages and family funerals, special paid vacation is given. Maternity leave is 42 days before and after birth and men are given 3 days' leave to be with their wives at the hospital. If an employee is permanently disabled in an industrial accident, he will be guaranteed his basic wage and bonus up to the retirement age.

In Japan, production line robots have become very popular. According to the White Paper on International Trade issued by MITI, Japan had 14,000 industrial robots, the United States 3,255, West Germany 850, and Great Britain 185 as of March 1979. Industrial robots have contributed greatly to enhancing the efficiency of manpower and to the high quality of industrial products produced in Japan. The spread of robots owes much to the attitude of in-company labor unions. As there exists a high degree of cooperation between management and labor, the introduction of robots can develop smoothly. Drawing upon the collective know-how in the company, efficiency in the production process can thus be greatly improved by shifting manpower as rationally as possible. However, it is still too early to predict how the spread of robots will influence employment problems in the future.

At Honda Motor, work is divided into three groups: suitable for men, suitable for men or robots, and suitable only for robots. The latter two categories are now being switched over entirely to robots. Welding, the heaviest labor for workers, is already being performed by robots. By the summer of 1981 the production of car bodies was automated up to 65 percent, and Honda Motor is now automating the assembly work. But the company has no plans to automate every process, for they understand the importance of leaving appropriate work for their employees to encourage the training of experts.

Honda Motor has introduced flexible systems that allow the workers to suggest technical improvements and job rotations. For example, three young engineers obtained a patent for eliminating air from the tube supplying brake fluid. If air remains in the tube, the brake loses its effectiveness and accidents could result. Under the newly patented technique, the air can be eliminated quickly and the process can be adjusted to the speed of the conveyor line. For this invention, each of the engineers received a special bonus of 320,000 yen, or approximately $1,500. Such innovations are not an everyday occurrence, but at Honda Motor more than 300,000 suggestions were submitted in 1981, and 90 percent of them were accepted. For major innovations, a bonus or funds to study abroad are awarded, but usually the prizes are quite modest. Those making suggestions are satisfied instead that the company will increase its profits, for they can expect good biannual bonuses from those increased earnings.

At Honda plants employees are usually divided into departments, such as body assembly, engine assembly, welding, chemicals, machines, quality control, and so on. The head of a department with around two hundred employees is called a manager and is not a member of the union. Under him are three or four assistant managers who are each responsible for about fifty men, and under the assistant managers are the foremen, with ten to fifteen men. Assistant managers and foremen are always union members. As for job rotation, each employee proposes his choice for a new job to the foreman. The manager of the department will carefully study these proposals and shift the workers whenever possible according to their wishes. The employees can thus keep a fresh and open mind in their everyday work.

In Japan, spontaneous quality control (QC) circles are very popular at production plants. QC circles registered at the Union of Japanese Scientists and Engineers at the end of 1979 numbered 103,644 (from 3,146 companies employing 980,000 workers), but it is estimated that there are five or six times that number which are unregistered. At Honda Motors NH circles (the equivalent of QC circles) are not officially organized by the company; they are managed spontaneously among employees during off-hours. In

Transportation ideas entered in Honda Motor's Idea Contest: a novel adaptation of rubber boots (*above*): a spokeless and hubless bicycle (*opposite, left*); a mechanical rikshaw man (*opposite, right*).

the United States and Western Europe, QC circles are usually associated with a payment system; in Japan this is rarely the case. NH circles propose and discuss various subjects, but are most effective in the areas of production innovations and the improvement of working life. At the Suzuka plant, one circle named *Kunta Kinte* studied sign language for six months, so they could work more smoothly with deaf-and-dumb workers. NH circles function as small communities to strengthen solidarity among employees. Once a year, all the NH circles meet together, reporting and discussing their activities. During the past few years, they have even received representatives from Honda Motor plants abroad. The company also has an event called an "Idea Contest" every eighteen months. Sponsored by an employee recreation association, workers can use the plant facilities and are given up to 400,000 yen (roughly $2,000) to build an original and sometimes outrageous machine. This event first started in 1970.

Honda Motor has other unique systems for encouraging their employees. The stock-sharing plan started in 1970. The company deposit plan began in 1954 with slightly higher interest rates than bank deposits, and at the same time this program is helping the company raise operating funds. In 1981, 80 percent of the employees had accounts and the average deposit was 350,000 yen (about $1,500). A mutual aid system for purchasing houses was started by the employees themselves in 1955, and a life insurance program began in 1962. Honda Motor also has such facilities as cafeterias, company apartments and dormitories, and vacation cottages for employees. At most plants there are athletic grounds, gymnasiums, swimming pools, exercise apparatus, libraries, study rooms, and hobby workshops. And some plants have even built mini-motorcross fields, where employees can enjoy bike trials after working hours.

The experience gained in Japan has been carefully applied to the motorcycle plant in Ohio. Honda Motor does not believe that every employee program and production process that has been successfully adopted in Japan can be applied with equal success in another country. Its management methods vary according to the specific requirements of a particular society and culture. Many people believe that the quality of American labor is poor. Officials at Honda Motor disagree, saying, "The problem does not lie in the quality of labor; it lies in the quality of management." They have become even more strongly convinced of this analysis when evaluating the success of the high-performance Honda GL-1100 motorcycle. Powered by a 1,100cc water-cooled engine, this bike is produced by the Ohio plant and exported to twenty-four countries in Europe and other parts of the world. The GL-1100 has been enthusiastically received by customers who would settle for nothing but the best in such a high-performance machine.

As Honda Motor's international strategies made progress, the company started reviewing the organizational structure of its top management. Basic corporate ideas are developed by the president and executive vice presidents, the organizational structure is developed accordingly, and individual board members are given specific tasks. The top management at Honda Motor is therefore quite flexible. In June 1979, regional task forces, which included many board members, were established, and were given the task of producing detailed and aggressive marketing strategies on an area-by-area basis. There were four such groups—for Japan, North America, Europe and Oceania, and developing countries—each headed by a senior managing director. Together with the three expert committees on personnel, equipment, and finance that were created earlier, the establishment of the task forces meant the completion of a matrix covering the entire range of corporate activities, both vertically and horizontally.

This system underwent a complete change in June 1981. The company first abolished the three expert committees on the grounds that they had completed their task of making an overall review of the corporate organizational structure. In their place, six regional "divisions" were formed under the *Senmu-kai* to devise and quickly implement market strategies. The six divisions are responsible for the domestic motorcycle market, the domestic car market, power products, Europe and Oceania, North America, and for developing countries. At the same time, board members were given the function of monitoring corporate activities horizontally rather than vertically. Specifically, their responsibilities were divided into such areas as administration, procurement, domestic motorcycle production, production engineering, parts and service, research and development, quality assurance, and certification. Each regional division is directly connected to regional sales departments and the head of each division has total responsibility for the entire territory he covers.

This "regional division" system of Honda Motor may appear to be similar to the "division" system, as it is commonly known in the United States, in which the head of each division is responsible for that division's profit picture independent of other divisions in the company. The latter system has been adopted by Matsushita Electric, whose products are marketed under the brand names of National, Quasar, and Panasonic. The system at Honda Motor, however, is different even from that of Matsushita, which is often regarded as a most typical Japanese company.

Some attribute the difference between the two companies to a difference in corporate size. But the fact is that Konosuke Matsushita, the founder of Matsushita Electric, adopted the division system when the company was still very small. He started his business in 1918 with three colleagues, first manufacturing light sockets, and then producing battery-powered lamps for bicycles, which proved to be a great success. When the company branched out into such products as electric irons and heaters, he decided to delegate these businesses to his colleagues because he was in poor health. This marked the beginning of the division system in Matsushita Electric, which was formalized in 1933. At the time, the company had three divisions, one for radios, another for batteries and lamps, and a third for power distributors and heaters. Matsushita Electric was the first Japanese firm to adopt the division system, and even in the United States this system was adopted by only a handful of corporations, such as General Motors and du Pont. Konosuke Matsushita sought and trained people who could be trusted to handle various divisions, and has thus succeeded in achieving overall corporate growth.

At Matsushita Electric today, there are some forty divisions covering such product ranges as televisions, radios, video tape recorders, refrigerators, and air conditioners. In contrast to this divisional decentralization, matters related to personnel, accounting, and finance are centralized in the corporate headquarters. Particular emphasis is placed on accounting, which extends even to the production lines, with a view to grasping the entire corporate position and securing a 10 percent profit.

Unlike Matsushita Electric, the top management of Honda Motor has no thought of adopting this kind of division system. At General Motors, Alfred P. Sloan, reputed to be one of the most outstanding corporate chiefs in history, introduced the division system in the 1920s, and it became the basis for the firm's growth to the largest automaker in the world. Based on a policy of marketing cars for every purpose and every pocketbook, General Motors developed five model ranges, from the luxurious Cadillac to the utilitarian Chevrolet. Each of these model ranges formed a division and was sold through independent channels under different pricing policies. For example, General Motors priced Cadillacs very high to give the owners a sense of status, while Chevrolets were sold as cheaply as possible for the mass market. Fujisawa understood that GM's strategy was possible because it was a huge company that had more than a 50 percent market share in the United States. Both Ford and Chrysler followed similar policies. It cannot be denied that an oligopoly by the "Big Three" allowed such a pricing policy. And while they enjoyed great profits from luxury cars, this policy could hardly be applied to the production of compact autos. Unlike its American counterparts, Honda Motor has evolved from the philosophy that every product has to maintain a competitive price, and to achieve that price, the production cost should be lowered as much as possible to meet the needs of consumers. This difference can be attributed to the position of General Motors as the world's largest automaker and that of Honda Motor as the latest entrant into the automobile field in Japan. Although Honda is the largest producer of motorcycles in the world, it has no intention of setting up separate divisions for cars and motorcycles. Rather, its motorcycle and car operations are structurally integrated, as exemplified by its plants in Ohio. Honda Motor follows a policy of complementation among motorcycles, cars, and power products, so that sluggishness in one sector can be compensated for by another, thus minimizing corporate risks and maximizing opportunities for growth.

This may lead to speculation that Honda Motor, instead of adopting decentralization through divisions, has a high degree of centralization with a strong grip on all corporate activities. But this is not the case. The function of the company's top management is to develop long-term and medium-term strategies, and not to concern itself with details, deciding who does what, or issuing specific orders. The upper management at Honda Motor is anxious to extract ideas, innovations, and enthusiasm from the lower echelons, and in this respect the expert system plays an important role. When a new project is launched, a project team of experts is created so that opinions from many different fields can be heard. This type of decentralization is quite different from that of the division system.

Such flexibility in corporate management and organization contains elements that may be difficult for Westerners to readily grasp. This probably stems from the great difference in culture. According to the leading oriental historian Konan Naito (1866–1934), the way in which Japanese culture manifests itself is similar to the process of fermenting cheese. When rennet is added to milk, the milk curdles and becomes cheese. Japanese culture is like milk, and when the rennet of foreign civilizations is added to it, the mixture "curdles" and takes on a specific shape. For more than a thousand years, the Chinese civilization served as the rennet; after the Meiji Restoration came Western European civilization; and following World War II the influence was American democracy, science, and technology. Just as milk can be made into many kinds of cheese depending on the process, Japanese culture can assume many different shapes. The culture is therefore inherently flexible and can be easily adjusted to changing circumstances.

Westerners have traditionally attached much importance to rationalism, which has been the basis for the development of science and technology. In the West in general, and in the United States in particular, efforts are made to manage a corporation on the principle of rationalism. In these countries, it is important to organize people of different races, religions, ideologies, and abilities. To accomplish this goal, rationalism is indispensable as a value common to all. In Japan, the people are homogeneous, which is why such importance is attached to the emotions as well as to rationalism.

The Japanese have very particular sentiments and emotions as a result of having been a closed island nation under the Tokugawa Shogunate. There is, for example, the expression, "a-un no kokyu." "A-un" comes from the Sanskrit word "ahum," meaning inhalation and expiration, and "no kokyu" means of breathing. In the Japanese national sport of sumo wrestling, the opponents first put their fists on the ground and study each other's face. They start the bout only when their inhalation and expiration match each other. There is a referee, but he does not give any signal to start the fight. Among sports involving more than one person, sumo is probably the only one in which the opponents decide when to start the match themselves.

"A-un no kokyu" also has the meaning of "two sides of a thing." In Japanese society, opposing opinions seldom remain in a state of confrontation and they are often regarded simply as two sides of the same problem. The Japanese are thus generally capable of understanding and appreciating each other's position. In corporate decision-making, meetings of the "a-un no kokyu" between management and the work force are regarded as being most important, rather than the top management unilaterally forcing its decisions on subordinates. The amicable and cooperative relations between labor and management in Japan are based on this type of cultural background.

In 1932, Konosuke Matsushita was greatly impressed by a religious person from a Shinto sect, and through him came to believe that the role of a businessman is to conquer poverty. During the Great Depression of 1929, Matsushita Electric faced the most serious crisis in its history, with sales plummeting by 50 percent. Matsushita declared, "The plants will work half a day every day and production will be cut in half. But not one single employee will be laid off and everybody will get paid their full salary. Instead, the employees will sacrifice their holidays and sell everything in the inventory." Faced by a similar situation most Western corporations, out of rationalism, would resort to laying off its employees. But the action taken by Matsushita served to enhance the sense of solidarity with the employees, led the work force to appreciate his sense of responsibility as an industrialist, and became a driving force behind the company's growth to what it is today. Now, Matsushita Electric has a clear-cut separation of responsibilities under its division system, and its employees fully appreciate the benefits of "Matsushita-ism." Matsushita Electric has thus developed a very flexible organization that is capable of organizing sometimes mediocre people under a common goal and extracting unusual ideas from them.

The corporate philosophy of Honda Motor is best expressed by Soichiro Honda himself, "Life is short, but by achieving greater speeds a man can make his life a little longer and more affluent." The company has attracted people who are dedicated to supplying vehicles powered by high-performance engines. Their enthusiasm and a flexible corporate organization should ensure that Honda Motor will continue to operate efficiently.

Recently, the Nikko Research Center issued a report comparing employee satisfaction at a large American auto plant (A) situated in the Midwest and a comparable Japanese automotive factory (B).[19] The research period was from November 1980 to March 1981. The multiple-choice answers to the questions were as follows: very satisfied, satisfied, satisfied in a way, unsatisfied in a way, not satisfied, and don't know.

In regard to wages, at the American plant, 42 percent were very satisfied and 33 percent were satisfied (75 percent in total), but at the Japanese factory, 3 percent were very satisfied and 5 percent were satisfied (8 percent in total). This extreme difference might be explained by the fact that U.S. auto workers receive almost twice the wages of the average Japanese automobile worker.

In regard to human relations in the company, at Plant A, 24 percent were very satisfied and 38 percent were satisfied, while at Plant B, 4 percent were very satisfied and 26 percent were satisfied, both being lower than at A. On decision-making rights given to the employees, at A, 20 percent were very satisfied and 26 percent were satisfied, but at Plant B, 3 percent were very satisfied and 7 percent were satisfied. And concerning promotion, at A, 16 percent were very satisfied and 22 percent were satisfied, as opposed to 1 percent being very satisfied and 5 percent being satisfied at Plant B.

Japanese management is said to afford decision-making rights equally to all employees, to produce harmony between labor and management, and to raise the morale of employees. But interestingly enough, the research conducted by the Nikko Research Center shows something quite to the contrary, and represents a situation that has also been observed widely in other Japanese industries. Evaluating this tendency, some critics now say that the highly rated Japanese management system is an illusion, and the so-called spontaneous employee involvement is simply the result of enforcement by management and peer group pressure by co-workers. In their view, this type of management is peculiar to Japan and will never work internationally.

But there is actually much evidence to suggest otherwise. IBM, Texas Instruments, Xerox, and others are doing very successful business in Japan by applying American high technology and Japanese-style management of Japanese workers. In the United States itself, more than 200 companies have introduced QC circles, which have strengthened the employees' morale and led to innovations in quality.

At Honda Motor's Ohio plant, some Japanese management ideas are currently being applied. For example, the system of proposing technical improvements has been very successful. As one employee at the plant said, "Americans can come up with good ideas in technology and production processes, but U.S. companies have never given us the chance." At the Ohio plant, by applying new types of management, employer and employee relations are quite harmonious and the turnover rate is low. And while there is no union at present, in the future there might be a conflict with the UAW.

What is the essential difference between U.S. and Japanese workers? In the U.S., where the paternal principle rules society, man must live independently and struggle to compete. In such a culture, people find satisfaction in being winners, and to be unsatisfied is to acknowledge failure. In Japan, where the maternal principle prevails, relationships of dependency are rather common and people hope to live in groups relying upon each other. In such a society, it is rather difficult to find satisfaction as an independent personality and many tend to feel persecuted. Japanese people have a psychology that is not easily satisfied, and they are always filled with complaints and frustrations, though perhaps they are also seeking satisfaction in a deeper psychological sense.

Recently, Japanese primary industries have been suffering from a decrease in exports, due to the rising protectionism of Western countries and trade frictions. In these circumstances, large Japanese enterprises are being forced to multinationalize but often have little idea how to manage overseas plants. Corporations that have evolved in the Japanese climate suffer the shortcomings of closed corporate management and group pressures inside the organization. This "closedness" has led many Japanese industries to step up production within Japan, to flood overseas markets with exports, and to create trade friction with respect to certain products. The group pressure, meanwhile, also has the effect of preventing the growth of unique individuals within an organization. Honda Motor has been largely successful in eliminating these problems by emphasizing strong leadership, a flexible organizational structure, and a sense of responsibility among people who are often tempted to rely on each other. This is the secret of Honda Motor's growth and has put the company one step ahead of its competitors in pursuing open-minded, international strategies.

SOURCES

(1) Raymond Vernon. *Sovereignty at Bay: The Multinational Spread of U.S. Enterprises.* New York, Basic Books,1971.

Raymond Vernon, Noritake Kobayashi, Jiro Tokuyama. *"Takokusekika o semarareru Nippon kigyo no akiresuken towa nanika"* ("Where is the heel of Achilles of Japanese firms urged to be multinational enterprises?"). *Asahi Journal Weekly,* Oct. 3, 1980.

(2) Takeo Kuwabara. *Yooroppa bunmei to Nippon* ("European civilization and Japan"). Tokyo, Asahi Shimbunsha, 1974.

(3) *Tokyo Nichinichi Shimbun,* June 26, 1936.

(4) *Tokyo Nichinichi Shimbun,* June 18, 1938.

(5) *Newsweek,* Sept. 29, 1975.

(6) Hayao Kawai. *Bosei-shakai Nihon no byori* ("Pathology of Japan, maternal society nation"). Tokyo, Chuokoronsha, 1976.

(7) Robert Lifton, Hayao Kawai. *"Fusei-shakai to bosei-shakai"* ("Paternal society and maternal society"). *Asahi Journal Weekly,* May 2, 1980.

(8) Otis Cary (ed.). *War-Wasted Asia.* Tokyo, Kodansha International, 1975.

(9) *Asahi Shimbun,* May 17, 1952.

(10) Takeo Doi. *Anatomy of Dependence.* Tokyo, Kodansha International, 1973.

(11) Daniel Bell, Ezra F. Vogel, Tetsuo Sakiya. *Kanosei no Nippon* ("Japan: It's capacity in the future"). Tokyo, Jitsugyo no Nihonsha, 1979.

(12) Chie Nakane. *"Toyo ni okeru kiso-bunka no seikaku"* (Basic cultural configuration of the Orient"). *Koza Toyoshiso, vol. 9.* Tokyo, University of Tokyo Press, 1967.

(13) Geoffrey Barraclough, Takeo Kuwabara. *"Sekai no unmei o sayusuru Chugoku no kisu"* ("The tendency of China, which affects the world"). *Asahi Journal Weekly,* Dec. 5, 1980.

(14) *Asahi Journal Weekly,* May 2, 1980.

(15) Daniel Bell, Ezra F. Vogel, Tetsuo Sakiya. *Kanosei no Nippon* ("Japan: Its capacity in the future"). Tokyo, Jitsugyo no Nihonsha, 1979.

(16) Chie Nakane. *Japanese Society.* Berkeley, University of California Press, 1972.

(17) *Asahi Journal Weekly,* May 2, 1980.

(18) *Ibid.*

(19) Nikko Research Center (ed.). *Japan's Cooperation for the Revitalization of American Industry.* Tokyo, Nikko Research Center, 1981.

CHRONOLOGY

1867

Oct. Restoration of imperial rule.

1868

Sept. Beginning of the Meiji period (1868–1912).

1872

Aug. Introduction of a system of compulsory primary education.

1877

Apr, Foundation of Tokyo Imperial University (present University of Tokyo).

1881

Oct. Declaration of foundation of National Assembly. Rush to form political parties,

1882

Oct. Establishment of the Bank of Japan.
Foundation of Waseda College (present Waseda University).

1889

Feb. Promulgation of the Dai Nippon Teikoku Kempo (Meiji Constitution).

1890

July First election of the House of Representatives.
Oct. Imperial Rescript on Education.
Nov. First assembly of the Imperial Diet.

	1894	
	Aug.	Sino-Japanese War begins.
	1895	
	Apr.	Treaty of Shimonoseki ends the Sino-Japanese War.
	1897	
	Feb.	Construction of Yahata steel mill begun.
	June	Foundation of Kyoto Imperial University.
	1902	
	Jan.	Anglo-Japanese alliance.
	1904	
	Feb.	Russo-Japanese War begins.
	1905	
	Sept.	Peace Treaty of Portsmouth ends the Russo-Japanese War. Frequent occurrence of strikes.
	1906	
Nov. Soichiro Honda born.	Feb.	Formation of Japan Socialist Party.
	1910	
Nov. Takeo Fujisawa born.	Aug.	Annexation of Korea.
	1912	
	Jan.	Foundation of Republic of China.
	July	Beginning of the Taisho period (1912–26).
	1914	
Apr. Honda enters Yamahigashi Primary School.	July	World War I begins.
	1917	
Apr. Fujisawa enters Koishikawa Primary School.	Oct.	Russian Revolution.
	1918	
	June	Versailles Peace Treaty ends World War I.
	1920	
	Jan.	League of Nations founded.
	May	First May Day in Japan.
	1921	
	Oct.	Foundation of Nihon Rodo Sodomei (Japan General Labor Federation).

1922

Mar. Honda leaves primary school to join Art Shokai in Tokyo as an apprentice.	July Foundation of Japan Communist Party.

1923

Apr. Fujisawa enters Keika Middle School.	Sept. Great Kanto Earthquake.

1926

	Dec. Beginning of Showa period (1926–). Foundation of Social Populace Party and Japan Labor–Farmer Party.

1927

	Mar. Financial panic in Japan.

1928

Honda opens Hamamatsu branch of Art Shokai. Mar. Fujisawa leaves middle school.	Oct. First 5-year plan of USSR.

1929

	Oct. The Depression begins.

1930

Dec. Fujisawa enters the 57th Infantry Regiment as a cadet.	Jan. Japan returns to the gold standard.

1931

Honda obtains a patent for his iron wheel. Nov. Fujisawa leaves the army.	Apr. Law to control key industries. Sept. Manchurian Incident.

1933

	Mar. Japan secedes from the League of Nations, May New Deal policy of President Roosevelt.

1934

Feb. Fujisawa joins Mitsuwa Shokai.	

1936

July Honda seriously injured in the All-Japan Speed Rally.	Feb. 2.26 Incident (military revolt on February 26 in Tokyo).

1937

Feb. Honda founds Tokai Seiki Heavy Industry Co. Nov. Honda succeeds in making a new piston ring.	July China Incident. Nov. Anti-Comintern Pact with Germany and Italy.

1938

	Apr. General mobilization. Sept. Munich Conference.

1939

Apr.	Fujisawa founds the Japan Machine and Tool Research Institute.	Aug.	Soviet-Nazi Pact.
		Sept.	World War II begins.

1940

Sept. Japan-German-Italian Tripartite Pact.

Oct. Foundation of the Imperial Rule Assistance Association.

Nov. Foundation of Great Japan Patriotic Labor Organization. All labor unions dissolved.

1941

Apr. Russo-Japanese Neutrality Pact.

Dec. Pacific War begins.

1942

Toyota acquires 40 percent of the stocks of Tokai Seiki Heavy Industry Co.

1945

Honda sells Tokai Seiki to Toyota for ¥450,000.

Aug. Fujisawa moves his company to Fukushima Prefecture.

June Dissolution of the Imperial Rule Assistance Association.

July Potsdam Declaration.

Aug. Atomic bombs dropped on Hiroshima and Nagasaki. Surrender of Japan.

Oct. Political prisoners released. Legalization of Japan Communist Party.

Nov. Dissolution of the *zaihatsu* by GHQ.
Foundation of Japan Socialist Party, Japan Liberal Party, and Japan Progressive Party.

Dec. Labor Union Act.
The first land reform.

1946

Oct. Honda Technical Research Institute established by Honda in Hamamatsu in Shizuoka Prefecture.

May Revival of May Day after eleven years.

Aug. Japan Federation of Labor and Congress of Industrial Labor Organizations established.

Sept. The second land reform.
Labor Relations Adjustment Law.

Nov. The Constitution of Japan promulgated.

1947

Mar. Kiyoshi Kawashima, who became president in 1973, enters the company.

Nov. Production of 2-stroke A-type engine (50cc) started.

Feb. General strike stopped by GHQ.

Apr. The Labor Standards Law and the Antimonopoly Law.

May The Constitution of Japan enacted.

1948

Sept. Honda Motor Co., Ltd., with capital of ¥1 million, established in Hamamatsu.

1949

Aug. Production of lightweight motorcycle D-type (2-stroke, 98cc), named "Dream."

Oct. Takeo Fujisawa joins Honda Motor.

Apr. North Atlantic Treaty.

Oct. Foundation of People's Republic of China.

1950

Mar. Tokyo branch set up.

Sept. Tokyo plant set up.

June Korean War begins.

July General Council of Japanese Labor Unions established

1951

July Dream E-type produced on an experimental basis. It undergoes a driving test at Hakone and records an average speed of 70 kph.

Oct. Dream E-type (4-stroke, 146cc) launched on the domestic market.

Apr. Japan Development Bank established.

Sept. Peace Treaty and U.S.–Japan Security Treaty signed.

1952

Mar. Shirako plant set up at Shirako, Saitama Prefecture.	Apr. Export-Import Bank of Japan established.
June F-type Cub (50cc) motorcycle marketed.	Aug. Japan joins the IMF.

1953

May Yamato plant set up at Niikura, Saitama Prefecture.	July Korean War ends.
June Labor union organized.	Aug. Law to restrict strikes in electric and coal industries enacted.
July Yamato plant expanded and renamed Saitama factory. Sumiyoshi plant set up at Hamamatsu.	
Aug. Benly J-type (90cc) announced.	

Dec. Employees' suggestion system started.

1954

Jan. Over-the-counter trade of Honda Motor's stock starts on Tokyo Stock Exchange. Juno K-type 200cc scooter marketed.	July Self-Defense Force established.

Mar. Honda Motor Co., Ltd. participates in São Paulo International Motorcycle Race in Brazil.
Honda Motor Co., Ltd. announces participation in the TT Race on the Isle of Man.

Apr. Construction of Aoi plant at Hamamatsu completed.

June	President Soichiro Honda makes a trip to attend the TT Race, and visits automobile manufacturers in Europe.		
Sept.	Juno scooter exported to U.S.		

1955

Apr.	Dream SB-type (350cc) marketed.	May	Warsaw Pact.
Sept.	Honda Motor Co., Ltd. takes the lead in annual domestic motorcycle production.	Oct.	Right and left socialist parties combine.
Nov.	Honda racing team participates in the 1st All-Japan Motorcycle Endurance Road Race.	Nov.	Foundation of Liberal Democratic Party.

1956

Jan.	Company management principles adopted.	Oct.	Suez War. Diplomatic relations between Japan and USSR resumed.
Feb.	Service Division established, and starts one-year guarantee system for customers.	Dec.	Japan joins the UN.

1957

June	R & D Center set up in Shirako plant.	Oct.	Sputnik launched by USSR.
Sept.	Dream C-70 (250cc, 4-stroke, 2-cylinder) marketed.	Dec.	Russo-Japanese Commercial Treaty.
Oct.	Honda racing team wins first place in 350cc class race in Mt. Asama Race.		
Dec.	Honda Motor Co., Ltd. listed on First Section of Tokyo Stock Exchange.		

1958

May	Test course completed near Arakawa River.	July	Oji Paper Co. union goes on strike for an indefinite period.
Aug.	Super Cub C-100 (50cc) marketed.	Oct.	Negotiations on revision of U.S.–Japan Security Treaty start.

1959

June	Honda racing team participates in the TT Race for the first time and wins 6th place (in 125cc class). American Honda Motor Co., Inc. established.	Mar.	National Congress against revision of U.S.–Japan Security Treaty formed by Japan Socialist Party, *Sohyo*, and the Japan Council against A- and H-bombs.

Aug.	Honda racing team wins Mt. Asama Race.	Aug.	Miike mines' struggle starts.
		Nov.	Trade liberalization policy of the Japanese government.

1960

Apr.	Suzuka factory starts operating in Suzuka, Mie Prefecture.	Jan.	Miike mines' union goes on strike for an indefinite period.
July	R & D Center becomes independent.	May	New U.S.–Japan Security Treaty pushed through by Liberal Democratic Party.
Nov.	Construction of new plant at Saitama factory completed.	June	New U.S.–Japan Security Treaty takes effect.
		Nov.	Miike mines' dispute ends.
		Dec.	Ikeda Cabinet launches the income-doubling program.

1961

June	Honda Deutschland GmbH established in Hamburg, West Germany. Honda racing team wins the TT Race in 125cc and 250cc classes.	Jan.	J. F. Kennedy inaugurated as president.
Aug.	Motorcycle sales top 100,000 units a month, unprecedented in the motorcycle industry.	Sept.	OECD formed.
Oct.	Overseas production started in Taiwan.		
Dec.	Honda racing team wins the manufacturer team prize in the 125cc and 250cc classes in the 1961 World Motorcycle Grand Prix Race.		

1962

June	Honda racing team wins 125cc and 250cc classes in the TT Race.	Oct.	Japanese trade liberalization reaches 88 percent.
Sept.	Honda Benelux N.V. established to assemble and sell motorcycles in the EEC. Construction of Suzuka Circuit completed. Honda Koki Engineering Factory set up, later incorporated as Honda Engineering Co., Ltd.		
Oct.	Lightweight truck T-360 and sports car S-360 introduced.		

Nov. All-Japan Motorcycle Championship Road Race held at Suzuka Circuit, and Honda racing team wins 50cc, 125cc, 250cc, and 350cc classes.
Dec. Honda issues ADR in U.S.A.

1963

May Assembly plant in Belgium completed.
June Honda racing team wins the TT Race in the 250cc and 350cc classes.
Aug. Lightweight truck T-360 marketed.
Sept. Annual exports are ¥10 billion.
Oct. Super Cub C-100 and C-110 awarded the Mode Coupe of France, one of the highest awards for a motorcycle.
Sports car S-500 marketed.

Nov. The World Grand Prix Road Race held at Suzuka Circuit for the first time in Japan. Honda racing team wins three classes (50cc, 250cc, and 350cc).

May Kennedy Round (general reduction of tariffs) started.

1964

Jan. Honda Motor Co., Ltd. announces participation in the F-I races.
Mar. Sports car S-600 marketed.

May Sayama factory completed in Sayama, Saitama Prefecture.
June Honda racing team wins the TT Race in 3 classes (125cc, 250cc, and 350cc).
General purpose engine G-45 marketed.

Apr. Japan shifted to IMF "Article 8" nation, and becomes member of OECD.
Aug. U.S. involvement in Vietnam increases.
Oct. Tokaido "Bullet Train" inaugurated.
Tokyo Olympic Games.
Nov. Foundation of Japanese Confederation of Labor.

Management system of Honda Motor Co., Ltd. substantially reorganized.

July Construction of Honda Service Factory system (S.F.) commenced throughout Japan.

Aug. Honda racing team participates in an F-I race (in 1,500cc class) for the first time in Germany.

Sept. Honda France S.A. established in Paris.

Oct. Asian Honda Motor Co., Ltd. established.

Dec. S.F. (Honda Service Factory) system inaugurated.

1965

Feb. Export of S-600 started.

July An alternate five-day work week adopted.

Aug. S-600 coupe wins the Nürburgring International Endurance Race in Germany.

Sept. Honda (U.K.) Ltd. established in London.

Oct. Honda wins the F-I Grand Prix in Mexico (in 1,500cc class).

Nov. Japanese government issues deficit bonds for the first time after the war.

1966

Apr. Honda Sales Research Co., Ltd. (dissolved in 1974), Honda Credit Service Co., Ltd., and Honda Used Vehicle Sales Co., Ltd. established.
Thai Honda Manufacturing Co., Ltd. (motorcycle production facility) established in Bangkok, Thailand.

Oct. Honda establishes a world record of eleven consecutive F-II victories.

Apr. Nissan Motor and Prince Motor merge.

1967

Mar. Lightweight passenger car N-360 marketed.

June Japanese government frees capital transactions.
Kennedy Round ends.

Sept. Honda wins the Italian F-I Grand Prix (in 3,000cc class).

Nov. Suzuka factory completed.
Automobile production starts
at Suzuka factory.

1968

June Honda specialist dealer system
adopted.
July Honda F-I takes second place in
the French Grand Prix.
Aug. Honda Motor Co., Ltd. signs a
contract for technical transfer
to the motorcycle industry of
Mexico and Spain.
Oct. Small passenger car Honda
1300 introduced.

1969

Feb. Honda Australia Pty., Ltd.
established in Melbourne.
Mar. Canadian Honda Motor Ltd.
established in Toronto.
Apr. Dream CB-750 Four, a large-
sized motorcycle, exported to
U.S. and Canada.
May Honda 1300 sedan marketed.
Nov. TN-360 Snowler marketed.

June U.S.–Japan textile trade negotiations start.

1970

Mar. Honda N-600 exported to U.S.
The first Idea Contest held at
Suzuka Circuit.
July Cumulative export of motor-
cycles exceeds 5 million units.
Automobiles exported to Italy.
Aug. Anti-pollution Countermeas-
ure Center established.
Sept. Honda Engineering Co., Ltd.
established.
Production of N-360 series ex-
ceeds 1 million units.

Mar. Yahata Iron and Steel and Fuji
Iron and Steel merge to form
Nippon Steel.

Oct. Honda Driving Safety Promotion Center established.
American Honda Motor Co., Inc. donates 10,000 minibikes to the YMCA of the U.S. to help to prevent juvenile delinquency.

1971

Feb. Honda CVCC (Compound Vortex Controlled Combustion) engine announced, the first to comply with U.S. 1975 Clean Air Act.

Apr. Kiyoshi Kawashima becomes president of Honda R & D Co., Ltd.

June Production of motorcycles started in Mexico.
Lightweight passenger car Honda Life, with water-cooled engine, marketed.

Aug. Honda Training Centers set up throughout Japan.

Nov. Honda Motor do Brazil Ltd. established in São Paulo.

Dec. New Z-360 with water-cooled engine marketed.

Apr. Capital transactions in motor industry freed.

June Return of Okinawa to Japan.

Aug. U.S. suspends the gold standard.

Oct. U.S.–Japan textile trade negotiations end.

1972

July Five-day work week adopted in all Honda factories.
Small passenger car Honda Civic 1200 marketed.

Dec. Honda Civic exported.

Feb. President Nixon visits China.

June Watergate affair.

Sept. Agreement on resumption of diplomatic relations between Japan and China.

1973

July A CVCC license agreement signed with Ford Motor Company.
P.T. Honda Federal Inc. established in Jakarta, Indonesia.

Sept. Honda Motor Co., Ltd. signs contracts with Isuzu Motors Ltd. and Chrysler Corporation granting CVCC engine technology.

Jan. Vietnam Peace Treaty.

Sept. Tokyo Round started.

Oct. The fourth Middle East War. The first "Oil Shock."

Oct. President Soichiro Honda and Executive Vice President Takeo Fujisawa retire and become supreme advisors.
Kiyoshi Kawashima becomes president.
First national motorcyclist festival held at Suzuka Circuit.

Dec. Civic CVCC 1500 and 4-door Civic CVCC 1500 marketed (both met the 1975 Japanese statutory exhaust emission standards).

1974

Mar. Honda Suisse S.A. established in Geneva, Switzerland.

May Component parts produced at P.T. Honda Federal, the first attempt at production overseas.

July Honda Engineering Co., Ltd. established.
Honda del Peru S.A. established in Lima.

Sept. International Association of Traffic and Safety Sciences (I.A.T.S.S.) established.

Oct. Production of all lightweight passenger cars curtailed.
Gold Wing GL-1000 marketed.

Nov. Civic CVCC passes the exhaust emission test of the EPA.

Apr. Declaration of New International Economic Order (NIEO) at UN.

Aug. President Nixon resigns.

1975

June Sales on credit started, called the "Honda Credit System."

Feb. Japanese government sets new exhaust emission standards.

July Moto Honda da Amazonia Limitada established in Brazil (an assembly plant for two-wheeled vehicles).

1976

Jan. Kumamoto factory completed.
Feb. NC-50 Roadpal (exported as Honda Express) marketed.

Apr. Civic assembly begins in New Zealand.
Honda International Technical School opened in Saitama Prefecture.
May Small passenger car Accord marketed.

July Cumulative production of Civic exceeds 1 million units in four years since production begun.
Sept. Honda racing team wins the Bol d'Or 24-Hour Race, the biggest endurance race in Europe.
Dec. ADR and EDR issued to an amount of $50 million.

May Liberalization in capital transactions complete except for agricultural products and a few industries.

1977

Jan. Motorcycle production begun at Moto Honda da Amazonia Limitada in Manaus, Brazil.
Mar. Civic CVCC ranked first in the Fuel Economy Test for 1977 models by EPA (Environmental Protection Agency) and FEA (Federal Energy Administration) of the U.S.
Sept. Civic 1500, meeting Japanese statutory emission standards, introduced.

Oct. Announcement that a motorcycle production facility would be
established in Ohio, U.S.A.
Dec. Honda Foundation established.

Feb. Announcement that a Distribution Center (for automobiles
and parts) would be established
in Ghent, Belgium.

Mar. Honda of America Mfg., Inc.
established to take charge of the
setting up and management of
the motorcycle production
facility in Ohio.

Apr. Honda Europe N.V. established in Ghent, Belgium as a part
of the program to improve local
procurement and distribution
system.

Nov. Prelude marketed.

May New Tokyo International Airport (Narita Airport) opened.

Aug. Japan–China Peace and Friend-
ship Treaty.

Sept. Iranian Revolution.

1979

Sept. Motorcycle production begins
in Ohio.

Oct. GL-1100 large-sized motorcycle for export marketed.

Dec. Agreement for technical collaboration with BL signed.

Mar. Egypt–Israel Peace Treaty.

Dec. USSR military intervention in
Afghanistan.
The second "Oil Shock."

1980

Jan. Announcement that a car
manufacturing plant would be
established in Ohio, U.S.A.

Feb. Small-sized passenger car
Quint marketed.

Aug. Ballade marketed.

Feb. Douglas Fraser, chairman of
UAW, visits Japan.

Nov. Ronald Reagan elected president.

Sept. Tact scooter marketed.

Dec. Construction of the car manufacturing plant in Ohio started.

1981

Sept. Small-sized passenger car Vigor
marketed.

Nov. City marketed.

Dec. Technical collaboration agreement on motorcycle production with China signed.

Apr. Voluntary restriction of car exports to U.S.

1982

Apr. Agreement with Cycles Peugeot for joint development and
production of motorcycles
signed.

Mar. Agreement to merge Toyota
Motor and Toyota Sales signed
(the new company, Toyota
Motor Corporation, to start in
July 1982).

POSTSCRIPT
Expansion and International Strategies, 1982–87

Since the original hardback edition of this book was published in 1982, Honda Motor has achieved great progress and considerable success in its international activities. I am thus taking this opportunity to outline the major developments of the last few years. T.S.

Honda Motor started out making motorcycles and has now become the world's largest manufacturer of them. Despite this, in recent years it is automobiles that have accounted for the great majority of the company's total sales. A sharp increase has also been achieved in what the company terms "power products," that is, lawn mowers, snow blowers, outboard motors, small generators, and water pumps, in stark contrast with a recent fall in motorcycle sales due to sluggish economic conditions. Virtually all of Honda Motor's motorcycles, cars, and power products are powered by engines of its own manufacture. This has made the company the world's largest manufacturer of engines in terms of volume.

The latest consolidated annual report, covering the twelve months ending in February 1987, shows that Honda Motor's gross turnover was 2,868,305 million yen, with automobiles accounting for 1,998,421 million yen, or 69.7 percent of the total; motorcycles 301,815 million yen, or 10.5 percent; power products 163,803 million yen, or 5.7 percent; and spare parts and others 404,266 million yen, or 14.1 percent.

One of the keys to Honda Motor's recent international strategies has been the completion of its automobile manufacturing plant in Ohio. Let us, therefore, briefly touch on events that led to this.

Nearly two decades ago, Honda Motor developed the mini passenger car model N-600 (with a 600cc engine), based on the popular N-360 model. This N-600 was first exported to Hawaii in 1969, and then to the mainland United States the following year. It was distributed by American Honda Motor Co., Inc., a wholly owned subsidiary, being sold through the network of motorcycle dealers that had been built up over the preceding years.

In 1973, Honda's first subcompact model, the Civic, powered by 1,200cc and 1,500cc engines, was exported to the United States. The launch of the Civic in the United States just about coincided with the first oil crisis, which encouraged Americans to buy more compact, fuel-efficient cars. The Civic attracted a great deal of attention and was rated the most economical in fuel by the U.S. Environmental Protection Agency for four straight years from 1974.

Around that time, Honda Motor also developed a low-pollution engine system called CVCC (compound vortex controlled combustion), which was capable of reducing toxic exhaust emissions without reliance on catalytic converters. With this system the company became the first automaker to clear the stringent 1975 emission standards established under the U.S. Clean Air Act. Other leading manufacturers, such as General Motors, Ford, Toyota, and Nissan, relied on catalytic converters, which had the major drawback that, to prevent overheating, only unleaded gasoline could be used. In the United States at that time the distribution of unleaded gasoline was inadequate, which caused huge numbers of catalyst-equipped cars to converge on a limited number of gas stations. Owners of the CVCC engine-powered Honda Civics, on the other hand, could use either leaded or unleaded fuel. The shortage of unleaded gasoline only lasted about a year, but it resulted in the huge success of the Civic.

The Civic was followed by the more luxurious Accord in 1976 and the sporty Prelude in 1978, both of which were soon launched in the United States. In the years following the first oil crisis, low sticker prices were no longer the major sales point of

Japanese automobiles in the United States. MIT's International Automobile Program reports: "The generation [of Japanese vehicles] after that, born around 1973, dropped the emphasis on low price and converted production cost advantages plus growing skill in vehicle design and packaging into a quality image. Although still sold as economy cars, the Japanese vehicles gained an image of craftsmanship and even luxury in a small package."[1]

The Accord, for example, was designed as a compact car with such an image of craftsmanship, and its quality won it a high reputation in America.

American Honda Motor had not able to set up a network of exclusive dealers when it was only selling the Civic, but with the addition of the Accord and the Prelude, many dealers throughout the country gladly became exclusive Honda dealers.

While the export from Japan of finished, assembled products is one major element in Honda Motor's international strategies, another is to produce outside Japan, wherever there is a major market. This principle is called "localization," and consists of the "localization of people," meaning hiring local people and assigning capable local employees to important positions, the "localization of products," meaning adaptation to local needs and the supply of products that satisfy local customers, the "localization of money," meaning the maximum reinvestment of profits locally, and the "localization of components." Immediately after setting up its exclusive dealer network in the United States, Honda Motor decided to physically produce cars there. It is significant that this decision was made before the trade frictions between Japan and the United States occurred.

In March 1978, Honda of America Manufacturing, Inc., was established in Marysville, Ohio, by Honda Motor and American Honda Motor jointly, opening the way for the construction of, first, the motorcycle plant and, subsequently, the automobile plant. Kazuo Nakagawa, Honda of America's founding president, wanted to operate the company as an American enterprise, free from any restrictions. He thus asked the Ohio State authorities to treat his company in the same way as any American company. James A. Rhodes, then governor of Ohio, has said that Nakagawa sought no particular advantages from the state, such as financial assistance.

Honda Motor's choice of Ohio was based on combination of various factors—good transportation systems, geographical proximity to component suppliers, and availability of high-quality labor. When founder Soichiro Honda was asked at an airport press interview why he chose Ohio, he jokingly answered, "It was a divine revelation." Indeed, the people in Ohio by and large are very religious and diligent. Shoichiro Irimajiri, who assumed the Honda of America presidency in June 1984, says the most gratifying thing in running his company is that he can hire outstanding people.

A ceremony commemorating automobile production start-up at Honda of America was held in November 1982, and the first car to come off the assembly line, with the license plate "USA 001," is still exhibited in the factory's lobby. This was the first car a Japanese manufacturer had ever built in the United States.

At present, the company has a work force of over 4,000, all recruited from among local residents—320 at the motorcycle plant and 3,700 at the automobile plant. They are called (and they call themselves) "associates," rather than the conventional "workers" or "employees." Associates and managers wear the same work clothes, eat at the same cafeteria, and are on a first-name basis, all of which contributes to the sense of unity. The automobile plant has the same personnel policy as that of the motorcycle plant described in Chapter 1.

As production start-up approached, around the summer of 1982, locally hired key production personnel returned from Japan where they had been given extensive training at the Sayama Plant of Honda Motor producing the Accord. They were joined by some engineers dispatched from Japan to teach and train the work force. Nakagawa's basic concern was to make sure that the cars built in Ohio were in no way inferior in quality to those shipped from Japan. Everybody was instructed to report to his or her superior immediately upon finding a component with any kind of defect. This quality-consciousness stemmed from unease on the part of dealers selling the Accord in the United States that production in America would inevitably result in a deterioration of quality. The dealers were encouraged, however, when they found that the quality of the Ohio-made Accord was just as good as that of cars built in Japan.

The Ohio car plant originally had a production capacity of 150,000 units per year, and reached full production in May 1984. Honda Motor had first aimed at breaking even in three years from production start-up and erasing cumulative deficits resulting from the initial investment within five years. But Honda of America had already started making profit by the final quarter of 1983, and the accumulated deficits were wiped out during the second and third quarters of 1984, or three years ahead of schedule. Although this was due in no small measure to good marketplace acceptance of the Accord for its high quality, President Reagan's investment tax reduction policy also helped, as did a steep increase in the price of Japanese automobiles resulting from Japan's voluntary restraint on car exports to the United States.

On the successful production of the Accord, Honda Motor launched a program of doubling the car production capacity in Ohio to 300,000 units per year by 1988 by establishing a second assembly line and adding the Civic to its production range. At a New Year's press conference in 1986, however, Honda Motor President Tadashi Kume declared, "We have now decided to increase the car production capacity in Ohio to 360,000 units per year without changing the target date. This will not require any additional production line, but will be done through improving the efficiency of the two existing assembly lines." The second line went into operation in April 1986. Today, the first line assembles the 4-door Accord, and the second line the 3-door Accord and the Civic.

"Experts from American automakers who visit us," says Honda of America President Irimajiri, "are first surprised by the shortness of our assembly lines. For example, where conventional methods would require four or five stages in the welding process, we use a general rotating-type welding machine that does the entire work in just one stage. We also use single-purpose welding robots, which are so small they are given nicknames."

Even at full operating capacity, neither of the assembly lines in Ohio will be producing more than 200,000 cars a year, less than half of the 400,000 cars being turned out per line at Honda Motor's plants in Japan. This is the reason why former President Kawashima instructed that each assembly line in Ohio be half as long as in Japan, that investment in each line in Ohio be half as much as in Japan, and that per unit production cost in Ohio be the same as that in Japan. The rotating-type welding machine was developed especially for Ohio by Honda Engineering Co., Ltd., a wholly owned subsidiary responsible for designing and supplying production tooling for all production facilities worldwide.

Soichiro Honda once denounced a playback robot with just one manipulator as "a one-armed monster," and showed little interest in such equipment. Honda Engineering succeeded in developing one playback robot to handle extremely complicated functions simultaneously, and another for simple, specific work. The former is represented by the rotating-type welding machine, which welds the two side panels, the roof panel, and the floor panel, completing most of the automobile's basic body structure. The latter, smaller robots function in the subsequent welding processes. At Ohio, six to eight of these robots are used in each station. In the second assembly line, welding is all but completely automated, as shown by the fact that the 90-meter(270-foot)-long welding line is staffed by only six people.

The Ohio plant has advanced equipment, some of which has not yet been used even at the parent plants in Japan. The effect of this is clearly seen in the amounts of money invested in Ohio. Investment for the first stage of the car plant construction totaled $250 million. Another $280 million was spent setting up the new assembly line. An additional $60 million was needed for improving production efficiency. In other words, Honda Motor has had to spend $590 million for a facility capable of producing 360,000 Accords and Civics per year in the United States. This sum would be regarded as incredibly small compared with the kind of investment that American automobile manufacturers would contemplate for construction of a comparable factory. This is ample proof that Honda Engineering plays a key role in Honda Motor's global strategies.

The following quote indicates that the Ohio car plant has achieved the lowest production cost in the entire American automobile industry. "Given that a considerable portion of the U.S. market will be protected in the long run it follows that Honda's strategy must be to become the low-cost, high-quality producer within that protected market. I think they are playing the smartest game of any manufacturer and have really stolen a lead on the rest of the Japanese in direct investment," says James P. Womack of MIT.[2]

"It is true," says Irimajiri, " that our plant has some of the most advanced machinery. But I've noticed there is a major difference in ways of thinking about machines between us Japanese and Westerners. Westerners tend to think that production equipment is destined to deteriorate as times goes by. For us, though, the installation of a machine is just the beginning, and we strive to improve it so the machine's performance will get better. This improvement is not just the responsibility of engineering experts alone. People on the shop floor know the machine better than anybody else, so they must cooperate with the engineers. This is the 'suggestion for improvement' system that we employ throughout our global operations. When we at Ohio started producing the Accord, our machines were more advanced than those in Japan. But our Japanese plant at Sayama made a much greater effort than we did to improve the machines, and as a result their efficiency has now become almost equal to ours. This clearly shows the importance of educating the work force."

Marysville, Ohio, is an agrarian region, with people who have had no connection with the auto industry. Hiring and educating such people is typical policy in Honda Motor's overseas manufacturing operations, for example in motorcycle plants in Belgium and Italy. This policy is now being adopted by American motor manufacturers, such as General Motors, which chose Greenhill, Tennessee, as the site for its Saturn program (though the scale of this has now been reduced) for the express purpose of going to "a greenfield site where there are no outdated social relationships either between workers and managers, engineers/designers and factory managers, the factory and the suppliers, or the factory and the dealers."[3]

In Honda of America, workers not only receive education in automobile production techniques but also are taught the "Honda Way" of corporate management that has been Honda Motor's philosophy ever since its foundation. The Ohio plant thus has been able to implement and expand the "suggestion for improvement" system, and a growing number of "associates" voluntarily take part in quality control circles. The UAW claims that controlling labor in this paternalistic manner is tantamount to sacrificing the rights of the workers for the good of the corporation. Because of this, the UAW has established an office near the Marysville plant in an effort to organize the workers. The plant management has taken a neutral attitude to this, saying that unionization is a matter to be determined by the work force, and has thus made no move to prevent union organization. So far, only a very small number of workers have joined the union.

As the Marysville plant is still expanding and new people are being hired, there has been no necessity for any lay-offs, and management has made it clear that in the future, should lay-offs be necessary, it will do all it can to minimize the number of people involved, a policy highly appreciated by the work force. In the spring of 1985, the company established what is known as the "Associate Review Panel" to determine whether the firing of a worker is fair. If the dismissed person lodges a protest, a meeting of this panel is called, consisting of a chairman and one corporate representative, both nominated by the management, and six other members, selected at random from among associates who have no particular relationship with the person dismissed. After the chairman declares the meeting open, the corporate representative states the reasons for dismissal and the person dismissed in turn is given an opportunity to defend himself or herself. Finally, the corporate representative and the six members of the jury hold a secret ballot. If four votes judge the dismissal unfair, the "defendant" is immediately returned to his or her job. This system has been instituted by Honda of America in an effort to adapt to the spirit of fair play that is the basis of American society.

One problem confronting Honda of America is the local procurement of component parts. The firm is purchasing steel sheets from Inland Steel, which is the fourth largest steelmaker in the United States, and has also contracted with suppliers in Ohio, Michigan, and Indiana for the purchase of glass, tires, batteries, and small plastic parts. The most serious problem is to insure adequately high quality. Honda of America once organized a team of both Japanese and Americans to conduct a far-reaching survey of American suppliers. This led them to believe that while suppliers were capable of achieving high quality on an experimental basis, their standards suffer in mass production. Honda of

America, therefore, is now working with the suppliers to improve quality.

Simulataneously with efforts to buy more from local suppliers, the company itself is investing to increase the local content ratio. Within the grounds of its own factory in Marysville, Ohio, for example, it has spent $42 million to set up plastic parts manufacturing facilities. At a new plant site near the village of Anna in Shelby County, Ohio, a sum of $70 million was invested as the initial step in manufacturing engines locally. The Anna plant at present produces motorcycle engines for the Marysville plant, and has also started what it calls the "pilot production" of the 1,500cc engine for installation in the Civic. In January 1987, Honda Motor announced that an additional huge sum of $450 million will be invested in Anna to expand the engine plant, which will eventually hire 800 new people and will carry out such processes as casting, machining, and assembling for full-scale production not only of car engines but also drive trains and brakes. Production is scheduled to get under way in the fall of 1988, and the plant will enter into full production of 360,000 units per year by mid-1990. As a result, the local content ratio of cars produced by Honda of America will exceed 66 percent.

Honda Motor has recently been moving some of its research and development activities overseas. Honda R & D Co., Ltd., was made autonomous in 1960 as a means of insuring freedom in research and development, regarded as the nucleus of all corporate activities. A "branch office" of Honda R & D was opened in Los Angeles in 1975, and this office was made autonomous in September 1984, as a wholly owned subsidiary called Honda Research of America, now known as Honda R & D of North America. One of its major goals is to utilize the "sense" of American people to promote research and come up with products best suited to the North American market. Needless to say, all this is being carried out in close cooperation with the R & D headquarters in Japan. The sporty-looking Civic CRX model, for example, was originally developed for sale exclusively in North America, but was so appealing that Honda Motor decided to market it in Japan. Another interesting example is the 4-door and 3-door versions of the Accord, both of which are being manufactured in Ohio. The concept for the 4-door sedan version had the complete support of both American and Japanese engineers and designers. But they totally disagreed about the 3-door hatchback version. As a result, the 3-door Accord is being sold today only in North America, and is not produced at any of Honda Motor's plants in Japan.

Most Americans and Europeans think that all Japanese cars are alike. Yet Honda Motor is always endeavoring to come up with something different. A few decades ago, many major car manufacturers of the world went for the "world car" concept with a view to developing and manufacturing stereotyped automobiles for sale throughout the world. Honda Motor, however, is obviously seeking to achieve market segmentation of vehicle designs.

Honda Motor started operations in Ohio with $35 million invested in its motorcycle plant. Its total investments will reach $1,187 million, including both car and motorcycle plants, a plastic injection shop, and engine production facilities. Eventually, it will employ some 5,000 people. After trying hard to become a fully fledged member of the American automobile industry, in June 1985 Honda of America succeeded in obtaining membership in the Motor Vehicle Manufacturers' Association (MVMA) of the United States. So far, no other Japanese automaker has yet become a member.

Honda Motor has also established a production base in Canada. Honda of Canada Mfg., Inc., was founded in the township of Tecumseth in the suburbs of Alliston, Ontario, in June 1984. With an investment of 200 million Canadian dollars, the plant started manufacturing the Accord model in November 1986. With the Civic to be added to its production range, the company is scheduled to have a production capacity of 80,000 units annually, and to employ some 700 local people by 1989.

The circumstances of auto manufacturers in Western Europe are distinctly different from those in the United States, mainly because all the big auto producers—Volkswagen, Renault, Peugeot, Fiat, Austin Rover, Ford, and General Motors—are faced with serious overcapacity and are engaged in fiercely competitive price-cutting. Of the nations of the European Economic Community (EEC), West Germany does not impose any quantitative restriction on cars imported from Japan because of West German car manufacturers' strong price competitiveness. Yet, it is quite likely that West Germany, too, will start curbing Japanese car imports should they rise dramatically. On the other hand, Great Britain limits Japanese imports to 11 percent of its domestic market through agreement between the Japan Automobile Manufacturers' Association (JAMA) and the British Society of Motor Manufacturers and Traders (SMMT). The French Government permits only 3 percent of the market to Japanese cars, while Italy virtually shuts out Japanese cars, only allowing 3,300 cars a year to be imported from Japan.

For all practical purposes, there is just no room for Japanese car makers to invest directly in Western Europe for local production, even if they wanted to do so to circumvent import restrictions. Nissan Motor today is the only Japanese automaker to have invested there, with a new plant recently starting operations in Britain.

For almost a decade Honda Motor has been collaborating with Austin Rover Group Limited (ARG), which is the volume car subsidiary of the Rover Group p.l.c. (formerly BL Limited). ARG approached Honda Motor with the idea of collaboration late in 1978. At that time, ARG urgently needed long-term technological collaboration to achieve revitalization. More specifically, it needed help to develop and produce a competitive new model in the lower-medium car sector. Honda Motor was the top of the list of potential partners for ARG, for the following reasons: it was not too big; its cars were different from those of other Japanese makers; and it had a global outlook in its international strategies. Preliminary discussions opened in Tokyo in March 1979. Contrary to ARG's fear that the talks might drag on for a long time, these preliminary discussions resulted in broad agreement after only two days. A formal agreement was signed in December 1979, giving ARG the license to produce and sell a new model based on Honda Motor's Ballade. The new car made its debut in Britain in October 1981, under the name of the Triumph Acclaim. This model subsequently underwent modifications, and was renamed the Rover 200 series, which was launched in June 1984. Simultaneously with this change, the production site was shifted from ARG's Cowley plant to that at Longbridge. The local content ratio started out at 70 percent, and it is intended to reach 80 percent in the future.

ARG has the exclusive right to market the licensed model in the EEC region, and Honda sells its own version elsewhere. In order to help ARG promote marketing of the licensed cars in the EEC area, Honda Motor has voluntarily refrained from selling its 4-door Civic or Ballade in the same area. In April 1986, the two companies signed another agreement, under which ARG is building the Honda Ballade 4-door sedan on a subcontract basis, and Honda Motor is selling it with its own emblem through its own dealers in Britain at the rate of 5,000 units per year. This enables Honda Motor to sell this model outside the import quota. Thus, Honda Motor has been able to obtain in Europe a production base, though very small in scale, without having to take any equity share in ARG.

In November 1981, meanwhile, Honda Motor and ARG signed a memorandum calling for jointly developing a new executive car dubbed "XX." This project culminated in the signing of a joint manufacturing agreement in April 1984. Norman Lamont, British minister of state at the Department of Trade and Industry, issued a statement welcoming this, saying: "The XX executive car is . . . a model which has been designed from the outset as a collaboration venture—probably the first of its kind in the world. The Government particularly welcomes this project as an example of collaboration between British and Japanese companies. . . . Within 18 months of the start of commercial production, average local content will be equivalent to a minimum of 80 percent, taking account for a transitional period of a further two and a half years of component exports for XX production in Japan."

Principal features of the joint manufacturing agreement were as follows:

(1) Honda Motor will produce not only its own version but also ARG's version of the XX model at its Sayama plant in Japan; ARG likewise will produce both versions of the model at its Cowley Plant in Britain.

(2) Production start-up is scheduled for the latter half of 1985.

(3) The subcontract-manufactured cars, namely, the ARG version to be built at Sayama and the Honda version at Cowley, will start coming off the respective assembly lines early in 1986.

(4) The XX with the Honda emblem to be produced at Cowley will be sold in Europe through Honda Motor's dealer networks. (5) The XX with the ARG emblem to be produced at Sayama will be sold in Japan and Australia through ARG's networks. (6) In all other markets, both companies will sell cars of their own manufacture.

The XX cars, powered by Honda Motor's V-6 engines displacing 2.0 and 2.5 liters, were unveiled in 1985, one named the Honda Legend and other the Rover Sterling. While they share technology, they look distinctly different, giving each company a separate corporate identity.

Strangely enough, the Legend and the Sterling, both produced at Cowley, are now competing with each other through the Honda Motor and ARG dealer networks in Europe. In the American market, the Japanese-built Legend and the British-made Rover Sterling are in competition.

In preparation for subcontract manufacture by ARG of the Legend, in February 1985 Honda Motor established Honda of the U.K. Manufacturing, Ltd., by acquiring a site occupied by the South Marston Airfield in the suburbs of Swindon, west of London. The facility, which was completed in the summer of 1986, assembles components to be sent to Cowley for incorporation into the Legend and carries out pre-delivery inspection of the cars built by ARG for quality checking purposes.

In June, 1985, meanwhile, Honda Motor and ARG signed another memorandum calling for joint development of a new model code-named "YY," which will be a sedan smaller than the XX, with engines displacing 1.3 to 1.6 liters. The target date is set for late in the 1980s. The two companies signed a formal agreement on this project in April 1987, clearing the way for production start-up in 1989.

"I have long been of the opinion," says Daniel Jones, senior research fellow at the University of Sussex, "that the Japanese would ultimately develop competitive products in the premium luxury and executive markets, dominated by companies such as BMW. When last in Japan people in Honda told us: 'we realize we cannot be a Daimler Benz—but we can and will become a BMW.' Everybody is targeting their next large car at BMW, having recognized that it is the larger European cars and not the larger American cars that were the target to aim for. The Honda HX and the Austin Rover AX are the first such vehicles to tackle BMW head on. This will ultimately be the biggest challenge to what was the greatest strength of the European auto industry, namely its lead in product technology and sophistication."[4]

The introduction of the Legend has also ushered in a new marketing strategy in North America for Honda Motor, as this model led American Honda Motor to create a new marketing network. Known as "Acura," this new network, along with the traditional Honda network, now enables American Honda Motor to sell automobiles through two channels. The Acura started in March 1986, with 60 retail dealers. The number is targeted to increase to 600 by 1990. At present, the Acura network handles two models, the luxury Legend car and the newly developed sporty Integra sedan, whereas the Honda network sells the Accord, Prelude, and Civic models. "Creation of the Acura network," says Cliff Schmillen, vice president of American Honda Motor, "is the biggest challenge our company has ever faced. The luxury and sporty car fields, which we are now entering, are the areas where highest growth rates are expected in the 1990s." The same Acura network is also being built up in Canada, with a target of 100 Acura dealers by 1990.

As its North American activities have become increasingly diversified to include production and marketing of motorcycles, cars, power products and components, as well as local procurement, Honda Motor in March, 1987, established a wholly owned subsidiary called Honda North America, Inc., in Torrance, California, as a means of expediting decision-making and coordinating production and marketing activities in the entire North American region, including Canada and Mexico. This reflects the company's attempt to institute more decentralization in decision-making.

Finally, Honda Motor's involvement in Formula I Grand Prix car racing must be touched upon. After a fifteen-year absence, the company returned to the undisputed pinnacle of motor racing, Formula I, in 1983. The following year, its team won a race. In 1985, it won four of the sixteen races. And in 1986, the cars developed by Williams of Britain and powered by Honda Motor's engines, won nine races, and the Williams-Honda Team won the constructors'championship. More pleased than anybody else, perhaps, was Soichiro Honda, who had been dreaming of winning this championship ever since his first entry in Formula I in 1964. In 1987, Honda Motor's engines are mounted on the cars of two racing teams—Williams and Lotus.

Needless to say, participation in Formula I requires the ultimate in automotive technology and helps refine technological skills. Perhaps more importantly, the racing activities benefit Honda Motor's international strategies as well, by elevating the corporate image internationally. In the minds of the Americans in particular, winning the Formula I represents Honda Motor's spirit of constant challenge.

SOURCES
(1) *The Future of the Automobile*, MIT Press, 1984, pp. 133–34.
(2) Tetsuo Sakiya, *Honda-shiki daiseiko e no kaigai senryaku* (Honda Motor's International Strategies), Jatech Press, 1986, p. 210.
(3) Sakiya, *op. cit.*, p. 212.
(4) Sakiya, *op. cit.*, p. 224.

INDEX

employee participation: in management, 207; in "Idea Contest," 209; in NH circles, 203, 208–9; in quality control (QC) circles, 203, 208–9, 216

employee satisfaction, 215–16

employment system, lifetime, 11, 108, 195

energy sources, "revolution" in, 105, 106

Environment Agency, Japanese, 182

Environmental Protection Agency, U.S., 181–82

equity ratio, 176

European Economic Community (EEC), limitation of auto exports to, 15, 31

exhaust gas recirculation (EGR), 183

expert committees, 199–200, 210

expert system, 169–72, 176–78

Express (Roadpal NC-50; motorcycle), 204

farmers, liberation of, 58–59, 195

Federation of Economic Organizations (Keidanren), 81, 128

Federation of Independent Unions, 107

Ferrari (Italy), 148

Ford Motor Corporation, 15, 16, 18, 212

Foreign Exchange and Foreign Trade Control Act (1949), 127; (1980), 131

Foreign exchange and foreign trade transactions, liberalization of, 128

Formula I and Formula II races, see racing, automotive

Fraser, Douglas, 14

French Grand Prix, 150

Friedman, Milton, 79, 138

front-wheel drive (FWD), 18, 157

Fuji Heavy Industries, 136

Fuji Iron and Steel, 78

Fujii Yoshinobu, 54

Fujisawa Hideshiro, 38, 39, 40, 41, 42

Fujisawa Takeo: and the Honda

Motor union, 90, 96–97, 103; as a cadet, 41–41; early career of, 42; early life of, 38, 41; in early days of Honda Motor, 68–74, 81–89; in postwar Japan, 64–65; management of, 139, 167–73; meeting with Soichiro Honda, 65–67; retirement of, 161, 162, 184–85

Furukawa *zaibatsu*, 195

General Agreement on Tariffs and Trade (GATT), 129, 130

General Headquarters (GHQ), 58, 63, 77, 79; *see also* Occupation, the

General Motors Corporation (GM), 15, 16–17, 18–19, 29, 122, 193, 212, 213

German Grand Prix, 143

Gilera (Italy), 111

Ginther, Richie, 144–47, 148

GL-1100 (motorcycle), 210

GM, *see* General Motors Corporation

Grand Prix races, *see* racing, automotive

Great Japan Patriotic Labor Organization, 91

Great Kanto Earthquake, *see* earthquake

Grey Advertising, Inc., 124–25

Hagerty, James C., 136

Hewlett-Packard, 12

Hillman (Great Britain), 24

Hinduism, 188

Hino Motors, 24, 164

hiring practices, 161

Hirohito, Emperor, 57, 64

Honda 1300 (automobile), 151, 158–59, 165, 187

Honda Benelux N.V. (Belgium), 19, 27, 125

Honda Foundation, 187, 189–91

Honda Gihei, 49

Honda Motor: and experts, 120, 123, 137; and racing, 110–15, 117, 141–51, 186; "Company

Principle" of, 19, 20–21; crises of, 95–97; employment conditions at, 204–7, 210; entry into auto manufacture, 134, 137, 193; entry into U.S. market, 121, 123–25; expert system of, 169–71, 176–78; organizational structure of, 167–73; over the counter trading of stocks of, 88; ownership of, 88, 161–62; regional division system of, 211; *senmukai* of, 199–201, 211; union of, 90, 96, 97, 98, 103; wage system at, 204–5; *see also* American Honda Motor Co., Honda Motor plants and offices

Honda Motor plants and offices: Aoi plant, 85; Hamamatsu plant, 98; Kumamoto plant, 201, 202–3; Marysville, Ohio, plant, 21, 28–29, 201–2, 210, 213; Shirako plant, 85, 90, 96, 97, 98, 103; Suzuka plant, 119, 139, 209; Tokyo plant, 69, 71, 85; Tokyo sales office, 69; Yamato (Wako) plant, 85, 97, 98, 103

Honda Sales Research Co., 180

Honda service factories, 180

Honda Soichiro: and air-cooled engines, 150–51, 158; and the Honda Motor union, 90, 99; as head of Honda Technical Research Institute, 62; as head of Tokai Seiki Industry, 53; as racing driver, 50–51, 52–53; early career of, 49, 50–51; early life of, 49; education of, 49, 54–55; in early days of Honda Motor, 68–74, 81–89; in postwar Japan, 62; retirement of , 161, 162, 184–85

Honda Technical Research Institute, 62–63, 67

Honda Used Vehicle Co., 180

house purchases, mutual aid system for, 210

IBM, 12, 216

Ikeda Hayato, 106, 129, 136

IMF-JC (International Metalworkers Federation, Japan Council), 108

imports and exports, dependence on, 126–27

International Association of Traffic and Safety Sciences, 189

International Monetary Fund (IMF), 129

Ishihara Takashi, 14

Ishizaka Taizo, 128

Isle of Man, *see* TT races

Isuzu Motors, 15, 17, 24, 29, 122

Italian Grand Prix, 144, 148

Ito Hirobumi, 36

Iwasaki family, *see* Mitsubishi *zaibatsu*

Jaguar (Britain), 143

Japan Automobile Users' Union, 163–64, 165

Japan Communist Party, 44, 93

Japan Development Bank, 80–81

Japanese women, 109

Japan Federation of Automobile Workers Unions, 14

Japan, Inc. theory, 137–38

Japan Machine and Tool Research Institute, 45, 48–49

Japan Socialist Party, 93, 94, 135

"J" cars (GM), 15, 17

Jialing Machine Factory (China), 27–28

Jitsueisha, 39

job rotation, 11, 21, 207, 208

Juno (scooter), 86, 94–95, 118

Kato Shuichi, 188

Kawai Hayao, 63–64

Kawasaki Steel, 78

Kawasaki *zaibatsu*, 195

Kawashima Kiyoshi, 21, 23, 28–29, 67, 71, 112, 120, 123, 147, 159, 183, 185, 193, 200, 201

"K" cars (Chrysler), 15

Keidanren, *see* Federation of Economic Organizations

Kennedy Round, 130

Nishiyama Yataro, 78
Nissan Motor Company, 14, 15, 24, 84, 86, 135, 136, 137, 162, 164, 180, 193
Nissan *zaibatsu*, 195
Nixon, Richard M., 131
non-tariff barriers (NTBs), 130, 132
NSU (W. Germany), 111

Occupation, the, 57, 58, 61, 62, 74, 76, 93, 99, 195; reforms of, 58; *see also* GHQ
Ohira Masayoshi, 14
oil crisis: (1973), 12, 13, 24, 130, 132, 178, 199, 200; (1979), 130
Okinawa, return of, 131
OPEC countries, 130
Orderly Marketing Agreement (OMA), 131–32
Organization for Economic Cooperation and Development, 129
overhead camshaft (OHC) engine, 119
overhead valve (OHV) engine, 71, 119

paternal society, 102–3, 185, 217
Pauley, Edwin W., 61–62
Peace Treaty, U.S.–Japan, 74, 76, 94
Pearl Harbor, 45
Perry, Matthew C., 36
plant facilities, age of, 12, 13, 18–19
priority production system, 76, 78
Proctor & Gamble, 12
production costs, reduction of, 173, 176, 200, 213
production index, 156
production processes, streamlining of, 173
protectionism, 217

QC circles, *see* employee participation
quality of working life (QWL), 18
QWL, *see* quality of working life

RA-270 (racing car), 142
RA-271 (racing car), 142–44
RA-272 (racing car), 145
RA-273 (racing car), 148
RA-300 (racing car), 148, 149
RA-301 (racing car), 149, 151
RA-302 (racing car), 150
racing, automotive, 53, 115, 141–47, 148–49, 150–51, 157, 183, 186, 187
racing, motorcycle, 110, 111, 112, 113, 114–15, 117, 142, 147
R & D Center, 113, 114, 141, 147, 149, 150, 151, 158, 160; autonomous status of, 168–71, 172–73
R & D laboratories, *see* R & D Center
"Rapid Response Control System," 183
rationalism, 188–89, 214
RC-142 (engine), 114
Reagan administration, 16
rebirth (*samsāra*), 188
recall system for defective automobiles, 163, 165
Reconstruction Financing Bank, 76, 77
Reich, Michael, 188
Renault (France), 24
retirement age, 195, 205
retirement grant, 205–6
Rhodes, James A., 21
Roadpal NC-50, *see* Express
robots, 206–7
Roosevelt, Theodore, 37
Russian Revolution (1917), 44
Russo-Japanese War (1904–05), 37–38, 49, 91

S-500 sports car, 142
S-600 sports car, 142
Sahashi Shigeru, 137
Sales, Engineering, and Development (SED) system, 203, 204
Sanbetsu (Congress of Industrial Labor Organizations), 93, 94, 107
Sangyo Hokoku-kai (Patriotic